PRAISE FOR
INTERNAL
COMMUNICATIONS

"This is a must-read for everyone responsible for developing or managing internal communications. It builds on the most important experience shared by leading experts over the past decades and elegantly summarizes this into a current overview of what internal communicators must do to add value to the business. I particularly enjoyed the focus on how communicators must increasingly leverage line managers to secure commitment to and not only awareness of business strategies and goals."
Torben Bundgaard, Head of Leadership Communication, Novo Nordisk

"A must-have for any internal communications practitioner – this book sets itself apart from others through its combination of theory and practical tips and templates. It is a joy to read – written in such an engaging, accessible way that anyone can understand it. From managing change communication to advising leaders and creating compelling messages, this book covers all the vital areas for any IC function. I'm sure it will become a well-used favourite of my team."
Saskia Jones, Head of Internal Communication, Oxfam GB

"Internal communication is more critical than ever and this book shows managers how to excel in their job and how to best deliver value to their organizations. It also provides practical insight on effective planning and delivery. The chapter on change was especially useful as it outlined clear and vital steps to follow."
Tim Cobb, Head of Group External Communications, UBS

"More and more companies are realizing that every meaningful conversation about their business begins with the people closest to it – employees. And yet, few have invested in the development of this practice. The book provides valuable insight to help with planning and delivery. I particularly found the chapter on measurement useful as it provided clear steps on the essential things to take into consideration on what can be a complex issue."
Rebecca Lowell Edwards, Chief Communications Officer, GE Oil & Gas

"I wish I'd had a guide like this when I started out in internal communication. Each chapter is easy to read and easy to understand. The templates and checklists are really helpful and the case studies really bring the guidance to life. I'd recommend this manual to anyone working in internal communication; it's a great reference point for the start of any new communication challenge!" **Jenny Clark, Head of Internal Communications, The De Beers Group of Companies**

"This is a very useful resource for everybody who works in internal communications. The book is very well structured, while easy and entertaining to read. FitzPatrick and Valskov provide practical and hands-on insights without neglecting the basic theoretical knowledge. It certainly helps professionals to develop a valid strategy and to hone it. Far from being highbrow, the book is demanding to the reader in a very positive sense – simply because the authors ask the right questions. I specifically like that the book is permanently focused on the very essential core of IC: adding value to the business." **Dr Jörg Kirchhoff, Director Associates Communications, Robert Bosch GmbH**

CIPR

Internal Communications

A manual for practitioners

PR in Practice

Liam FitzPatrick and Klavs Valskov
with Pamela Mounter

KoganPage

Publisher's note

Every possible effort has been made to ensure that the information contained in this book is accurate at the time of going to press, and the publishers and authors cannot accept responsibility for any errors or omissions, however caused. No responsibility for loss or damage occasioned to any person acting, or refraining from action, as a result of the material in this publication can be accepted by the editor, the publisher or any of the authors.

First published in Great Britain and the United States in 2014 by Kogan Page Limited

2nd Floor, 45 Gee Street
London EC1V 3RS
United Kingdom
www.koganpage.com

1518 Walnut Street, Suite 1100
Philadelphia PA 19102
USA

4737/23 Ansari Road
Daryaganj
New Delhi 110002
India

© Liam FitzPatrick and Klavs Valskov, 2014

ISBN   978 0 7494 6932 0
E-ISBN   978 0 7494 6933 7

British Library Cataloguing-in-Publication Data

A CIP record for this book is available from the British Library.

Library of Congress Cataloging-in-Publication Data

FitzPatrick, Liam.
   Internal communications : a manual for practitioners / Liam FitzPatrick and Klavs Valskov.
      pages cm. – (PR in practice)
   ISBN 978-0-7494-6932-0 (paperback) – ISBN 978-0-7494-6933-7 (ebk)   1. Communication in management.   2. Communication in organizations.   3. Business communication.
I. Valskov, Klavs.   II. Title.
   HD30.3.F554 2014
   658.4′5–dc23

                                                                         2014023526

Typeset by Graphicraft Limited, Hong Kong
Print production managed by Jellyfish
Printed and bound by CPI Group (UK) Ltd, Croydon, CR0 4YY

CONTENTS

LIST OF FIGURES

LIST OF TABLES

PR in Practice Series
Published in association with the Chartered Institute of Public Relations
Series Editor: Anne Gregory

Kogan Page has joined forces with the Chartered Institute of Public Relations to publish this unique series, which is designed specifically to meet the needs of the increasing numbers of people seeking to enter the public relations profession and the large band of existing PR professionals. Taking a practical, action-oriented approach, the books in the series concentrate on the day-to-day issues of public relations practice and management rather than academic history. They provide ideal primers for all those on CIPR, CAM and CIM courses or those taking NVQs in PR. For PR practitioners, they provide useful refreshers and ensure that their knowledge and skills are kept up to date.

Professor Anne Gregory PhD is Director of the Centre for Public Relations Studies at Leeds Metropolitan University, UK. She has authored over 70 publications; as well as being editor of the Kogan Page/CIPR series of books which she initiated, she is Editor-in-Chief of the *Journal of Communication Management*. Anne also leads specialist commercial research and consultancy projects from the Centre working with prestigious public and private sector clients. She is a non-executive director of Airedale NHS Foundation Trust. Originally a broadcast journalist, Anne spent 12 years as a senior practitioner before moving on to academia. She was President of the Chartered Institute of Public Relations (CIPR) in 2004, leading it to Chartered status and was awarded the CIPR's Sir Stephen Tallents Medal for her outstanding contribution to public relations in 2010. In June 2012 she became Chair of the Global Alliance of Public Relations and Communications Management, the umbrella organization of over 60 public relations institutes from around the world.

Other titles in the series:
Creativity in Public Relations by Andy Green
Crisis, Issues and Reputation Management by Andrew Griffin
Effective Internal Communication by Lyn Smith and Pamela Mounter
Effective Media Relations by Michael Bland, Alison Theaker and David Wragg
Ethics in Public Relations by Patricia J Parsons
Evaluating Public Relations by Tom Watson and Paul Noble
Online Public Relations by David Phillips and Philip Young
Planning and Managing Public Relations Campaigns by Anne Gregory
PR and Communication in Local Government and Public Services by John Brown, Pat Gaudin and Wendy Moran
The PR Professional's Handbook by Caroline Black
Public Relations in Practice edited by Anne Gregory
Risk Issues and Crisis Management in Public Relations by Michael Regester and Judy Larkin
Running a Public Relations Department by Mike Beard
Writing Skills for Public Relations by John Foster

The above titles are available from all good bookshops. To obtain further information, please go to the CIPR website (**www.cipr.co.uk/books**) or contact the publishers at the address below:
Kogan Page Ltd
2nd Floor, 45 Gee Street
London EC1V 3RS
United Kingdom
Tel: 020 7278 0433
www.koganpage.com

FOREWORD
BY ANNE GREGORY

As the authors of this powerful and practical book say, 'leaders around the world have come to acknowledge that good communication is part of the success for any organization' and the story of success begins on the inside.

Talk to any enlightened chief executive and they will put their workforce at the top of their list of priorities and mean it. They know that having well-motivated staff who understand what they are doing and why, and indeed who have been involved in determining the what and the why, is their most powerful asset. The intellectual capital, focused effort and good will of employees is a resource of immense worth and the relationships they form, both internally and externally are the basis of the brand's integrity. At the heart of harnessing and nurturing that resource is communication. Organizations are social entities: without communication they cannot exist.

This book unpacks in detail the process and value of internal communication. It starts with eight golden rules which frame the main contents of the book. Rule number one makes the point that 'activity' on its own is pointless. A focus on what the activity is meant to achieve is what really counts. This no-nonsense approach characterizes the book. What follows the eight rules is a systematic exploration of what internal communication is and why it matters, how it should be organized, how it dovetails with and into the line manager's role and working with senior managers including the CEO.

Then the detail of communication planning is examined, with each element dealt with comprehensively, from understanding and segmenting audiences, to designing appropriate messages and content, to determining the most appropriate channels, and finishing with research and evaluation.

Two other chapters complement these topics – change and developing the team. Change and managing change is almost the mantra of senior managers in today's world. Events are fast moving, globalization is a current reality and the speed of technological developments compress time and geography at an ever-increasing rate. Organizations need to be responsive and adaptable not only to deal with an increasingly complex and speeded-up world, but to try to be influential in shaping it. The ability to change is a core capability and hence this topic fully merits a chapter of its own. Likewise, self and staff development for the internal communication team. To manage and to help others to manage this change requires a team at the top of its game. The days of the amateur are over. Professionals of the highest skill, knowledge and behaviour are required as trusted advisers to managers and as role models and coaches to others.

Liam FitzPatrick and Klavs Valskov have subtitled this book *A Manual for Practitioners*, but it's more than that: it is a must-read for all managers who understand that communication is essential to whole-organization success and who want to understand how professional communicators can work with them to achieve that. It's also a must-read for professional communicators who are not directly involved in managing and implementing internal communication programmes. It is an area of increasing importance and this book will give you the insights you need to partner with internal communication colleagues more intelligently to the benefit of your organization and our profession more generally.

Professor Anne Gregory
Series Editor

FOREWORD
BY JAMES HARKNESS

As former Chair of CIPR Inside, the Chartered Institute of Public Relations' (CIPR) sector group for internal communication professionals, I believe that this is an important time for internal communications.

Once, organizations paid lip service to the need to communicate with their people – now there can be few CEOs and leaders who don't see communication as vital to their role. Once, internal communication was a role without influence or kudos – now people actively choose our sector for the opportunity to make a real difference. Once, employee communication was an add-on to other disciplines like HR, PR or marketing – now it is recognized as a key foundation stone for the achievement of organizational strategy and business goals.

The reason for this transformation is simple. As a body of practitioners, we have learnt to take ourselves seriously and we have developed tools, techniques and approaches that actually work. We have matured to the extent that we have our own qualifications, evidence of our effectiveness and a confidence that we have a place at the centre of decision making in organizations large and small.

Crucially we have moved from focusing on channels and processes to focusing on results. Mature professionals begin every conversation with the outcome and not with outputs, which is what this book sets out to underline.

Klavs and Liam take a very pragmatic approach and seek to provide practical advice. But running through everything they say is the belief that the impact or results of communication should be the central concern of a communicator.

In the CIPR Inside Group we celebrate this approach – it is core to our profession. And we stress the need to keep learning and developing as individuals and practitioners. Through events, debate, awards, campaigning and mentoring we hope to support the ever-growing cadre of specialists who are proud to be known as internal communicators.

If you find this book useful, come and meet us online at **www.ciprinside.co.uk**. You'll find people who share your passion and are ready to take you further on your journey to help build your skills and the difference that our profession makes.

James Harkness
Partner
HarknessKennett

ACKNOWLEDGEMENTS

We would like to acknowledge the inspiration, help and support that we have had in writing this book.

There are a number of great writers whose work is reflected in this book. They include Roger D'Aprix, Jim Shaffer, Shel Holtz, Gary Grates, Sue Dewhurst, John Smythe, Angela Sinickas, Kathryn Yates and Bill Quirke. We have tried to credit them where appropriate but their influence is such that much of their wisdom is now commonly accepted as good practice and so may not always be directly referenced. Likewise we acknowledge the influence of Melcrum, whose publications and training have done so much to inspire people in our profession. And thanks to Anne Eriksen who brought us together.

We should also mention a number of people who have helped us to write this book, not least Dan Grafton, whose thoughts on the early drafts of a couple of chapters were invaluable. Likewise Sue Dewhurst's contributions to the chapter on skills was very helpful. Our friends, including Tony Quinlan, Ezri Carlebach, James Harkness, Tracy Playle, Ellen Hall, Andy Brown, Naomi Goodman and Robert Berrier should all take credit for a number of improvements – and for none of the flaws – in this book.

Finally we thank our families, particularly Francesca, John and Juliet for their continuing support.

Before we start

We have written this book to help people who are getting started in internal and change communication. We have tried to work through the essentials of practice, highlight some important theory and suggest some simple templates for thinking through common problems.

However, these will only get you so far.

There will be times when you need inspiration, when the advice we have given doesn't quite cover the situation facing you or you need to sound clever in that job interview or appraisal meeting.

At such times we suggest you come back to some golden rules. These are, we believe, fundamental truths about the practice of internal communication and will last at least a few more years. If in doubt, apply one of these rules and the solution to your problem should seem a bit clearer.

Rule 1: It's about results and outcomes, not activity

No matter how tempting it is to hide yourself in a flurry of activity and how appealing it is to generate beautiful films and websites, if nothing changes as a result of your work why are you doing it? Every conversation in internal communication begins with 'What do we want people to *do?*'

Rule 2: It's about the business

Whatever we want people to do, it should be rooted in the needs of the business or organization. Party organizers and entertainers do things because they are fun, professionals do things because it helps deliver a strategy or plan. If we can't show the linkage back to the needs of the business then we are probably not adding any real value.

Rule 3: We don't drive with our eyes shut

A communicator who doesn't know their audience inside out, who doesn't know how they are thinking and might react is of little use to anyone. Our job is to be the bridge between two worlds – a job that calls for us to spend as much time as we can away from our desks, talking and listening. No one else can do it for us because what we know is what makes us valuable and without it how can you produce communications that will interest anyone or talk to their concerns?

Rule 4: People have two ears and one mouth – so should organizations

People are much more connected and committed at work when they feel they are in a conversation. Internal communication that is a one-way broadcast isn't just rude, it's ineffective. We make sure the organization shuts up long enough to listen!

Rule 5: Come with data, leave with respect

Senior managers generally live in a world of facts and spreadsheets. If you want to help them make good communications decisions, meet them halfway. Gather data about process and outcomes and present it simply. Use evidence to predict scenarios and base your advice on insight. Your credibility will rise instantly.

Rule 6: Line managers matter

Line managers are not the universal solution to every communication problem, but they hold the key to a lot of the answers. In organizations where local leaders care about communication, can explain how events and plans affect their people and feel listened to, people work harder and are more committed. If you have few resources and little time, after you have decided what you want people to do you can do a lot worse by starting your communications plan with the question 'What do we need managers to discuss with their teams?'

Rule 7: There is no silver bullet

Continually we are told that some technology or idea is going to transform internal communication. This has yet to be proven to be true – the telephone, e-mail, intranets and even social media might bring improvements, but not revolution. We could be proven wrong, but until then stick with rules 1 and 2!

Rule 8: What we do matters

Our job puts us in a privileged position. We get to stick our nose where we like and what we do has an impact on people's lives. Best of all, we get the chance to change things at work in small and large ways. Not many people can say that.

The immutable truths set out by writers like Roger D'Aprix, Bill Quirke and Kathryn Yates remain: we want someone to tell us what our job is, how we're doing and how it relates to the bigger picture. Organizations want good staff to stay, do their best, be flexible and say nice things to their family and friends. People do that when they feel involved and valued, when leaders at every level take time to listen and explain the connection between their job and their vision of the organization.

01
What internal communication is and why it matters

What you will learn from this chapter

We believe that internal or employee communication is now a widely accepted part of any organization. Much has changed in a short space of time as leaders around the world have come to acknowledge that good communication is part of the secret of success for any organization.

Once upon a time, talking to employees was not really something that concerned anyone much outside the personnel department and may have been seen as the preserve of trade unions. Now, we argue, communication is a well-established feature of modern organizations. But we argue that the role of the internal communication effort can be much more than a glorified postal service or town crier. At the heart of this chapter and this book is the belief that internal communication should be about adding value to the core mission of the business or project that it supports. If you read nothing else in this book remember this: internal communication is not about making noise for the sake of it – as a maturing profession we have the responsibility to make a difference and share responsibility for the strategic goals of our employers.

In this chapter we take a look at the recent history of the profession and practice. Then we introduce the idea that there are five generic purposes to internal communication. Finally we raise the issue of ethics – the concern of a professional.

Internal communication is coming of age

The word has finally got out that successful organizations communicate with their employees. It has been a while in coming, but over the last 20 years, discussion about internal communication (IC) has moved from its role in the context of industrial relations[1] to its importance in the CEO's armoury of leadership skills.[2,3] We have come a long way from the world described by Roger D'Aprix in 1982[4] where IC suffered from poor budgets, a lack of professionalism and a short-sighted approach.

As this journey has unfolded we have seen the evolution of a professional class of internal communicators and the growth of a new category of consultancy. There have been turf wars about where IC should sit within an organization: is its natural home inside marketing or HR or perhaps as an integrated part of the CEO's front office?

Whatever the right answer is, the question would be irrelevant without the widespread acceptance that good IC is essential for the health of every organization – be that in the private, public or voluntary sectors. Once, the challenge was to find a senior manager who thought there was a need for a dedicated IC team – now these senior managers are crying out for help.

Less and less often it seems that IC managers need evidence to justify their existence, although there is quite a lot around if you care to look. A study in the United Kingdom into employee engagement was awash with data[5] and consultants Towers Watson have done some impressive work looking at the links between good communication and business performance.[6] Other writers point to benefits such as lower costs, fewer industrial disputes, more innovation, quality improvements, reduced absenteeism and generally higher productivity.[7]

Once, 'Internal Communication Manager' was the title you gave a loyal and blameless employee nearing retirement when you wanted to put him or her out to grass. Now, leaders can call on the support of an army of strategically-minded professionals who have spent years developing and refining the ability to translate business strategies into meaningful concepts for employees.

Once, IC was all about the media: company magazines, newspapers and even, in large corporations, sponsored films. Now practitioners are preoccupied with messages and providing counsel to leaders on their internal profile, progress on strategy implementation and running large-scale engagement campaigns based on real insight.

Once, belief in the power of good IC was the province of a few zealots. Now it seems close to becoming orthodoxy. Standing in its way is a simple challenge. Leaders know that good IC matters – but they don't always know what good looks like. This is a massive opportunity for our profession and is what is behind our urge to write this book.

Definitions

Before we start we should clear up a few things with a couple of definitions.

Definitions matter for a number of reasons. Not least, we still remember our university lecturers challenging us to always start by defining our terms.

We are aware that we operate in a field that is rich with confusion. There is very little agreement in our craft about what different things mean, not just among practitioners but among the people with whom we work. And academics seem as confused. Multiple learned articles on the subject seem to spend ages wrestling with definitions before ending disappointingly with a call for further research.

In real life, confusion about communication is a convenient social device. We all love to blame everything on poor communication because the alternative may be to admit that we disagree with someone else or find their opinions offensive. Thus, failures in communication make a great all-purpose excuse when employees reject management attempts to cut wages, double hours and make life generally miserable.

A communication professional needs to get a few things straight otherwise we'll be forever apologizing for things that are not our fault or having strange conversations with friends who think we're experts in IT and telecoms or colleagues who think of us as secretaries for the executives.

So here are some semi-definitions which we will try to follow throughout the rest of this book.

Organizational communication

When friends moan about the colleagues who sit three cubicles away but never actually tell them important things, or you hear tales of whole departments not sharing vital information with each other, that is probably within the realm of organizational communication.

Communication is the day-to-day lifeblood of any organization. Without communication (and probably coffee) your organization would grind to a halt. Orders wouldn't be processed, salaries wouldn't be paid and it would be even more difficult to get the IT helpdesk to understand that you need help.[8] Some organizations are very effective at communication and others are dreadful. There are whole books written on the subject and they make fascinating reading.[9]

However, is organizational communication the concern of the IC manager?

In most cases the answer is no. Everyone who comes to work is responsible for the communications they send to their co-workers. If people don't want to share information or are careless about the quality of their communications, we would argue that this is not the concern of the IC function. In the same way that IT are not responsible for your e-mail mistakes and the switchboard can't stop you being rude on the telephone, the IC team is not responsible for the failings of its colleagues – in general.

On the other hand, misunderstandings or poor interpersonal communication are often the result of people having different views of the world. If you think the most important thing in your workplace is the Christmas raffle and your colleague feels that customer service matters most you may discover a certain friction in your relationships.

Internal communication can help here. Writers such as Quirke[10] talk about 'connections' and other writers[11] mention integration as an important part of the discipline. Although the challenge of getting everyone talking nicely to everyone else is probably beyond the ability of a single team, we can help ensure that people have the tools to collaborate or at least share the same view of the world.

However, this book is mostly not about organizational communication. It is about making people have a shared context, see things in the same light and work in an engaged way together towards a common purpose.

Internal communication

Internal (or employee) communication is concerned with sharing information, building understanding, creating excitement and commitment and, ideally, achieving a desirable result. A popular academic definition from a standard textbook goes like this:

> The planned use of communication actions to systematically influence the knowledge, attitudes and behaviours of current employees.[12]

The main point that comes up when writing a definition is that internal (or employee) communication is:

- Planned – ie this is not a haphazard or accidental process.

- Systematic – ie it is a process that applies some science and discipline.

- About influence – ie employees can't always be forced to do things: they have a choice about what they do and how well they do it so they have to be persuaded.

- More than 'telling' – ie although awareness is an essential starting point for any communications campaign, we are also concerned with affecting attitudes and behaviours. Later we will explore what it means to win over 'heads, hearts and hands'. These are the essentials of communications planning, reflecting the widespread belief that professional communication advisers are not in the business of making noise for the sake of it.

- Multi-disciplinary – it is difficult to avoid the fact that information alone is not a strong driver of behaviour in the workplace. Communicators expect to work closely with colleagues across their organization to ensure that staff are trained, rewarded, motivated and resourced to do the job being asked of them. We need to understand that we're only one of the cogs in the wheel and therefore we need to be excellent in working with colleagues in other teams to be successful.

You will see that we have been using the terms *employee communication* and *internal communication* interchangeably. *Employee communication* is more widely used in North America and *internal communication* is used elsewhere, but we do not think there is much difference between the two. We will mainly be using internal communication or 'IC' in this book and only refer to employee communication for stylistic reasons.

Employee engagement

You will hear the term 'employee engagement' thrown around a lot. This is a tricky one and we tend to avoid it because it can be taken to mean so many different things that it is often unhelpful. You will hear people talk about communications that are engaging when they mean arresting or eye-catching. Other people will talk about employee engagement as shorthand for reducing absenteeism or staff turnover while other people use it when they are talking about getting employees to work harder because they have a commitment to a shared organizational goal.

If you find yourself drawn into a conversation about engagement, asking people exactly what they mean saves a lot of confusion (and can lead people to assume that you are pretty smart for spotting a potential misunderstanding).

It's not about telling – it's a two-way thing

One of the articles of faith in IC is that one-way communication has very little impact.

For a long time, writing and research on the subject has talked about having a range of styles that can be used at different times.[13] Practitioners have long made a distinction between communications designed to instruct, to inform, to consult and to involve and writers like Quirke[14] have famously highlighted that different channels should be used for different purposes. Essentially, Quirke made the point that if you want people to change the way they behave you have to do more than send them a memo.

A core idea in our profession is that communication works best when it is a conversation. Many practitioners believe that pushing information at people has a limited usefulness and that staff are more likely to hear what you are saying if you allow them to ask questions, listen to their opinions and respect their right to make their own minds up about something.

That is not to say that the role of IC is to make every office or factory run like a workers' cooperative. But it does imply that staff may be more receptive to a new idea if they believe that someone cares about what they think and that their reasonable and constructive criticisms are being taken into account. Modern communicators are expected to be adept at developing channels and practices within their organizations that allow employees to ask questions, to test understanding and to be trusted by the senior leaders to feed back reactions and suggestions.

In Chapter 6 we will talk about the range of channels that is available to internal communicators. We shall highlight which channels are best for building awareness and which are more useful for creating involvement and excitement.

The essential point here is that one-way communication is a very limited approach. In fact, many practitioners would insist that any definition of employee communication includes a reference to mutual understanding.

Getting strategic

IC teams should be busy. However, busyness can happen for the wrong reasons as much as the right ones.

We all have tales to tell about colleagues who think we are responsible for everything from sending out their Christmas cards to ensuring the CEO secretary's laptop can talk to the projector in the boardroom. If we are not careful, IC becomes the catch-all department responsible for the things no one else wants to do. And that is on top of the random calls that the switchboard directs our way because no one else's job title quite covers the issue!

Countless management books advise having a defined mission as the route to success, fame and fortune. And with good reason. If you do not know where you add value it is hard to make choices about where you are going to invest your time, deploy your resources or what issues you are going to lose sleep over. A straightforward articulation tells colleagues where they can expect your support and it guides your team towards the things that matter.

This is the difference between operating as a postal service and as a function that is of strategic importance.

Essentially, the IC team has a duty to distil down the endless mission statements, strategic imperatives, core values and 'must-win battles' into something that makes sense to the employee, helping them to actually do something that makes a difference.

A good practitioner has a clear idea of their role and where it adds value. Without a clear *raison d'être* you are likely to be subject to every whim and bizarre demand that finds its way to your desk. In short, we advise communication managers to articulate a core purpose. It is a reference point that enables you to make choices: clear boundaries save you wasting countless hours.

Start by understanding your organization and its challenges

As strategic advisers you should begin by understanding the nature of the challenges facing your organization or your project. Very often this boils down to a few things like:

- retaining skilled staff;
- selling more products to customers;
- making a bigger margin in what you sell;
- operating effectively with lower costs;
- hurting fewer people in the workplace;
- reducing impacts on the environment;
- finding better ways of doing things;
- treating customers or users nicely;
- winning the trust of your community.

Sometimes it will be obvious, but in fact very often organizations do a brilliant job of making life complicated and confusing themselves.

If you find yourself working for the sort of place that wraps its mission up in thousands of words of verbiage you will know what your job is. As an IC professional, your first task is to make sure people have a pretty good idea of what your employer is trying to do, which rather implies you have to understand it yourself first.

The obvious way to begin your research is to ask the most senior people in your organization (you might want to do this before you accept the job as you will be surprised by the variety of answers you will get from many executive teams). The annual review and external statements to major stakeholders should also help fill in the gaps.

The next task is to decide where IC can help with those challenges. It is our experience that there are five main reasons (laid out in Figure 1.1) why we can make a contribution.[15]

1. It is the law

Almost everywhere in the world, the law requires employers to talk to their staff. Sadly, this rarely extends to making workers feel valued but tends to concern issues like basic safety instructions, explaining why sites are being closed or jobs cut.

Within the European Union, works councils are a legal requirement (depending on the size of the organization) where staff representatives should have the opportunity to debate company policy and direction.

Just because the law requires that communication takes place, there is no reason why the message should be poorly presented or delivered grudgingly. The role of the IC manager should at the very least include making sure that messages are clear, consistent, appropriate and accurate.

Importantly, we have often found that there can be confusion in organizations about the exact nature of legal obligations to communicate. While we are not suggesting that the IC team take on the mantle of corporate lawyers, they should at least understand the basic legal requirements in their country for things like redundancy consultation and dismissals.

FIGURE 1.1   Why internal communication matters

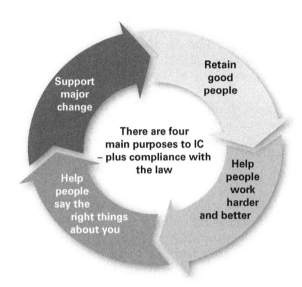

Having a basic awareness of the law will enable communicators to spot when legal or regulatory requirements have been missed. Also it helps you to tell when the lawyers are giving legal advice and when they are making stylistic suggestions (which you may want to ignore).

2. Holding onto good people

One of the biggest problems facing organizations today is finding good people with the right skills. When they have been recruited, IC has a role in making sure that they want to stick around and feel good about doing so.

We are not planning to go into a long description of what motivates people at work – writers like Dan Pink do it so much better than we can – but we should highlight a few things to illustrate the job that IC has to do.

There seems to be a consensus that material rewards are not so very powerful as positive motivators – in fact money tends to matter mostly in a negative way. People only worry about salary when they think they are not getting enough: once they feel fairly rewarded, extra money or a trip to Hawaii seems to stop having any effect.

Things that make us stick around include the esteem of our peers, the chance to do great work, being part of a community and being involved in something that will make a difference. This last thing is in fact the driving ethos in many Japanese companies: they prioritize making the world a better place – with the balance sheet often a lower priority.

A communication manager should understand what special motivators might matter in his or her workplace and, most importantly, where communication fits in.

For example, we can do a lot to celebrate the contributions made by individuals and teams – perhaps by writing them up on the intranet or running an awards programme. People might want to learn about how they are helping to change the world so communications can ensure that external voices are heard in the in-house newspaper or perhaps recruit employee bloggers to report customer experiences. We can help nurture the sense of internal society in so many ways – by organizing the summer barbecue, helping recruit volunteers for a community project or publicizing the fundraising efforts of the obsessive cyclists in the finance department.

Often communication managers fear being seen as empty-headed party organizers and yearn to be asked for their views on the latest version of the corporate strategy. However, being a community builder could well be the major strategic contribution in a sector where skilled help is hard to find, where the work offers little intrinsic excitement or where staff turnover has a massive impact on customer service.

The box below contains a case study from China where one company has built a strong customer-responsive community of employees not by giving them extra money but by asking them to help others and celebrating what they did.

3. Working harder and on the right things

When you talk about motivation at work you should very soon find yourself discussing the concept of 'discretionary effort'. If you think about your contract of employment or your job description you will quickly realise that it actually describes a tiny proportion of your job. If you look around a large department you will see that some people seem to get through far more work than their peers with similar skills or experience. The difference between people only doing exactly what is asked of them and those who go the extra mile is their discretionary effort.

What motivates people to make that extra contribution varies from workplace to workplace. However, there are two major deciding factors – trust and purpose.

If you believe that your hard work always goes unnoticed or that your boss will overlook you when it comes to bonus or promotion time you are simply going to stop trying. The communicator has a role in ensuring that people feel that they can depend on their employer to value their additional contributions. While the local manager is responsible for ensuring that the hardworking employee gets the occasional Friday off or perhaps is encouraged to apply for promotion, the communication team can do a lot to reinforce a climate of trust.

This might be as simple as reporting colleagues who have won recognition on the intranet or more complex activities such as ensuring that people have a chance to connect with the CEO.

Allied to this role is the need to help people feel that there is a purpose to their work. Not everyone is lucky enough to work for a charity finding a cure for cancer or trying to save whales but we all hope to make some difference in some small way. That might be about making a customer happy, helping a colleague with a tricky problem or finding a way of buying pencils more cheaply.

The communicator is responsible for ensuring that everyone has a clear view of the connection between their daily work and the overall mission of their team, department or organization. In the jargon of our craft this is often known as the 'line of sight'.

Having an understanding of how your job contributes, enables you to make day-to-day and minute-to-minute choices in your work. If excellent customer service is the *raison d'être* of your work group you are more likely to answer the telephone before you change the cartridge in the printer. Someone who understands running a low-cost organization won't need to be told to book their travel on a cheaper train.

The communicator has to ensure that people understand the core purpose of the organization and find ways of illustrating how individuals 10 layers down in the hierarchy can see their contribution.

They also have a major part to play in explaining how things should be done.

This might involve creating understanding about safety rules, showing what good customer service looks like or helping a project team explain new operating procedures. Our role is to act as the bridge between the organization and its employees and ensure that a message is delivered in a way that makes sense and is attractive. Rather than letting managers send out imperious memos, we exist to show them how to explain in terms that are clear, motivating and effective.

4. Helping people say the right things

Some years ago research organization Ipsos MORI looked at the drivers of corporate reputation and they came to a simple conclusion. Advertising and media relations might reach large numbers of people but they actually have a small impact on what those people think about the organization being mentioned compared to having an actual experience of the products or services supplied by that organization. If someone has a dreadful experience with your company, advertising will have an uphill struggle to convince them that there is anything admirable about your firm. However, knowing 'someone who works there' can overwhelmingly counter a direct negative experience and any amount of advertising. Someone might read in the paper that your company is disgraceful because of the products it sells, but might ignore all the bad press because their neighbour or friend has had a positive story to tell about their job with them.

When you think about your personal life you probably can think of an organization you hold in low esteem simply because one of your friends had a horrible time when they worked there.

Employees are potentially your biggest advocates and can help you win regulatory approval, shape local attitudes to your planned expansion or demonstrate your commitment to corporate social responsibility.

A communicator therefore worries about ensuring employees hear the company's side of the story before it is covered in the media. When there is a piece of negative publicity we should, as a courtesy at the very least, make sure employees have the facts at their fingertips. Your hospital might have been attacked for poor hygiene, so get the CEO to talk to staff about the steps being taken to remedy things. Your soft drinks company may have been criticized for the high sugar content of its cola, so supply workers with a factsheet on healthy drinking choices to share with their families and communities.

Clearly your employees are not mindless drones who will quote the company line no matter how ridiculous. But they expect to be treated like adults and given an answer they can support when challenged around the dinner table or in the bar.

Any PR campaign that does not seek to at least keep employees informed ahead of the media is probably missing a significant opportunity.

CASE STUDY   The Blue Horizon Group and the 'Drop of Water' initiative

(with thanks to Belinda Liu, Cardiff University MA student)

The Blue Horizon Group, a small group of luxury hotels in China, was founded in 1994 in Dongying, Shandong Province. Today it comprises 14 highly rated hotels, three restaurants, a vocational school, a food factory and a construction company. Together they employ hundreds of thousands of employees.

As the Group expanded it became clear that the youth and poor education of some new employees was cause for concern. Consequently, they accomplished less when faced with parents, colleagues and even guests. Some lacked the sense of cooperation, care and responsibility that influenced the building of internal harmony in the company. Poor quality service potentially led to unnecessary complaints and damage to BHG's reputation.

Internal communication and culture building had started with the Secretary of the Party Committee of BHG (Blue Horizon Group) launching a hotline in March 2003, giving her contact information so employees could send problems or suggestions to her via texts or phone calls. In 2005 the Corporate Culture department was founded, reporting directly to the Secretary of the Party Committee of BHG and the CEO to ensure communication was 'short, true and fast'.

In 2008 the department started working on behaviour change and a year later, following consultation at all levels of BHG on a proposal from the Secretary of the Party Committee of BHG, the 'Drop of Water Group' was launched. The aim was to improve employee behaviour through education, help them to think positively and cultivate their merits through activities.

The only condition for joining the 'Drop of Water Group' was to help a guest or even a passer-by, no matter what your position, age or gender.

The Corporate Culture department drafted an overall plan and led the project. Branches participated, verified and reported cases to the department once a month.

In less than six months the Corporate Culture department received more than 1,000 typical examples, including offering seats to others on buses, helping to push a van and returning a large sum of money left by mistake. This initiative has clearly inspired employees. It is going from strength to strength thanks to the videos of the best cases shown on the BHG TV programme *BHG Monthly* (*Lan Hai Yue Bo Bao* in Chinese) and reports in BHG newspaper *BHG View* (*Lan Hai Feng* in Chinese). 'Drop of Water Group' mugs and pins are awarded to outstanding employees and branches now compete against each other to be chosen.

And the return on investment? Better behaviour means doing a better job, like the employee who was always late for work but changed his ways and as a result won 'Drop of Water Group' recognition.

'These benefits are priceless,' says the Corporate Culture department's Ms An Ying, 'members of the "Drop of Water Group" are promoting the popularity and reputation of BHG, which cannot be bought by money.'

5. Supporting major change

Change is the subject of a whole chapter later in this book so we will keep our comments here brief.

It should be enough to say that any transformation would be impossible if people were ignorant about the planned changes, simply didn't understand them, were uninterested, puzzled about what they were supposed to do or couldn't see the progress of the change.

As communicators, our interest is broadly in ensuring that people who are facing change in the workplace:

- are aware that it is coming;
- understand the rationale, what it involves and how it will affect them;
- are excited or at least not hostile to the change;
- feel able to do the things that are asked of them;
- have a sense of how things are developing and perhaps can see the change working.

There are possibly a number of other reasons for great internal communication, but we think we have drawn these five general categories loosely enough to cover most situations and provide a framework for thinking about the purpose of your communication function. As a starting point, we need to step away from thinking our job exists just to 'send out stuff' and ask the question: 'What shapes the success of my organization and what can I do to help?'

A clear answer to that question should then shape every other choice a communicator makes. When you know how you add value it becomes easier to decide what media to use, how to craft your messages and what campaigns you need to run. What you need to evaluate becomes more straightforward.

Best of all, a communicator who knows how they add value and shares that view with their masters will have a happier life!

Ethics

If you think of yourself as a professional you will probably subscribe to some notion of ethics, maybe one defined by your professional body.

The UK's Chartered Institute of Public Relations (CIPR) makes it a condition of membership that practitioners agree to uphold a code, which is set out in Appendix 1. Simply put, the code requires communication professionals to:

- act with integrity, discretion and propriety;
- operate fairly and honestly;
- protect the reputation of their profession;
- be up to the job – ie keep up to date and commit to continuing development.

For internal communicators these are very relevant standards simply because our job would be impossible if we could not be trusted to respect confidences, give advice impartially or tell the truth. Having the clarity of a professional code is useful because most internal communicators have had the experience of being asked to be dishonest to the workforce at some stage of their career. If you haven't been asked to 'spin' a story at some stage you probably haven't been doing the job for very long!

It would be tempting for organizations to manipulate their employees with the connivance of the IC department. We have access to slick tools and techniques designed to persuade and convince. However, our role extends to ensuring that our skills are not used to deceive or mislead.

If we lived in a world where everything was black and white, being ethical would be equally straightforward. But life isn't like that. Organizations and their leaders have to navigate through multiple shades of grey: a challenge that isn't helped when leaders become remote from their employees or simply stop seeing things in the same way as the rest of the world. A communicator can be very quickly sucked into blurring the story about why the CEO has been asked to spend more time with their family or why 1,000 people need to lose their jobs despite the company declaring record profits.

Even if there is not a cavalier attitude to the truth, organizations often mislead their staff unintentionally. Messages can go through several stages of editing and approval before they are finally transmitted, a process that can allow serious mistakes or misleading statements to creep in. The communication manager is often the last person to see something before it goes live and so has the responsibility to check and challenge if something isn't right.

Standing by a set of professional values is also important because of the impact of the work we do. Colleagues make life-changing decisions based on what they are told at work. People rely on workplace communication when they make choices about where to live, what schools to send their children to, how to save for retirement or whether or not to change jobs. The integrity of what we tell them matters.

Sadly, the law is rarely a sufficient guide to what is right or wrong, especially when it comes to employment relations. The fact is that we all need to have a clear idea of the line we will not cross. Identifying that line and our responsibilities is always better done before it is tested.

A professional set of ethics defined by a professional body is a useful starting point when deciding your own standards and seeing how your values apply in your job.

The CIPR code has relatively few absolute rules and is open to some interpretation. Its core assumption is that we need to be consistent in applying our values and understand that expectations of behaviour are also dependent on culture and social norms. However, these are only baselines – we have to have a personal understanding of how they apply to us and how we meet our responsibilities.

In our experience, internal communicators are most commonly tested in relatively few ways. For example, it is wise to have a view about the boundary between honesty and candour. There may be times – such as when managing a crisis – when telling everything you know could accelerate the collapse of a company with attendant job losses, or during a health panic when it is in everyone's interest not to add to general concern.

Finally, a communicator should be up to the job they have signed up to do. If you are reading this book you have probably got some form of commitment to learning and development. The recent past has shown how quickly the tools of our profession can change – we view staying up to date as a question of professional standards.

The key learning points from this chapter

Internal communication has come of age. It's no longer simply a case of producing 'stuff' like newsletters and videos, or an intranet. It's now about outcomes, ie the result of what you produced, not just what you produced. It's about:

- listening and engaging rather than telling;
- supporting senior managers to deliver the appropriate messages, to the appropriate employee audiences, in the appropriate ways, that will influence employee behaviour in ways that propel the business forward;
- committing to continuous professional development;
- following the law, retaining good people, helping people work harder and better, enabling people to say the right things about you and supporting major change;
- being ethical personally;
- having the influencing skills to persuade management to behave ethically.

Above all, becoming a professional internal communicator is about being a strategic adviser capable of taking a place in the boardroom.

Notes and references

1 Bland, M (1980) *Employee Communication in the 1980s: A personnel manager's guide*, Kogan Page, London. This book offers an insight into how relationships with staff decades ago were still largely formal and often managed through trade unions.
2 Murray, K (2012) *The Language of Leaders*, Kogan Page, London. This book reports the views of over 50 very senior leaders and reflects their firm belief that employee communication is an essential core skill at the top.
3 Murray, K (2012) *The Language of Leaders*, Kogan Page, London
4 D'Aprix, R (1982) The oldest (and best) way to communicate with employees, *Harvard Business Review*, Sept–Oct, pp 30–32. Roger D'Aprix remains one of the most influential commentators in our field and many of his ideas have passed into standard thinking.

5 MacLeod, D and Clarke, N (2009) *Engaging for Success: Enhancing performance through employee engagement* – a report to Government, Department for Business, Innovation and Skills, London

6 Anything by Kathryn Yates is worth reading including Yates, K (2008) Becoming an ROI builder: delivering effective employee communication, *Employee Relations Today*, **35**, pp 19–23.

7 Clampitt, P G and Downs, C W (1993) Employee perceptions of the relationship between communication and productivity: a field study, *Journal of Business Communication*, **30** (1), pp 5–28, cited in Hargie, Owen, Dickson, David, Tourish and Dennis (2004) *Communication Skills for Effective Management*, Palgrave Macmillan, London.

8 Management writer Henry Mintzberg has long talked about communication as the essence of a manager's job. Mintzberg, H (1971) Managerial work: analysis from observation, *Management Science*, **18** (2), B-97.

9 Clampitt, P G (2009) *Communicating for Managerial Effectiveness: Problems/strategies/solutions*, Sage Publications, London. An excellent introduction to the subject for the practitioner.

10 Quirke, B (2002) *Making the Connections*, Gower, Aldershot

11 Kalla, H A (2005) Integrated internal communications: a multidisciplinary perspective, *Corporate Communications*, **10** (4)

12 Tench, R and Yeomans, L (2006) *Exploring Public Relations*, Pearson, Harlow (quoting Strauss and Hoffman)

13 Smythe, J, Dorward, C and Reback, J (1992) *Corporate Reputation: Managing the new strategic asset*, Century Business, London

14 Quirke, B (1996) *Communicating Corporate Change: A practical guide to communication and corporate strategy*, McGraw-Hill, Berkshire

15 See also FitzPatrick in Theaker, A (2011) *The Public Relations Handbook*, Routledge, London

02
Organizing internal communication

What you will learn from this chapter

Whenever internal communicators get together, sooner or later the issue of how to organize the team comes up. Should we be part of HR? Should we have a direct reporting line to the CEO? How can we be expected to be both a news service and strategic advisers?

The reality is that every staff function from finance to HR, from legal to strategy, has similar questions and the answer to all of these questions is: 'It depends...'

This chapter looks at the factors that help you decide how your internal communication team should be organized. We examine the reasons why IC might report to one function or another. We look at the main business issues that define the shape of your team.

We also look at three classical roles that a communication function should contain and help you think about how you should resource your team. Given that most internal communication teams are small operations we take a look at the advantages (and the disadvantages) of using external support.

At the heart of what we describe is our constant refrain that great communications are about making a difference to the underlying direction of the organization they support. This is no less true when it comes to issues of organization. Our starting question is always: 'What value does the organization need from internal communication?' From the answer to that question, all decisions about the shape and focus of the communication team follow.

A little history

Once upon a time, employee communication was an activity that was probably managed either by the managing director's secretary or, in large organizations, by the editor of the staff newspaper. In either case, few people got very worked up about IC – it was often seen as little more than a welfare function, designed to make sure that staff felt appreciated.

Much of the real conversation that went on in the workplace was often managed by trade unions. Indeed, in many workplaces, attempts by management to directly address the workforce were viewed with suspicion and were likely to be confined to uncontentious issues.

During the 1980s, management thinking underwent a quiet revolution. Personnel departments transformed into Human Resources, a change that was greater than an act of self-aggrandizing marketing. It reflected an awakening that if labour was a valuable asset it should be properly nurtured and managed. And, for better or worse, that meant actually talking to the workforce.[1]

With time came the realization that good managers were also good communicators and that employees had a significant impact on the external reputation of an organization. In a matter of a few decades employee communication has gone from a subject that interested no one much to an issue that looms large in everyone's thinking. Once, internal communication was a lonely wallflower at the dance. Now it has bloomed into a function with many suitors.

Now, few business functions are at the centre of so many turf wars as internal communication. HR people think that they should own it because it is so close to the central mission of people management. PR people think they own it because it should align with external messaging. The marketing team just want staff to know what they are meant to say to customers.

The big answer

Behind all these turf wars is a question. What is the natural home for internal communication in an organization?

Sadly the answer isn't very simple.

The answer is that it depends on a number of factors. The main issue is understanding what the purpose of internal communication in your organization is.

In the previous chapter we talked about the strategic roles of internal communication. We said that it boiled down to:

- meeting legal obligations;
- holding onto good people (by making them feel part of something worthwhile);
- helping people work harder and better;
- helping people to say the right things about you;
- supporting major change.

If the role of internal communication is to build external advocates then it would make sense that the team is based alongside their colleagues working on external reputation. If the job is all about building an employer brand of which people feel proud enough to stay, then maybe the IC function should be closely aligned with HR.

In short, there is no natural home for employee communication. It belongs where it can fulfil its mission. However, wherever the function sits, IC should be able to work across organizational boundaries. An IC manager who deals only with colleagues in one department or is seen as a representative of a particular community in the organization is likely to have a tough time doing their job. A team that thinks only in marketing terms is bound, sooner or later, to be pulled into line by HR. A team that thinks it is only interested in people management issues will wake up to find that IT have created their own communication function behind their backs!

The other issue is that some commentators suggest splitting up the tasks of the internal communication department. For example, some people might think that HR has the job of deciding what has to be said and when, and then it falls to the communication team to decide how to deliver the message.[2] Such an approach is unlikely to deliver a coherent communication strategy in our experience and will do little to develop the capabilities of the communication team.

When should IC sit within HR?

HR is one of the main homes for employee communication. This is for a large number of reasons, not all of them particularly strategic. Sometimes it is the HR director who has the vision to see the possibility of IC, or it might be that the first IC manager was originally an HR professional, or the IC function might have developed from a specific HR project back in the distant past.

There are strengths and questions associated with the IC function within HR and these are summarized in Table 2.1.

TABLE 2.1   Why sitting in HR is a good idea

Why sitting in HR is a good idea	Questions
• Can be close to wider people management strategy and thinking. • HR leaders commonly see their mission as being an agent of transformation and as a voice of employee concerns – key interests of an internal communication manager. • HR always have a natural interest in the tough issues like reorganization or job losses. • HR has a mission to build the capabilities of leaders – which has to include sharing IC's agenda of building communication skills. • HR people may be expected to naturally see the benefit of good communication. • HR is often responsible for issues like engagement and behaviour change. • HR should have a natural understanding of the audiences and own data about demographics. • HR will naturally own the legal responsibilities for employee consultation or supporting Works Councils.	• Within HR, would IC be a subordinate function – confined to tactical execution of strategy decided by others and would that matter? • Do senior managers in HR need to understand how to manage IC and creative approaches? • Can HR business partners take a brief from their internal clients that asks the right questions needed to shape a good IC plan? • Does HR have a particular reputation in your organization – a reputation that affects the credibility of your messages or the willingness of employees to be candid in their feedback? • Does HR's agenda for developing leaders have space for communication training? • Will HR people naturally understand external reputational issues where IC has an impact? • Is HR taken seriously at the top of your organization? Who wants to be the sidekick to the laughing stock?

We would argue that HR is a good home for the IC function when:

- employee engagement is a central concern for the organization;
- HR is closely aligned with the day-to-day workings of the organization – rather than being a centralized department;
- building managers' skills is central to the mission of HR;
- senior HR managers are open to feedback from the organization and do not see communication as a one-way process.

In order for IC to work effectively as a part of the HR department, communication practitioners need to ensure that the value they offer is fully understood by their peers in the HR team. People who have made a success of working with HR colleagues highlight the importance of understanding respective areas of expertise, proactively offering solutions and having strong independent feedback mechanisms. In particular, IC professionals need to be ready to suggest how to improve results and to highlight how messages are landing, in other words, demonstrating their value beyond simply producing and distributing messages.

Should IC sit in external communications or marketing?

When IC is not owned directly by HR it is most commonly found in the external communications or marketing department. This makes a lot of sense when the organization is facing significant stakeholder issues and especially in the age of social media when the organization needs to speak with a consistent voice. Messages relayed internally have to match what is said outside.

Many organizations realize that their employees are their most potent channel of communication with the outside world. Imagine how a retailer would cope if their staff routinely badmouthed their employer and think how powerful a message it sends when workers go out of their way to defend or promote the organizations for which they work. The employee advocate is a valuable asset in all sorts of situations ranging from crises to consumer campaigns. The steady proliferation of social media makes this increasingly important.

TABLE 2.2   Why sitting in marketing or external communications is a good idea

Why sitting in marketing or external comms is a good idea	Questions
• When there is a strong need to align internal and external messages. • When it makes sense, perhaps across digital channels, for there to be collaboration in skills and content. • When communications can benefit from a highly creative input. • When it is efficient to manage creative services, such as writing or design, in one place. • When the skills of managing external creative and project management agencies are needed.	• Do external communication people see communications as a matter of 'spin' or message control? • How important is an integrated reputation to your organization – media, financial audiences, employees and political stakeholders – getting a consistent story? • How central to the success of the organization is the brand? In a consumer organization it is likely to be integral, perhaps less so in a public sector body.

Regular surveys from people like the publisher Melcrum or the UK's Chartered Institute of Personnel and Development (CIPD) suggest that the trend for HR or some other function to own IC is waxing and waning. From our own experience as practitioners, we have come across substantial communication teams sitting within IT, strategy, health and safety and facilities. Organizing around such functions is often the result of history or a response to a specific short-term need.

It is always worthwhile looking at your own organization and trying to understand the business logic for where the communication function is housed. You may find that understanding the history of the decision gives you a powerful insight into the psyche of your employer.

It might also be logical to have dual reporting lines or a foot in more than one camp. Perhaps there is sense in reporting to the director of communications while also being a member of the HR leadership team?

Stop worrying about control – get realistic

When you are thinking about the way you organize communication it is easy to fall into the trap of believing that there is a natural need to control or shape all communication. Anyone who thinks about this for five minutes will realize very quickly that this is either an impossible task or a quick route to insanity!

The fact is that internal communication happens regardless of where the central team is based. Some writers argue that communication is the core life force in organizations and that an organization is actually defined by the act of communication that humans do – it defies control or ownership. This doesn't just apply to the day-to-day interactions of colleagues but also to the urge to communicate that arises in every functional silo.

As we said above, we've seen organizations with dedicated communication teams supporting operations, IT or health and safety. In organizations of all sizes, we frequently have conversations with senior communication managers who freely admit that they have no idea how many people in their workplace have communication management as a significant part of their responsibilities. And that is not because they are stupid! How can you know how many people have the job of managing communication in the far-flung reaches of your organization?

As an increasing number of leaders see the value of having resources dedicated to running communications, the ability to control the conversation from a central place becomes harder and harder. Internal communication, unlike other staff functions, rarely has significant power or authority. A corporate counsel will normally have the defined role of handling legal issues and the finance department will have the job of creating a single set of accounts or providing advice on financial matters. Good communication should be the concern of everyone in a leadership role and therefore it is potentially futile to believe that a single team can control or manage what is said internally.[3]

In planning how to manage central communication operations there are a few questions that will help you decide the best or ideal balance between a central and a local focus.

- Is it useful and possible to define a core message or narrative that runs through the whole business? If the organization is too diverse, perhaps there is little need for a big central team. If we can see a common thread that needs to run across all communications, have we been clear about how local communications should reflect this?

- Can we be clear about the competencies of people working in communication around the organization? Do we have a defined operating model where the organization's communication professionals can see their role clearly? If we can drive the types of people doing the job or provide training, will a common mindset ensure both quality and a consistent narrative for people who work here?

- Do we need a capability to run central campaigns perhaps supporting Corporate Social Responsibility or IT? Or can we rely on these functions to develop their own suitable approaches?

- Do we need a single hand overseeing central channels such as the intranet or do local teams need a tailored approach?

Whatever the pressure to decentralize, a communication manager should bear in mind the considerable benefits of having resources consolidated in a single place. There can be sound economic reasons for having a team in one place, but perhaps more important is the ability to foster a common professional ethos. Also, dispersed teams can struggle to offer development opportunities to people in the way that larger central teams might find possible.

Solo practitioners trade freedom from central control for a limited local support network. Working alone in a business means being the sole standard bearer for good practice and potentially being cut off from the inspiration and expertise of colleagues with different experiences in the field of communication. On the other hand, central teams have to work hard to prove their value to the departments or dispersed clients who they serve. There is a constant battle to reassure people around the company that a team based at company headquarters has their best interests at heart.

The approach that central teams tend to take in such situations is to ensure that local communicators are competent rather than directly controlled, often achieving this by defining person specifications, training and ways of working.

The communicating organization

In recent years we have begun to understand more clearly that communication adds value to organizations when it has a number of components. This has been the subject of work by Roger D'Aprix, Bill Quirke and others.

However, some of the biggest strides have been made by Kathryn Yates,[4] who developed a model that suggests that profitability in commercial organizations can be linked to having the right combination of communication activities. She bases her work on a large-scale analysis of profitability levels in different businesses and by looking to see what types of communications or HR practices they have in place.

While there is room for debate about the relative importance of each type of communication activity, she makes the significant point that the basics of communication, such as having working channels or a skilled team, are actually only opening contributors to the success of the organization. The big prizes come when the communication team can influence managers and senior leaders to listen to feedback and communicate personally.

FIGURE 2.1   Where does communication add value?

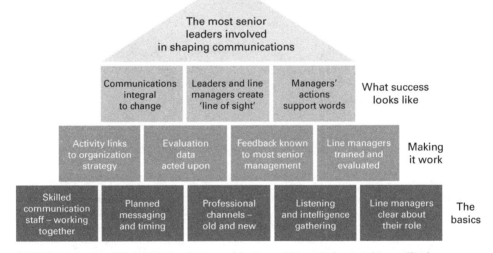

SOURCE: Dewhurst and FitzPatrick, drawing on work by Towers Watson, Melcrum and Roger D'Aprix

This is partly reflected in the model in Figure 2.1 developed by Sue Dewhurst and Liam FitzPatrick as part of their work on the Black Belt training program with Melcrum, which draws on ideas from a number of practitioners, especially Kathryn Yates of Towers Watson.

The argument here is that an effective communication team needs to do much more than deliver great plans, manage excellent tools, gather intelligence and work with line managers. The added benefits start to be realized when communications reflects the organizational strategy, when senior leaders have feedback they can act on and when line managers are supported and measured for their communications.

The greatest value is delivered when communication is recognized as a key element of change, when leaders help employees see the vision and their personal contribution (what is often called 'line of sight') and when messages are consistent with the actions of the organization.

In effect, a communication function makes a difference when it can deliver excellent plans and tools, when it can partner with the business to explain strategy and help managers listen and communicate and when it can deliver strategic advice around change, setting a vision and challenging when words are not consistent with the actions of the organization. We call these three areas the internal communication 'Value Spaces'.

Understanding your Value Spaces

There are essentially three core areas, or Value Spaces, where a communication team brings benefit to their organization:

- delivery excellence;
- business partnering;
- strategic advice.

Delivery excellence

At the most basic level, a communication team needs to be a reliable creator of content and tools. No matter how strategic we aspire to be, if we cannot get material on the intranet, make the leadership conference fly or set up a CEO webex we will quickly find ourselves replaced!

FIGURE 2.2   Matching tasks to value

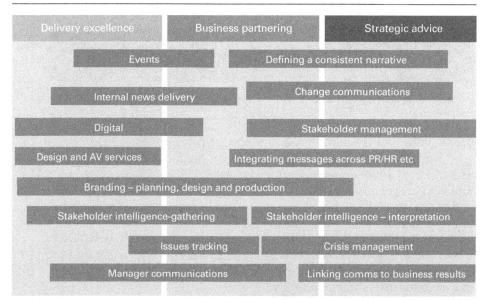

At some point or another, a communication function will be asked to operate as a production facility. Being the reliable point where colleagues can get material or collateral produced is an often-neglected or undervalued capability and it is our experience that teams that are weak on delivery will struggle to be heard when they want to talk about wider issues or bring a more strategic focus to bear.

Teams that are managed around the production house model will typically invest in craft skills such as writing, design, digital and project management and will sometimes need processes and practices that are very similar to those used in design agencies. These might include well-developed procedures for taking briefs from internal customers, rules about formal approvals and budgeting.

Commonly, such teams will also have clear responsibility for a number of core channels such as the intranet, a newsletter or a cascade brief. This responsibility brings a need for strong planning and forward news management, a role that also assumes a responsibility for intelligence and data gathering.

Bear in mind that it is in delivery excellence teams that you will often encounter the most experienced and seasoned professionals. This role is about more than junior production tasks and provides a home for many people who enjoy developing a specialist skill such as writing or want space to explore their creativity or new tools.

Business partnering

Increasingly, internal communicators are adapting the business partnering model first developed in HR functions – working with individual leaders or teams across the business to address specific problems.

Much like account directors in agencies, a business partner is the point of entry for a business manager and will draw upon the expertise from delivery excellence colleagues when crafting and delivering compelling solutions.

For example, this might involve working with an IT director to understand his or her business challenges and suggesting communication solutions. Perhaps communication can help make an IT network more secure by explaining password rules better or maybe helping to improve satisfaction ratings for the helpdesk by setting clearer expectations among users.

In these roles the IC team needs to be adept at understanding the detailed strategic and operational needs of the parts of the organization they are supporting. At their most effective, a communicator is proactive at suggesting strategies and plans designed to support specific business challenges or targets. To fulfil this role, the communicator will be closely involved in the planning and the management of the department which they are supporting.

Underlying this is the need to apply a consistent narrative about the wider organization. Is there a simple, understandable idea that unifies all communications regardless of the immediate preoccupations of local leaders? Can you bring a golden thread to the story that employees hear that introduces the overall strategy message into news about change or operational information for example?

A business partner has the dual role of helping local leaders achieve their objectives and of ensuring that the underlying focus of the organization is not lost in the day-to-day noise.

Strategic advice

The role of strategic adviser is principally about helping leaders deliver their vision. This calls on not just communication expertise but also insight into what else drives the success of the organization. With deep awareness of what really matters to the most senior leaders in your department or organization you can step beyond the simple role of being the person who produces communications plans and tools.

Working at this level means that you need to bring some core capabilities. Having data-based knowledge of how stakeholders are thinking and reacting, providing predictive analysis and scenarios, being a persuasive advocate for ideas and being clear about your impact on overall business results are all vital. It is essential that the function can be relied upon to deliver the basics. As we explain in Chapter 8 on senior leader communication, the ability to provide collateral to a high standard is the ticket that gets you into the conversation with senior leaders. If you fail to keep providing high-quality tools, leaders will start to look elsewhere.

Taking the example of the communication manager supporting an IT function, they will need to deliver things like the intranet or the higher manager conference excellently. They will need to be able to apply consistent messages as they help the Chief Information Officer (CIO) use communications to achieve his or her objectives. They will need to develop a trusted relationship based on an understanding of the business so they can proactively suggest activities that no one else thought of. The team needs to build on excellent delivery but think like a member of the senior leadership team.

Although few people's roles are entirely clear cut – even the most strategic adviser has to deliver things – we find these general headings to be a useful guide when thinking about the type of work a team needs to do and the resources required in order to deliver for the organization. We all have to fulfil some or all of these roles from time to time. We need to understand what each role requires us to prioritize at any given moment.

How do you decide what you need?

In our experience there are a few simple steps you need to consider when planning your function:

- understand the business;
- identify communication needs and core purpose;
- what needs to be done centrally and what can happen locally;

- establish core processes and channels;
- define the competencies you need;
- agree your metrics;
- match it to resources.

You will see that resources comes at the end of our list and you will see from Figure 2.3 that our approach is circular. This is because it is always better to start by defining what you need and then adapting to what is possible given your budget rather than the other way around. This approach gives you a vision to aim for. We'll discuss this in more detail below but you should not think of this as a linear or fixed chain of decisions. When you are doing your thinking you will go backwards and forwards and revisit different elements as your thoughts evolve.

FIGURE 2.3 What do you need?

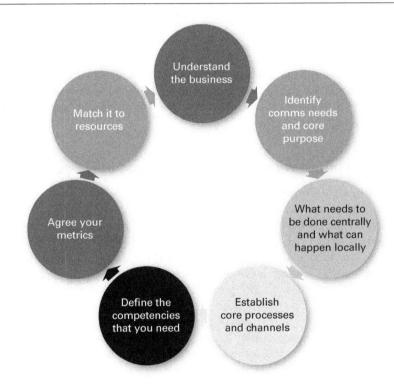

Understand the business

By now you should have got the message that everything begins with the business or the organization and what it will take for it to succeed. While it is tempting to jump straight into designing communication tools and processes you will always find them hard to develop if your thinking is not grounded in the central purpose of the organization, its strategy and its challenges.

In Chapter 1 we have talked about this issue but would add that when you start asking about the strategic issues be prepared for some raised eyebrows. Many managers would not think of communicators as people who are interested in the fundamental workings of the organization but you are about to change that!

If you are struggling to engage a stakeholder in a conversation beyond communications, a useful technique is to ask them to help you draw up two lists: communication activities that are important and unimportant and communication activities that are delivered well or delivered poorly. Asking, as you compile the first list together, why they think some things matter more than others should get you some useful insights but then cross-reference the two lists and see what you find. You should be able to see areas where you are underperforming on things that matter (or over-delivering on things of less value).

How businesses think changes from sector to sector and the unique combination of circumstances that your organization finds itself in will give you a set of challenges and opportunities that are special to you. You need to avoid a generic approach that assumes that all public bodies are the same and that if you have worked in one bank you can transplant your learning without any adaptation.

Identify communication needs and core purpose

Understanding the business and its challenges should help you identify where communication can make a difference. You should therefore begin the task of defining the purpose and focus of your communications.

Having a clear sense of your priorities in this area will influence the shape of your communication organization from the word go. If you are only concerned with meeting legal obligations you won't need many people (or probably anyone with any personality or soul!). Where retention and community matter, a communication function will need close links with HR, possibly building a strength in event management and creating a social intranet and strong capabilities for showing leaders when their words are out of alignment with their actions. Where promoting more and better work is the challenge, you would expect to have a developed business partner network. An advocacy-focused team would work closely with external relations and a change-supporting communication team would need very specific skillsets as well.

These are not prescriptions of how to set up every communication function but illustrations to make the point that a clarity of your contribution to organizational success should be shaping how you organize.

What needs to be done centrally and what can happen locally?

A very simple question needs to be addressed quite quickly in this process. Should we have a central team or do we need people spread around the organization?

Clearly this is most relevant in a large organization or somewhere that has diverse operations or multiple locations. We have discussed some of the issues above and won't repeat ourselves now. It is enough to say that as part of your thinking you should consider how you ensure a consistent story when you have a dispersed communication operation. Your options are normally associated with clarity of the message, control or core channels and influence over the recruitment and development of practitioners.

Establish core processes and channels

Earlier we talked about the split between delivery excellence, business partnering and giving strategic advice. We would argue that all communication teams need to operate in each of these spaces, but thinking through the needs of your organization and its mission and the overall focus of your team will help you understand where to prioritize your effort – at least in the initial stages.

However, every communications team needs a certain number of core processes and tools regardless of the prioritization of your work. These are:

- **Planning and governance.** Every communication team needs to be clear about the processes by which they create an annual plan and the more specific plans underpinning it. This is largely the subject of Chapter 3. You also need to be clear about your processes for getting stakeholders engaged in your planning processes. At its most crude this is about having clear procedures for getting materials signed off but at the more rewarding end of the scale it is a strategy for involving leaders in conversations about their business needs. You might want a regular meeting with a particular internal customer or a more informal way of staying connected with a key senior influencer.

- **Messaging, identity and brand.** At the core of any strong communication function there is a strong message set that endures and talks to the core purpose of the organization rather than the day-to-day pressures of the latest clever initiative or fad. We are the guardians of the internally-facing portion of the brand and we need to be able to fulfil this role. This calls for a process for being tied into the overall brand management procedure. This could be a formal relationship with the brand or identity stewards in your workplace or a more simple discussion about how the identity and brand guidelines are applied.

Perhaps more significantly, we need a discipline for ensuring that our communications delivers a consistent story across the organization, regardless of location, function or grade. This will involve a common approach to when and how messages are to be defined. In Chapter 5 we discuss this in more detail but the point is that having control over the story you tell changes you from a noise-maker to a communicator.

- **Channel development and management.** We will not spend a lot of time here covering ground that is explored in more detail in Chapter 6 but rather will make a couple of points.

  You will need a standard set of channels to allow you to function. You need to be able to send out news and information: people need somewhere they can come back to for reference, there needs to be a space for discussion and engagement somewhere in the organization as well as a place that promotes a sense of community. There may be dozens of channels or just a small number but you need to cover the bases somehow.

  Importantly, and allied to your planning, you will need a mechanism for planning what will appear in which channel at what time. Bill Quirke coined the phrase 'Air Traffic Control' to describe this communications process of identifying what needs to be said and when and it sums up the issue very well.

  This mechanism need not be very sophisticated and may be a simple discipline to keep track of what is coming, what is missing and what could cause a mid-air collision. Without some structure and organization around your pipeline of activities, you could have long spells where nothing appears on the intranet and you miss publication dates. Your audience will assume communication is an ad-hoc activity and your stakeholders won't automatically associate your name with reliability or delivery!

- **Line manager approaches.** Closely allied to the channel regime you need a way of managing your line manager needs. We said above that at every step of the IC value chain, line managers are a crucial factor and that is why we have devoted Chapter 7 to the subject.

Below we set out five challenges that every communication team needs to consider and, referring back to the pyramid of IC value that we looked at in Figure 2.1, you will see the logic of making sure you have mechanisms for:

- showing managers that it is their job;
- treating them as a special audience needing additional care and information;
- training and developing their skills;
- supplying tools to help them;
- showing that someone is interested in their feedback.

Senior leader support

In Chapter 8 we explore this issue in greater depth, but communication teams need a way to ensure that senior leaders are given the service, support and guidance that they need.

It might take time to build a relationship of trust from the beginning but the communication team should know what activities the most senior leaders would like to do and be on hand to make sure those activities go brilliantly.

Change advisory

All communication teams get involved with change to a greater or lesser extent, so should be ready to advise on good practice and have processes in place to ensure the best outcomes when a change or a transformation process arrives demanding your undivided attention! This is the subject of Chapter 9 so we will not explore it in more detail here.

The main impact though will be to prepare your team to move at speed, be excited working with uncertain plans that change without reason and be able to experiment with new tools and techniques. All of these will call on your ability to maintain great relationships across the organization and have control of the intelligence tools.

Although supporting major change might not immediately seem to be one of the core purposes in your communication team, it is unavoidable at some stage or another. If your other disciplines and habits are robust – strong planning capabilities, channels that work, knowing the organization backwards and working with senior leaders – your change experience will be heroic and rewarding. Without tools, intelligence, friends and organization it will be nasty, brutish and short.

Intelligence gathering, analysis and reporting

A communication team that doesn't know what is going on is of little use to anyone. If you do not invest regular and frequent time in gathering data and feedback and have a deep understanding of your audience it will take a miracle for you to be effective!

We discuss this more in Chapter 10 but at the very least you need a process for:

- reporting what the mood of the organization is monthly or quarterly to senior leaders and what plans you have in place for communications in the coming weeks;
- gathering feedback quickly and informally on an ad-hoc basis;
- managing your own formalized data collection such as quick polls on intranet stories or online surveys;
- analysing the feedback and data to generate insights that guide your communications decisions and the advice you give leaders;
- an informal way of regularly walking the floor so you can remain close to the grassroots, which is, after all, one of the main benefits for a CEO of hiring people like you!

Resource management

If you hope to be given decent budgets and resources you had better know from day one how you are going to manage it. We are not really concerned about making sure that invoices match purchase orders or that the team are not fiddling their expenses – the finance department will have whole teams devoted to that sort of joy-filled worrying. Rather, you need to understand what it is you have to do to get your resources approved, how you protect them in the annual round of teeth-sucking and headshaking that the CFO loves to run and how you get the best value from the money and people that you have.

We are not planning on going into detail in this book but will make a couple of points.

You will need a process for defining the value that any resource should be adding. This isn't about looking for hard numerical data on return on investment, but about knowing that if your colleagues expect you to help them get results they are going to have to pay for it! This begins with being able to agree the outcome value they want to achieve rather than starting the conversation with how cheaply they can buy a video for. No one wants to waste money but moving the conversation to investment rather than cost helps shape thinking in a more strategic way.

There are few really reliable benchmarks for team size in internal communication. The numbers employed seem to vary by industry profitability (for example, pharmaceutical companies have more communication staff in general than retailers), complexity (if you are a diverse business producing in multiple countries you will have a bigger team than a single service based in one place) and decentralization (companies that allow managers a greater degree of autonomy tend to have more staff in communication – although this is often wasteful).

Finally, in Europe at least, there is a thriving market for freelance and interim staff who are happy to be employed for short periods of time. This means that factoring in skilled temporary staff can make a world of difference but beware the cost of inducting them into the organization, investing in their internal networking and the damage done when they take their knowledge and experience with them at the end of their contract.

Working with suppliers

The world of internal and change communication is well supplied with contractors and consultants who will help you with almost every problem. However, the market is not always very well delineated so it is easy to make the mistake of being sold a strategy by a videomaker or wondering why that poster design you bought off the HR strategy adviser was so expensive!

You therefore need to understand what you can get from where.

In-house and consultancy

In-house people have a massive advantage when it comes to running internal communication in that they should know their audiences and processes better than anyone else. A consultant coming in to work on a project has to learn the core business of the organization, understand the people who work there and build an internal network normally under considerable time pressure.

When you retain a consultant, you therefore need to be very clear where you hope that they will add value.

If you just want a body to work at your direction, you should consider hiring an interim contractor (see below): they will cost less in general and if you are giving all the instructions you don't need to pay for plans and insights you already have.

Where a consultant can make a real difference is in three main areas: expertise, energy and challenge.

You may have a project or situation arise that is just outside your area of expertise. Perhaps there is a change project that needs someone who knows how to facilitate relationships with a programme management office. Maybe the change needs someone who understands that the first third of your energy will be devoted to aligning senior stakeholders or has previously developed complex messaging around a reorganization. Often consultants are asked to share their experience of other organizations and good practice.

The need for energy is also a popular reason for bringing in a consultancy to support a specific initiative. Perhaps the existing team is worn out or has too much invested in old ways of working. Or maybe you need a team of people to get things moving, train up the existing team and step away again.

Many communication managers use a consultant as someone who will challenge them or other senior managers. Having an outside view is either refreshing for the communicator or a way of getting a senior leader to hear advice that is being ignored because it comes from a familiar source.

The trick is to be very clear at the start of the assignment where you would like an external supplier to bring you an advantage. The phrase that is used is 'added value': ask what the benefit of bringing in an outsider is. Naturally, great consultants end up adding more than you originally imagined, but brilliant relationships begin with clarity of both parties about where things are meant to lead.

Get the right supplier

There is a large number of great suppliers who specialize in internal communication, be that design, video, events or web. Because they have experience of working inside organizations they understand the challenges of things like story generation, stakeholder management or the fun to be had selling a new idea to an IT department.

In our experience it is wise to be wary of suppliers who think that they can impose a solution that they have worked on in the outside world on an internal environment. It can be painful, stressful and often expensive. A supplier who understands you and what it means to work in internal communication is worth their weight in gold and is worth hanging on to.

Outsourcing

An increasing trend for organizations is to outsource large-scale activities such as event management, design services and running the intranet. This is very similar to what we have seen happen in areas like HR, with the outsourcing of payroll management, or in finance where invoicing is commonly handled by a third party.

So far, the drive in internal communication has been limited by the volumes of work to be contracted out but it does have considerable advantages. Importantly, cost does not seem to be a prime motivator in many outsourcing projects: the drive for improved services and availability can be front of mind.

Getting the best from a consultancy

If you ever want to get a conversation going among internal communication managers, ask them what they love or hate about consultants! You will quickly get a list of names but you'll find that one client's nightmare was another's salvation. How come some clients get more out of their consultants and contractors than others do?

There are a few golden rules to remember on both sides which should help oil the wheels.

- **It's a win-win game.** Clients and consultants only look good when they both look good. If you have taken the client on or hired the consultant you have made an investment. The consultant needs a delighted client so that the bills get paid and the next contract comes along. The client wants his or her boss to applaud their wisdom for bringing in such smart, hard-working people.

- **If you're paying the bill make it easy for them to do the job.** When you engage make sure the admin is right at the start. Building passes, IT access, meetings set up: if these are all arranged at the start of the assignment valuable time isn't lost. Also understand why some team members won't collaborate with the people you have hired to help.

- **Everyone needs to be clear at the beginning.** A consultant should ask you to agree a list of tasks and deliverables before they start work. That's your signal to check the price and your obligations for enabling them to keep their part of the bargain. Time spent discussing this is rarely wasted. As well as contractual matters you should cover your unspoken needs (such as getting the CEO to look good) and issues like confidentiality and security.

- **Use someone who knows.** You wouldn't normally ask your gardener to rewire your house but you will find plenty of suppliers who would claim that they can solve your problem. If you need proper internal communication advice ask a specialist and remember that internal communication isn't the same as PR, advertising, marketing or HR. Be proud of your profession and don't be patronized by people who think it can't be so difficult. If you have to work with a centralized supplier without IC experience, work with them to find someone they can hire to support you. Otherwise you will spend your life explaining to an increasingly frustrated supplier why their latest brilliant idea won't work!

- **Use your supplier.** Consultants are a loyal breed and you want them to be loyal to you, not a project leader who is paying the bills and asking for some strange newsletters and websites. If a budget becomes available for communication support, ensure that the commissioning comes through you.

- **Always read the ingredients.** When you buy a consultancy you are essentially buying the knowledge of the leader plus the skills and experience of the consultants. Read the résumés very carefully and ensure that the job they are being offered matches their skills. It is not rude to say that you'd prefer to pay more for someone with more experience. If you don't take a hard look at the team you might find that nothing ever happens when the lead consultant isn't around to give orders.

- **It's not about the money.** Of course, everyone needs to make a living, and consultants and contractors are no different. However, just like regular employees, consultants, contractors and freelancers are motivated by more than material rewards. They want to do interesting work, be appreciated for it, and feel like they are part of something exciting. Playing to these motivations gets better results than you might expect!

The key learning points from this chapter

This chapter has explored in general some of the approaches that people apply to how they organize their internal communication function. We looked briefly at the issue of whether the team should sit in HR, marketing or somewhere else. However, our view is based on a very simple mantra: all organizational decisions are based on understanding what the organization needs communication to change.

A communication manager begins designing their team by exploring the question of where value needs to be added. From there it is possible to understand that most communication teams need to be able to:

- excellently deliver;
- partner with the business;
- provide high-level advice.

This is because great communication is about more than well-created tools, articles and collateral. Great communication is about the most senior leadership bringing their staff on a journey: a task that requires strong intelligence and coaching.

The challenge facing many practitioners is that they operate in small teams, often as solo practitioners. We all have to attempt to be a combination of the reliable technician, the thoughtful and informed account manager and the trusted adviser.

Notes and references

1 For an interesting discussion of the recent history of internal communication, it is worth reading a short paper by Kevin Ruck and Heather Yaxley: Ruck, K, and Yaxley, H (2013) Tracking the rise and rise of internal communication from the 1980s.

2 See Sinčić, D and Pološki Vokić, N (2007) Integrating internal communications, human resource management and marketing concepts into the new internal marketing philosophy, *Faculty of Economics and Business*, *No. 0712*, University of Zagreb.

3 See Diane M Gayeski's work in Gillis, T (ed) *The IABC Handbook of Organizational Communication: A guide to internal communication, public relations, marketing, and leadership*, Jossey-Bass, San Francisco.

4 Yates, K (2006) Internal communication effectiveness enhances bottom-line results, *Journal of Organizational Excellence*, **25** (3), pp 71–79

03
Planning

'Communication works, for those who work at it,' said the British film score composer John Powell. But to get communication to work you need to plan it. Too often communication happens as an afterthought or turns into a routine exercise, giving the illusion that communication has taken place when it has not.

Information distributed top-down or despatched with little thought of the intended audience is not communication. It is noise. Effective communication happens when you think through the value you want to add to your organization, target the people you should be addressing, work out how to get them on board and consider how to follow up. In short, communication only happens when you plan it.

What you will learn from this chapter

In this chapter you will find the essential tools for planning. It explains the steps you should take when faced with a communication issue and how to take control of it. As a bonus for planning properly you will earn the respect of your stakeholders and customers because you have shown them how to get from A to B with a properly constructed plan, with timescales.

Building a detailed and structured plan is a skill that some communication professionals disregard. After many years of experience, what needs doing will sometimes feel instinctive. Yet analysing an issue and planning the solution is imperative for practitioners who want to remain trusted advisers of business leaders: the language of leaders also revolves around the language of plans, overviews and timelines.

The essential steps of planning

It is easy to communicate badly, it is very difficult to communicate well. The difference is often just a matter of planning.

When communications is done poorly, you can generate widespread confusion and employees will switch to other channels or become irritated at what they see as 'corporate propaganda'. In the worst cases you fuel the rumour mill, building suspicion and even anger. That is because internal communication is often political and/or sensitive and relies on the audience's interpretation for it to have meaning. It therefore succeeds only when various audiences hear what you intended them to, interpret it how you hoped and respond as you need them to – a tall order!

Many professionals will recognize the constant frustration of getting hung up on delivery with too little time to think through an entire flow. The risk is that you simply don't have a clear understanding from the outset of what you want people to do as a result of hearing a message. A bit like sitting in the cockpit of an airplane without a destination.

There are several models, templates and suggestions to pick and choose from when planning communication. However, here are the six essential questions that are common to all plans.

TABLE 3.1   The six essential questions

Why	What is your overall business or organizational objective or goal? Knowing how your communications are to add value is the most important question, and all other answers have to support it.
Who	Who is this relevant for? Will they understand? What do they know and think now? What do you want each audience group to actually DO differently?
What	What are we actually asking people to engage with? What is in it for them?
When	Are there any timing conflicts with other messages or events? Is speed important? Or can you wait for complete information?
How	What medium or channels are most appropriate for the content and the audience? What style is most suitable?
Feedback	How will you track whether or not you are having the intended impact?

As a simple guide, we use this model to help take us through our thinking:

FIGURE 3.1   Elements of a plan

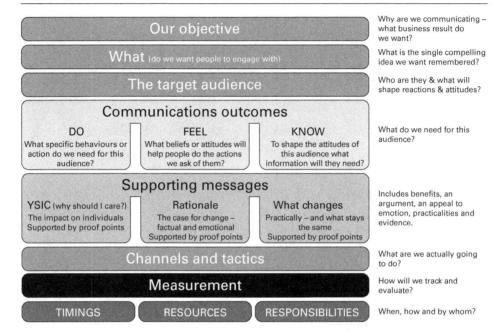

Why communicate – setting your overall business objective

The critical first step in your planning is to ask: 'Why do we want to communicate this and what are we hoping to get out of it?' Important communication can fail because the project team or executive group behind it think they all agree on the end goal, without appreciating the different views in the room. These undeclared misalignments will magnify into inconsistency, doubt and lack of coordination when communicated.

Is it about, as we said in Chapter 1, helping people work harder and better, helping people say the right thing about the organization, supporting major change or retaining good people? Perhaps it is something less fundamental but, if you believe in the importance of tying messages back to the mission of the organization, you have to have a clear linkage at the very beginning of your communication planning.

Many conversations about communication action plans turn quickly to discussing what content is needed and which media should be used. But before leaping into the content, you need to ask yourself why it is important and establish that every team around you, including the executives, agrees on the imperatives (what is most important for the organization; limit yourself to a list of no more than three) and the outcomes (what actually happens as a result of the communication; again, limit your list to no more than three). If there are gaps and inconsistencies it is the communication professional's role to facilitate finding a common ground and formulate a set of objectives that can be agreed and written.

We say that the detail should be kept focused. In our experience if you are trying to load too much into a communication the likelihood of success is limited. People just don't absorb complex or multiple messages easily and it is our job to help our colleagues get their point over. That sometimes means being harsh about the volume of communications they are attempting to pull off!

The key questions you need to ask your stakeholders are:

- What is the business need underlying the communication?
- What are the broad goals?
- What do we want to see happening as a result?
- What specific outcomes do we want to see? (ie what behaviours, actions or attitudes will we see if it is successful? What will we see if it is unsuccessful?)
- What is the single main goal of this communication?
- What is its principal relevance to the organization's strategy?
- What are the three most important specific actions/processes you want to see?

The objectives or goals are absolutely fundamental. These are what the communication effort will be measured against – and how your effort will be evaluated. The upside is that clear objectives make the rest of planning – and especially the tracking – a whole lot easier. You will find you are saving time, you will feel motivated because you know you are doing the right thing, and you will know your precise criteria for success.

Who is it for?

As we have said in several other places in this book, a deep understanding of your audiences is one of the essential attributes of the internal communicator. It is the source of our influence and planning any programme is impossible without reference to the people with whom you want to connect.

Although we have dedicated an entire chapter to talking about audiences, there are a few points we should draw out briefly here.

In the previous step we asked *why* we need to communicate and spoke about the importance of setting clear objectives. Now you need to ask: *who* am I hoping to connect with and how do I make it relevant for them?

At the very least, clarity about the target of your communications avoids adding to the information overload. It is human nature to want more information but there comes a point at which people will switch off. If we understand the audience, the volume of information they are already getting and what they would be interested in receiving, we can tailor our communications accordingly.

This calls for expertise in segmentation. Appreciating that not everyone needs the same treatment allows you to focus your channels and adapt your messages. Your segmentation might be simple – such as looking at the different needs of departments or professions, or it might call on more sophisticated thinking such as dividing your audience by behaviour or attitude.

For example, pensions communications will need to have specific approaches for people just starting their careers and those reaching retirement. HR messages might have to cater for managers who don't value performance reviews as much as managers who see staff appraisals as central to their role. Each group will have different needs, be at different points on a change curve (see more in Chapter 9 on change) and they will want to get the information in different ways and through different channels.

Your audience analysis should outline what you want each stakeholder group to do or think differently as a result of the communication effort. Of course this is only possible if you can link back to your initial question – why do we need to communicate and what is the value we are trying to add to the organization by doing so?

The audience analysis will tell you if a group needs to be brought into a process, needs to change their mindset or needs to be motivated. The key factor in any communications is the *desired outcome for the audience*. If you cannot articulate any actual change wanted as a result of the communications, why do it? You would just be adding to the volume of noise in the organization.

The key questions to ask are:

- Which are the crucial audiences for this communication?
- Are they all the same or will they need to participate in different ways? (eg are they in the office or off-site? Are they culturally different?)
- Is there a history to consider? (eg has one audience group been through similar situations in the past? Have they just gone through a mass redundancy programme and therefore be likely to be highly cynical?)
- What behaviours do you want them to exhibit as a result? What actions? How will you get this across or achieve it?

Figure 3.2 offers a simple template for your audience analysis:

FIGURE 3.2   Audiences template

Audiences		Group 1	Group 2	Group X
Employee needs	How well does each audience know the issue already?			
Risks	What is their current history and sentiment?			
Outcomes	What specific behaviours or actions would you see if this is successful?	KNOW: FEEL: DO:	KNOW: FEEL: DO:	KNOW: FEEL: DO:

When you come to creating your plan, all your communications will have to be structured from a perspective that many find surprisingly difficult to work with: the audience's perspective, not your own.

It is easy to talk about what you are doing, what engages you and what you want employees to know. That is what most business leaders do when they communicate. But that will not work for your audiences. So in the planning phases, you would do well to spend a great deal of your time thinking about all their information needs.

Be clear about the KNOW – FEEL – DO continuum:

- What do they need to **KNOW** if they are to believe or feel the right attitude or hold a supporting opinion?
- What do they need to **FEEL** or believe in order to get them to do what we need of them?
- And finally, what is it that we want them to **DO** as a result of our communication?

This simple discipline reinforces a couple of essential points.

First, very few communications are conducted just to tell people things. We nearly always have a specific action in mind. A communicator who begins with that action in their planning asks tough questions at every step of the way and is more realistic about the likelihood of success. They also make better choices about channels and tactics. As Bill Quirke says, a memo is unlikely to change behaviour, whereas a chance to be involved might.

Second, it distinguishes between information and opinion. Just because the CEO or the project team thinks something is a great idea, doesn't mean you have a guarantee that other people will form the same opinion, even if they see exactly the same data or evidence. Thinking about beliefs and attitudes at the planning stage shapes your choices of activity and messaging.

Keeping it real

While employees may understand the concepts in the communication, they may not necessarily change their behaviours. A further factor is whether what they hear matches what they already know or believe. You need to consider:

- the day-to-day reality of their job;

- the other projects and changes happening around them.

A communication manager therefore needs to have some insight into what is going on in the world of the audience – insight that can only be gained by spending time out in the organization. One communication manager we know who worked for a trucking company spent her first month on the job riding in the cabs of lorries, seeing first-hand what it meant to be a driver. We've seen communicators fail spectacularly because they never left head office and were reduced to making wild guesses about how an audience might interpret information.

In our consulting work we always say that a good communication manager is at their desk as little as possible.

What is the communication?

Deciding *what* to communicate is usually the point in the process when leaders and project teams call in the communication team saying: 'We are ready to communicate what the strategy is about – we'd like you to organize a video/town hall meeting/laser beam show in the night sky'. It is decidedly not the ideal starting point for an IC professional who, in a perfect world, would be involved much earlier in the thinking process.

So this is the moment where you will have to backtrack and take people through the previous steps. It is very possible you and your stakeholders will realize that the 'what' needs to be carefully restructured if it is to truly engage people.

In short, 'what' is not what you want to say – it is what you want to engage people in, framed in the context of the audience's needs, and what you want to achieve from the communication.

This is a subtle and important point. We are not talking about content here. We are talking about the core idea with which you hope to connect or excite people. It's not about a well-crafted piece of copy or a beautiful video yet, it's about the essential point you want to share, the light bulb you want to switch on in people's heads!

We explore messaging in more detail in Chapter 5 but there are a couple of general principles we need to underline at this point.

Earlier we said you need to distil down your point. If your message is hidden behind layers of other points the audience has to be highly motivated to dig it out. This is not about cutting back the jargon and using simple language: it is about being very clear about what it is you need to say and removing extraneous ideas or noise.

We also need to stress that great communications work because they are framed for the audience – not the sender. We have to craft our messages in terms of the audience's 'What's in it for me?'

'What's in it for me?' (WIIFM) and 'Why should I care?' (YSIC)

In any communication – big or small – employees will constantly be placing what you are saying into the context of what it means for them. This is not just an 'employee thing', it is a human quality true of all communication. Think about what goes through your mind as you listen to your own business leaders, or to a government announcement, or to news from your friends and family. You listen to the words... but what you hear is how it will affect you.

With the employee audience listening so critically, you need to structure your communication around their information needs and how they will be listening to you. If the first 75 per cent of your communication is about a new brilliant process, you will fail. Instead, start the communication by focusing on the outcomes for the audience. No matter what you are saying to them, no matter how brilliant and inspirational it is to you, employees will be constantly interpreting everything you're saying into:

- How will this affect me?
- Is it going to hurt?
- Will I lose my job?
- Will I have to change the way I work?
- Is this going to make things easier?
- Will this take the challenges out of my job?
- What do I need to know?
- What is your hidden agenda in telling me this?
- Is this just another example of a bright idea from head office?

In Chapter 5 on messaging we describe this is as the *YSIC question* – 'why should I care?' Remember that people are presented with millions of pieces of information every day and they have to choose to ignore some and pay attention to others. One of the simplest tests we use in our heads is whether a piece of information is something that impacts us.

If you ignore this human trait and only talk about what is important to you or the company, you can only blame yourself when no one hears your exciting news. Think about it in advance and work out how you can centre your communication around the outcomes for the audience, such as:

- their job will become easier;
- decision making will be improved;
- they will spend less time correcting things;
- everyone will be using one global system;
- etc.

Sometimes this is referred to as the WIIFM question – 'What's in it for me?' – however we think this is not always a helpful way of framing it because you can be fooled into thinking that every communication has to imply a positive benefit. Plainly, in many work situations the communication is about the exact opposite: if you always try to put a positive spin on every communication, you'll eventually find yourself telling people that job loss is a chance to take up a hobby or that the CEO's desertion to a competitor is a vote of confidence in the hard work the rest of the team has been doing.

When is the communication?

Good communication is frequently about timing, especially when the message is difficult, relates to a project or change with a specific timeline or comes during a busy period (for example during the holiday season or coinciding with quarterly results) when attention may be focused elsewhere. Time it too early and you risk not having enough information, giving the feeling you are being evasive or are ill-informed and unreliable as the communicator.

Time it too late and you will be fighting an uphill struggle against rumours, suspicion and cynicism. We always say the person who tells it first is usually the most credible.

There are some key questions you could ask when thinking about timing:

- Is the timing of the communication impacted by other events?
- Will it compete unnecessarily with other key messages?
- If you must wait (eg for final decisions to be made or for regulatory reasons) what early information can you give out to pre-empt or quell rumours? Remember: it is always better to communicate that you cannot say anything, yet, than to say nothing at all.

Structure your communication flow into phases. In Chapter 9 we take you through some fundamental steps and suggest some ideas about what it is best to do when.

How will you communicate?

Many a conversation about communications in our experience starts with: 'I think we need a newsletter and a town hall'. Sound familiar? The intentions are probably right and it is indeed positive that someone – or even anyone – is eager to communicate. But as you will have gathered by now, the 'how' comes after we have analysed the challenge.

Choosing the right channel is crucial. IC people need to know which ones are appropriate and when to use them. Do you know the difference between channels that push, pull, talk, engage, build commitment or provide intelligence? This is so important we have dedicated an entire chapter (Chapter 6) to the subject. However, as part of the overview of the planning process, we outline some of the key points here.

This is the phase where you can unleash your creativity and introduce new ideas and ways of engaging people. Most important of all, this is where you make the deliberate choice of channel because you know which is the most effective.

TABLE 3.2   Thinking about your channels

Purpose	Style	Channel	Example
Create awareness or inform	Factual, using frequent and varied media	Mass, impersonal	E-mail Newsletter Group meetings
Influence opinion or attitudes	Persuasion	Targeted, personal	Face-to-face meetings Personal memos
Secure commitment	Motivational	Personal, peer or opinion leader	One-to-one meetings Personal phone calls

SOURCE: Adapted from Roger D'Aprix:[1] *Communication in the 21st Century Workplace*

Feedback on communication efforts

The final core element in your communication planning process is how you intend to track and measure progress to prove whether or not objectives have been reached.

Failing to include it is a recipe for damage to your own reputation and an opportunity lost. Being able to show your peers in management that the actions you pursue have an impact on the business helps win support for your next plan. Further, you will need data to tell you if your plan is going off course and to help you reflect and improve on your work in the future.

Tracking and evaluation

There are two essential issues to keep in mind when it comes to measurement plans:

- **Tracking** (how will we know we are progressing towards our goal?) – this might be as simple as having a timed list of activities or a number of data points from a pulse survey that you hope to see at different stages of your communication plan.

- **Evaluation** (how will we know when we have got there and what impact we have had?) – this can be a statement of evidence reflecting your defined objective and a way of understanding what people think and are doing as a result of what you have communicated.

These are reflected more fully in Chapter 10 on measurement.

Having your objectives clearly formulated and agreed makes the process of measuring a lot less daunting. It is also helps to have decided what methods to use to collect the intelligence: do you use quantitative or qualitative methods, what types of questions do you ask, should you use a panel or do a focus group, and so on. Look at Chapter 10 for a more thorough walkthrough of how to track and evaluate performance.

Resources and responsibilities

One of the defining characteristics of a communication professional is the ability to make things happen. Central to this is having clarity about the resources you will need to deliver your plan and a statement of who is actually going to be responsible for each component.

How you define these will largely depend on practice in your organization, the complexity of the task in hand and the role you need different stakeholders to fulfil. Suffice to say, at this point you need to have done the work to define this element and this should be reflected in any written statement of your intentions.

As a sanity check it is always worth reviewing the objectives you have set yourself and seeing if they can be described as SMART. Follow this well-loved template and your objectives will always be more robust.

TABLE 3.3   SMART objectives template

Specific	Is it clear what we are setting out to do – will it be clear rather than vague?
Measureable	How will we know when we've achieved the objective? Ideally can we see how close we are getting to it?
Agreed	Have we signed up all the relevant stakeholders? Does everyone in the team buy in where necessary?
Realistic	Is it actually achievable? Are we setting a goal that is a dream or can it practically be done?
Time-bound	When are we actually going to do it?

Example of a SMART objective

Work with the executive team to explain their new strategy to the top 100 leaders in the organization so that they feel they understand it well enough to explain to their teams at local roll-out sessions following the November conference. The roll-out sessions are to be held before year end.

Analysing the objective using the SMART criteria raises some useful questions:

Specific: It says specifically what we need to achieve – a level of understanding that will equip leaders to run sessions.

Measureable: We can measure both how equipped the leaders feel and whether the roll-out sessions happen. Perhaps we can ask them how comfortable they feel explaining the new strategy?

Agreed: It is implicit here that the executive team want this to happen, but perhaps we need a formal sign off of this as an objective?

Realistic: We can deliver a conference and roll-out packs, but can we guarantee that leaders will conduct the roll-out sessions? Is there something else we need to worry about to make sure it happens?

Time-bound: The roll-out sessions are to be conducted before year end.

Templates for a communication plan

Now we have taken you through the core steps of communication planning. We treat the various elements in more depth later in the book. There are probably as many ways of structuring a communication plan as there are IC practitioners so we are not claiming definitive status! Crucially you will need to take into account how best to present your thinking to your stakeholders – what works for one may not work for another. You can then choose to implement your plan based on your analysis, following the above. Or you can turn it into a flow chart that looks more like an action plan – which is recommended. Senior leaders like action plans. This could look something like:

FIGURE 3.3   Timed flow chart

Month 0	Month 1	Month 2	Month 3	Month 4	Month 5	Month 6	Month 7 Go live
Planning	Prepare leaders	CEO road show	Awareness communications	Understanding communications	Media and customer	Track sentiment	Launch
	Launch to customers	Track sentiment		Track sentiment	Training of staff	Adjustment communications	Hypercare

Then for each month you expand on what actually takes place, what is being developed, who is doing it and who is responsible. Again, this is meant to inspire you to come up with your own plan to match the issue you are facing.

It is often useful to think about how you are going to present your plan. After all, you will need to engage stakeholders and get approval and resources in order to implement it. Often those stakeholders may not be IC professionals with the patience to work through your thinking or understand the detail of your segmentation. You might want to attempt to lay it out on a single page. See over for an example of a simple plan for a safety communication programme.

FIGURE 3.4 Plan on a page example – safety

OUR OBJECTIVE	• Supporting XYZ PROJECT to make us respected for our safety culture • Explaining safety to the XYZ division and minimizing incidents
MASTER TAKEAWAY	• Safety matters here – we all have a responsibility and are empowered to put safety above all other issues

TARGET AUDIENCES

Communications outcomes

Production	Supervisors	General staff
• KNOW: Safety equipment is free and must be used • FEEL: Safety should be taken seriously • DO: Use equipment and speak up when they see unsafe practices	• KNOW: What safety involves • FEEL: Empowered and accountable • DO: Attend 'Leading Safety' training and apply learning	• KNOW: Safety rules • FEEL: They have a role in making us safe • DO: 'Act, report and support'

Channels and tactics

GENERAL	ENGAGE	CELEBRATE
• Video – explaining empowerment • New style tool box talk • New style 'Driving Safety' dashboard	• 'Leading Safety' programme • 'Safety Masters' series	• Mystery guardian programme • Near miss report of the month

KEY DATES

For an example of a communication plan for change, see Chapter 9.

TABLE 3.4 Essential dos and don'ts

Dos	Don'ts
Plan the content	Let content be the only thing you think about
Make it relevant to the audience	Do it just because your business manager told you to
Base your plan around the underlying business need	Leave it at board level – plan how you will relate the business need to the employees' daily experience
Have a clear idea of what outcomes you want	Confuse specific outcomes with broad and general goals
Choose the most appropriate channel for the audience	Choose the most convenient channel for you/the manager
Measure it	Hope the results will speak for themselves

Below is a real example of highly effective planning. It's a case study of the communication that deservedly won a CIPR Excellence award for best internal communication campaign. It wasn't executed by a well-funded, large corporation, but by the UK's Glasgow Housing Association (GHA). The GHA is a not-for-profit housing association, part of a group of organizations that work together to provide affordable housing, community regeneration and property management services.

CASE STUDY   Think yes! CIPR Excellence 2013 award winner Glasgow Housing Association

GHA has around 1,650 staff in more than 60 locations. Around 70 per cent of its staff work on the frontline either in housing or in neighbourhood environmental roles with the remainder in Support Services.

The brief from the Executive Team was to take customer service to a new level through a programme of empowering staff to deliver tailored service to customers at the first point of contact.

The Marketing Service Team took the brief from inception to conception, creating the idea of 'Think Yes', the brand and the visuals in consultation with a staff focus group. The Communication Team then translated the idea into a suite of communications and led the charge towards better customer service. They made it accessible, understandable and they kept it alive when staff interest in it could have flagged.

The Think Yes campaign was first introduced to GHA staff as a pilot project in July 2011. The objective of Think Yes was to raise customer satisfaction levels by asking staff to think positively when faced with a customer request. The pilots were a runaway success and Think Yes was rolled out across the entire organization in May 2012. Customer satisfaction has increased significantly along with staff satisfaction.

Strategy and tactics

Martin Armstrong, the Chief Executive, visited staff in the pilot areas to explain the aims of Think Yes face to face with staff. He told staff they were empowered to 'think yes' in the face of customer requests, to take pride in their work, and take action to delight customers. The pilots were a huge success.

At this point, the Communication Team stepped in to tell the story of Think Yes. They spoke to the leaders who designed the programme and the staff who had made it a success. They had to find a way to explain both what Think Yes was and how it could be emulated by everyone.

These conversations culminated in the first Think Yes dedicated edition of the staff newsletter, a Think Yes microsite on the old intranet and a suite of all-staff e-mails. Think Yes was introduced to the organization in the February 2012 edition of *YourNews*, the staff newsletter. It was the first time, other than in leadership meetings, that the distinctive Think Yes 'tick' appeared.

The Marketing Services Team, along with the design team, had already created a brand and a suite of marketing materials which were distributed to the network. This included posters, screen savers and branding elements that could be used in communications.

Initial communications in staff newsletters set the scene, explaining what had happened in the pilots and how it had improved customer satisfaction and, more importantly for colleagues, how it empowered staff to make the right decisions.

Implementation

Better Futures week in April was the official launch of Think Yes for all staff. The Marketing Services Team immersed the organization in Think Yes – rebranding the training academy as the hub of Think Yes. The question posed to all employees was: 'Why do we say no to the people who (in paying their rents) pay our wages?'

Through careful scheduling and targeted communications, all GHA staff members attended one of the sessions. At the end they received their own Think Yes pack and a personal e-mail from the Chief Executive thanking them – all put together by the team to keep Think Yes in their minds at all times and to underline their personal role.

Staff were also introduced to the 'blockage buster': an internal website and phone line where staff could report a blockage which was stopping them from thinking yes. Over time this led to over 60 specific 'blockages' being removed and services improved as a result.

Evaluation

Overall tenant satisfaction for GHA rose to 87 per cent, up from 85 per cent the previous year and a rise of 20 percentage points over eight years! The tenant satisfaction survey also showed that the number of tenants very satisfied with GHA as their landlord had increased from 16 per cent in 2009 to an all-time high of 42 per cent. In 2012 the tenant survey showed that levels of customer dissatisfaction with GHA had remained stubborn, fixed at 8 per cent since 2009. But the 2013 survey results showed GHA had made progress on this, with only 6 per cent of tenants dissatisfied.

The key learning points from this chapter

A robust plan will help ensure the success of your communication. Poorly planned communications that ignore the basic question 'What's in it for me?' are doomed to cynicism at best and failure at worst. The key to effective communication is seeing it from the audience's viewpoint and especially from a particular audience's viewpoint, because even within the same organization there will be different cultures responding differently to a particular message. Most importantly, if you can't answer the question: 'Why are we doing this?' then don't do it.

Reference

1 D'Aprix, R (2001) *Communication in the 21st Century Workplace: The challenges, the needs and the answers*, International Association of Business Communicators

04
Audiences

What you will learn from this chapter

Some time back, we went to a presentation by research expert Robert Berrier, who opened by showing a picture of the Voyager Spacecraft, saying:

> Right now, the Voyager Spacecraft is flying through outer space and it carries a message about Earth and its inhabitants. A message written in binary code: ones and zeros. We have no idea where the message will land, who will find it, whether they will understand it and, if they understand it, what they will do as a result.

Robert was making the simple point that much of our communication is like this: simply sending out a message without any care for the ability of the audience to digest it. In order to be a great communicator, you should always have your audiences in mind from the very beginning of your planning. If you don't you will just be shouting into the darkness.

This chapter looks at why an internal communicator really needs to understand their audience. We argue that there is a technical reason but additionally that it's at the core of our professionalism. We look at ways of breaking down or segmenting your audience. The aim is to give you some idea about the things you need to know about the workforce.

Why understanding your audience is important

Communication is a two-way process and whatever model you use, there is an implication that you need to have some sense that your message is getting through. If you can't see how your audience is reacting, how can you hope to adapt your message, know when to repeat it or build upon it? As someone who is responsible for delivering an effective communications operation, you know that you cannot function without knowing your people.

The defining role of the professional communicator is to build a bridge of understanding between an audience and the people who wish to communicate with it. A media relations professional understands how journalists think, an advertising specialist understands how potential consumers think. An internal communicator has to understand how employees think.

Furthermore, few audiences are homogeneous. A communicator needs to be able to see how different sections of the workforce should receive communications. This process of segmentation allows a communicator to focus messages and direct them to the right people at the right time. If you have no sense of the subtle differences within the people who work in your organization, communications becomes inefficient and probably ineffective.

In our roles as advisers or business partners we have to be able to advise on how to reach audiences. A deep understanding lets us explain to our stakeholders which messages will work and which will fail. When we understand the preferences of our audience we can show why an expensive video isn't necessarily the right approach or make sure that a manager cascade has the right elements to make it work.

This knowledge is a source of power. In other chapters in this book we have said time and again that an influential communicator is a knowledgeable communicator. Being able to advise stakeholders on what an audience group is really thinking is highly valuable in most organizations. If you are investing considerable time in developing this understanding you will quickly find yourself in a unique position.

Yet understanding the audience has value way beyond the needs of delivering well-understood messages. How people are going to react is essential information for a change programme. We can advise not just on how to explain things to a programme office but also how much time to schedule to achieve understanding together with the approaches needed to build acceptance and get people following new behaviours. Specifically we can explain why some aspects of the planned change might never work because the audience cannot accept them. Audience knowledge is key to your organization's communication team being more than a waiter serving up whatever strange requests come its way. Audience knowledge is key to having a voice in strategic discussions.

Audiences or publics?

We use the word 'audience' in this book because that is what we believe most of our colleagues in business think is the right term for the recipients of communications. In academic circles, the word 'publics' is often used instead because good communications doesn't happen if one party is passive. Talking about 'publics' shows you understand that the people with whom you communicate bring their own opinions, history and experience and that the relationship between the participants in communications is richer than simply sending out information and expecting it to be heard.

However, in our opinion 'publics' is an example of our professional jargon that is yet to cross over into everyday speech. Communicators use terms that their audience understand and the majority of people with whom we work understand 'audiences'. So, without apology, we talk about audiences.

The basics – the demographics every internal communicator needs to know

It is inconceivable that a good internal communicator would not understand the complexity of the workforce in their organization. You can't produce an interesting newsletter if you don't understand what different people want to hear. If you're trying to build employee commitment and loyalty you need to understand how motivations vary in different groups of employees.

So, on their first day in the job, what are the essentials that every communicator needs to know? At the very least we should be able to list out:

- how many people work here;
- where they are and in what numbers;
- what they do;
- what languages they speak;
- what channels reach them;
- what their recent history is.

In our experience we have found it useful to create a simple map or organization chart to hang on the wall of the internal communication office. We have seen posters including such things as contact details for local communication support and time differences.

However, be under no illusion about the difficulty of compiling a schedule of the basic information. Many organizations do not actually know how many people work for them, have poor records about where they work or may not have consistent procedures for differentiation between full-time and part-time staff and between permanent employees and contractors. Getting to the bottom of this information may actually take some time and may never be fully accurate.

Understanding what people do is crucial and can often only be fully appreciated by going out and seeing the work done for yourself.

As consultants we often ask clients if we can start assignments by conducting a few focus groups with regular employees. This gives us the opportunity to hear how people speak, the context that they apply to communications and, most importantly, talk about their work and what they think is important.

If, at the end of the conversations we can get one of the focus group participants to show us around the office or factory so much the better. On one assignment the client insisted that we worked shifts in a hamburger restaurant and we have found it useful to spend time observing on cargo ships or cleaning hotel bedrooms.

The need to understand the job is one of the reasons some of the most effective internal communicators come up from the shop floor rather than through a communication route. We've met ex-cabin crew running communication for airlines, ex-bank managers talking to bank staff and ex-constables advising police forces on messaging.

You should therefore start by asking yourself what you really know about the people who work in your organization. Can you write down some basic facts and how often can you get out and meet people? On starting a new role it is always worthwhile running a few simple focus groups and repeating the process periodically. If you have consultants working with you, insist that they have some form of internal induction and never miss an opportunity to talk to colleagues outside your office.

In short, no one should know the workforce better than you. Without a full understanding you cannot do the basic parts of your job and your advice will be little better than guesswork with no added value.

Segmentation: One size does not fit all!

Internal communication is a craft that demands subtlety. Even in relatively small organizations a 'one size fits all' approach just doesn't work. Even though they work for the same organization, do similar jobs and have a similar experience, your colleagues just don't consume or react to communications in the same ways.

A communicator has to be able to segment their audience. They have to recognize the sub-groups that exist within their organizations and consider their communication needs.

The need to segment is actually not obvious at all to many people. As a communicator you will meet people who assume that a single message phrased properly will reach and be understood by everyone. Therefore being able to explain how segmentation works and is of value in your organization is important.

At its heart your segmentation approach will be about finding patterns or commonalities within groups in your workforce. It might be that the natural groups within your organization are around locations or craft. It might be that people can be organized by attitude or behaviour.

Below we discuss a number of different approaches. You will naturally find approaches that are right for your organization and you will want to incorporate them into your everyday thinking. However, there will come a time when elements of all of these models can help you solve a communication problem. For example, you might organize your regular communications around locations or departmental structures but when facing a change perhaps you might want to communicate to people based on attitude or according to their level of involvement in the change you are describing.

Remember that you do not have a choice. You will always need to perform some sort of segmentation.

The immediate problem is that some information just cannot be universally shared. Market-sensitive plans or proprietary designs and ideas have to be restricted – and even discussing their existence is sometimes not possible or even legal. There are times when sharing information can take a public company dangerously close to unfair competition or breaking privacy rules.

Even in a relatively open or unregulated environment, different people will see information differently. Senior managers may be excited by the prospect of change, for example, while junior colleagues may feel threatened or nervous by promises of disruption and uncertainty. Investors might be delighted at the Board's aggressive plans to cut unprofitable product lines – factory hands might welcome the news with less glee.

Failure to segment leaves employees overwhelmed. They suffer from message fatigue which ultimately means they may view important messages as company spam and just delete or ignore it.

There are a number of different approaches which we will explain in more detail but they generally fall under these headings:

- organization;
- demographics;
- access;
- attitude;
- outcome.

Organization

Most communication teams will begin their segmentation around the natural shape of their organization. When we spoke about basic demographics above we implied that a communication manager has to have some basic understanding of the shape of the organization for which they work.

The default position is therefore to organize communication either by geography or function (or a combination of both). This is an obvious thing to do because, as any student of organization theory will tell you, organizations are essentially defined by communication flows. When people sit down to design an organization their thoughts are all about how communication will work, who needs to give orders to whom, who needs to talk to whom. Issues such as office design or team size are driven by the needs of day-to-day communication.

In theory, at least, if we follow the grain of our organization messages should flow easily.

The other attraction is that organization structures have a boss with whom we can work: someone we can get to act as a figurehead, someone who can approve our messages and who can instruct middle managers to discuss issues with their staff. They might be a director of a function such as the Chief Finance Officer or maybe a country manager.

Staff may naturally identify with their place within the organization or hierarchy well before they see themselves as part of a larger entity or as members of another sub-group. People can be very loyal to their site, country or division and will respond to communications that touch on that sense of identity. Indeed, in complex conglomerates that have multiple service or product lines there may be little point in trying to talk about the wider organization, especially if employees support sub-brands. A communicator has to work with the affinities that employees recognize.

Within an organizational model of segmentation there is usually some differentiation of hierarchy, commonly around three main categories:

- the CEO (or most senior leader in the population) and senior leadership team;
- their next level of reports – sometimes defined by a number rather than an organizational chart;
- the rest.

This clearly is only relevant for some communications – it is nonsensical to plan a hierarchical approach for all messages. News of a better canteen menu or changes to safety rules apply equally regardless of status, but you may wish to add additional responsibilities into your messaging, for example leaders may need guidance on how to explain the new safety rules.

However, sticking with organizational boundaries is far from perfect as a model for managing effective communication.

The organization model can introduce gatekeepers who may not always be helpful. For example, the head of marketing may insist that any communications sent to her staff is cleared with her first – regardless of the relevance of her permission. Many internal communicators have experience of dealing with the site manager who has strong ideas about the value of a CEO's town hall or how it should be organized. Notional 'ownership' of a segment of the population is often seen to confer the right to modify, delay or even block messages even when there is no reason to do so. Hence the importance of insight and data to help build your mandate.

Finally, the biggest difficulty is that whatever structure you choose, it will assume that the groupings within it are homogeneous as well. If all your communications are organized around location, how well will it meet the differing needs of accountants, researchers or marketers who happen to work at the same place? Just because you are a member of a particular group doesn't mean that you are identical in every respect to every other member of that group.

Every communicator will need to understand the structure of their organization, the reasons for it being shaped the way it is, the leadership structures and the locations where people are based. We just need to be aware of the shortcomings of organization structures as a model for effective communication planning.

Social demographics

In recent years we have heard a lot about how people at different life stages consume communications differently. People talk about 'baby boomers', 'Generations X and Y' and 'digital natives' to highlight how people who joined the workforce in different eras have different expectations of the communications experience.

Age is sadly not a particularly useful tool for segmenting communications in general and in some cultures is likely to cause offence if used too overtly. In our experience there are actually few issues apart from compensation and benefits where tailoring communications according to age has any real purpose or value.

In recent years employers have become more understanding of the diversity within their workforce in other ways. It is not uncommon within some larger workplaces to see networks of varying degrees of formality organized around gender, ethnicity, sexuality or religion. For a communicator such groups are very attractive opportunities because they involve people who have taken the trouble to discuss issues within the organization. They are networks of people who have engaged with the idea that the organization could be better, which means they are probably interested in talking about it.

If such networks exist, the communicator should find a way to be involved.

A communicator will also be interested in issues such as educational levels. For example, in a pharmaceutical company there will be a mix of highly-educated researchers with PhDs and factory staff with perhaps less formal education. Attempting to talk in the same terms about the same issues to both these groups would be tricky and might provoke thoughts of different channels.

In multi-national companies an awareness of language groups may also define how communications are managed. While many organizations insist that there is a single company language (in the West it is normally English), others accept that factory workers in Brazil or China may have never had the opportunity or seen the need to learn a second language. When your communications are only aimed at senior managers you might be able to use a single language, but for campaigns to the whole workforce the choice might be different.

Although some intranets now have translator tools, the results of these are frequently confusing or even hilarious. There is no alternative to paying for translators. But always have an internal reviewer, as your suppliers may not naturally understand your business or your own way of talking. If you find yourself needing to plan communications around linguistic groups you need to understand the impact this has on things like the complexity of the basic message, planning extra time for translation and how linguistic groups are linked to cultural interpretations.

Naturally, an internationally diverse workforce brings the need to understand cultural differences. A manager in Europe might expect a communication to allow them flexibility to implement a change as they see fit. Their counterpart in China might consider the same communication to be vague because it does not come with detailed instructions. A communication manager has to understand these nuances.

Using archetypes to shape your plans

In large organizations with sizable communication teams it can be useful to create some stereotypical profiles of employees.

Creating the profiles can be as subjective or as scientific as you need. A team workshop identifying the main characters with whom you will need to communicate can be as effective as a statistically-derived model based on the annual employee survey. The aim is to come up with a profile of a fictional but typical employee who personifies a particular segment.

Draw up a sheet for each stereotype, perhaps consider giving them a name and maybe add a photograph. On each profile add information like average length of service, where they are based, what they like about the job, what interests them at work, the channels that reach them and how they like to hear news. Consider adding data from the employee survey and information about the number of them in the organization.

When you are happy with your stereotypes you can use them in a couple of ways.

Refer to them when you are considering any communications. Ask yourself how your imaginary colleague might be interested in an article you are writing for the intranet or how they might react to a piece of news. Perhaps you might want to think about the right channel to reach them for your latest internal campaign.

When you are working with a stakeholder to plan a communications campaign, consider showing them the stereotypes and asking: 'What is going to excite this character about your initiative?' or 'What do you need this person to do differently as a result of your project?'

Using simple stereotypes in this way brings your segmentation to life and reminds your stakeholders that you understand the audiences they wish to reach.

Some organizations cope by providing tools in several different formats. For example, a 'manager toolkit' based around annual targets might come with detailed slides for the managers who expect to issue clear instructions or a video with discussion notes for managers who have to win the support of staff through debate.

Of course culture is not just shaped by geography. Within countries you can find a variety of different cultures. In a university, for example, academic staff might expect multiple opportunities to share their thoughts on a well-argued paper about change, while administration staff might be happy just to be shown what to do next. A communication manager needs to be able to factor the needs of different internal cultures into their thinking when planning, if this is necessary.

Finally, some organizations have begun to experiment with psychological profiling as a way of segmenting audiences. We are aware of organizations that have tried to apply tools such as Myers-Briggs or similar trait-based models to communications with varying degrees of success. They use them for example to review content for the intranet to ensure that the content's messages appeal to the different types of employees that are to be found in the company. However, it is hard to apply such models to general communications because very few people are a perfect match between the archetypes and the work involved in matching communications to 16 or more categories of people is beyond the resources of most teams.

Access

A communicator needs to understand which channels reach which people. This might be an issue of being aware that factory workers rarely look at the intranet, or seeing that staff who are driving around all day do not have time to read the company newsletter on their rare visits to the depot.

Every internal communicator today will know which of their people have access to e-mail and who needs a paper communication. They can usually tell you who can reach the intranet and who cannot.

However, segmentation by means of communication behaviour often goes much further – and often without any deliberate design. Every internal communicator knows of times when a key piece of information has only been provided through a particular channel, such as the intranet, meaning that only people who have looked at the intranet have received it. This approach is to be avoided for anything that is likely to be controversial – if people think you've tried to make an announcement by the back door it will seriously undermine any hope you have of being seen as proactive or candid in your communications.

Yet there are times when discussing issues with only the users of one channel or another makes sense. You may actually decide that you only want to debate a specific topic with people who are interested enough to attend a meeting on the subject, or you would prefer to test initial reactions to something with the small group of people who use a particular forum on the internet.

Interestingly, marketers often say that adventurous or innovative consumers are marked by their exposure to multiple media. Apparently, people who watch more television, read more magazines and spend more time on the web are more likely to experiment with new products. There may be some lessons here for the internal communicator!

Attitude

Understanding the attitudes of your workforce and communicating with them accordingly is an important development on top of understanding organizational structures.

Two colleagues sitting in the same office working on similar work may have completely different attitudes to the workplace and those attitudes will lead them to make different choices about the communications to which they expose themselves, how they interpret messages and the actions they decide to take as a result.

Sometimes attitude can be predicted by grade or job type. An employee paid by the hour working in a warehouse may see the world very differently to a senior executive who is part of the share option scheme. However, a simple look at the results of your last employee attitude survey will quickly highlight how unreliable such assumptions can be. Working on a production line does not prevent someone from having high hopes for their company and many executive teams include time-serving cynics who care little for the organization they lead.

There are a number of different approaches that people use to develop a model of their organization.

Bill Quirke talks about classifying people according to their exposure to change. His model[1] divides people on two axes: 'impact' and 'interest/concern' and he suggests generic strategies for communicating with them. People who have a low interest but could be highly impacted should receive communications designed to deliver a 'wake up'. Staff who are highly concerned and probably likely to be greatly affected should be exposed to communications that are about engagement. Colleagues who have high concern but are likely to be largely unaffected need reassurance and people with little concern or impact should be educated.

Quirke and also D'Aprix talk about classifying people according to their knowledge and enthusiasm. Essentially, Quirke's approach identifies four general attitudes: 'unguided missiles' (excited but uninformed), 'hot shots' (excited and knowledgeable), 'slow burners' (uninformed and unexcited) and 'refuseniks' (well informed but disinterested).

Another attitudinal approach was reported by employer branding experts Simon Barrow and Richard Mosley.[2] They explain that market researchers TNS created a simple model which defined ordinary employees in terms of their commitment to their employer cross-referenced with their commitment to their career. This model divides the world into 'ambassadors', 'career oriented', 'company oriented' or 'ambivalents'.

Mosely talks about UK retailer Tesco's project using data to model employees' attitudes to career development, reward and work in general.

You might find this approach useful, especially in areas such as compensation and benefits, for producing different messages designed to meet the needs of people with different attitudes to things like pensions. For example, if you were offering employees a range of choices around flexible benefits – where they might choose additional leave, extra pension contributions or training – you might produce communications that appeal to staff interested in taking more holidays, concerned about personal security or motivated by career advancement.

While TNS use a simple two-dimensional model, more advanced statistical techniques can generate even deeper insights into the real attitudes of your people. Using techniques that owe much to political polling and consumer research, Dr Robert Berrier of US specialists Spring International develops factor-based models for clients (see case study opposite). This approach involves looking more deeply at survey data and exploring the underlying connections between staff attitudes and how they cluster together. This approach allows you to identify segments defined by a common mindset.

In work for one company,[3] Berrier was able to show that communications during a crisis were being directed at staff who were likely to leave the organization anyway while staff who potentially could be long-term advocates were being neglected.

In the same way that a politician understands how to position their messages to appeal to potential voters, a model for your workforce will highlight what communications will engage different groups of your people. Importantly it will show that people are probably not defined by their location or function – you will probably see that employees in certain groups are spread across your whole organization, meaning that you will have to develop approaches that do not depend on hierarchies or existing structures.

On top of the value that attitudinal segmentation provides to crafting messages, it also helps the internal communicator fulfil one of their most important roles – that of organizational sense-talker. When senior colleagues are advocating decisions or communication, having an alternative map of attitudes helps enormously to test the wisdom of the proposal under consideration. By stepping away from normal organizational boundaries and the political issues they bring, looking at clusters of attitudes allows an alternative perspective to be aired.

Letting the data segmentation explain the issues

Working with US-based researchers Spring International, a high-tech company was experiencing falling engagement scores, about a point a year, and was wondering what they should do to reverse the trend. The president wanted to make a commitment to the board to not just improve but to become a stronger leader so wanted to understand what lay behind the scores.

The most recent engagement score was 71, which for some leaders in the company was still a good score and not a cause for real concern. Others used anecdotal information, usually focusing on bad managers, to make an argument that engagement was an issue. The loss of some staff considered to have high potential further reinforced the concerns about engagement.

The question for the president was: 'What score was possible?' Or to put it differently, what level of engagement could he commit to achieving to his board of directors?

A segmentation analysis of the data identified a number of similarly-minded groups of employees. Their differing attitudes seemed to hold the clue about how to repair engagement.

The company had a group of positive people characterized as 'Cheerleaders', but they had several issues that mattered to them and that were shared with the next group characterized as 'Casual Fans'. These issues included career development and work-life related issues concerned with too many conflicting priorities and always feeling like they were on call. The Casual Fans were more negative on these issues, but also felt a lack of involvement in decisions that affected their work.

There was also a segment called 'Stymied Fans' whose one issue was the quality of their local manager, but otherwise they were as positive as the Cheerleaders about the company. Then there was a group of 'Disillusioned Employees'.

Understanding the changes in the population showed on the one hand engagement was taking a significant hit, as Cheerleaders became disillusioned. But, at the same time, the company was expanding and many of the new hires were Cheerleaders, at least for the first two years. These two trends – one increasing engagement with new recruits and one decreasing as they lost faith – were, in the aggregate, resulting in slightly falling scores.

By addressing the issues that were leading Cheerleaders to become disillusioned and improving the performance of local management, the company could not only reverse falling engagement scores, but set a goal of becoming known for its exciting employee experience and positive work environment. This reputation would help to retain and attract the best employees.

Segmentation analysis showed not just what issues were driving engagement scores but the groupings of staff whose satisfaction needed to be addressed in order to bring about change.

Outcome

We have talked elsewhere about Bill Quirke's writing on the subject, but his idea is a potent tool when discussing communications approaches with stakeholders. He suggests that when discussing communications for a change programme you should break down the workforce according to whether you wish them to be merely informed, understanding or involved. When a colleague comes to you asking for help with an internal communication problem, getting them to think about who they really need to change helps them reach more sensible conclusions about the focus of communication.

For example, consider the implementation of a new IT platform. It might be that the vast majority of staff need only know that there is to be a change in how the IT system works and that perhaps there may be times when the network is unavailable. Some other colleagues may perhaps be more directly affected because the customer service tools are going to change so they may need training and support. A final population of developers in the business may need to be directly involved in the project team planning the implementation.

Each group needs to be identified and have a communications approach tailored to help them. Asking questions about the differing behaviours of sections of the workforce and their respective contribution to the success of the project nearly always adds considerable value.

Choosing your approaches to segmentation

The internal communicator needs to be able to use a number of different approaches to segmentation. This will very much depend on your unique organizational culture, structure and environment. Whichever approach is considered, a balance is always needed between the competing pressures to draw up a complete picture and to arrive at a sensible model.

One could attempt to create a model which perhaps allows the organization to be defined in terms of site, craft, gender and age. Undoubtedly this would allow highly-targeted messages. But would the groups so identified be too small to have any value for an efficient communication team?

The following grid can help you decide which approaches to segmentation to use in your organization.

TABLE 4.1 Approaches to segmentation

Type of segmentation	Strengths	Weaknesses
Geographic location	• Easy to operationalize as follows existing organizational boundaries • Efficient to run as staff familiar with groupings • Taps into existing informal networks	• Not all groupings are homogeneous • Hard to get network to action messages which require differentiation • Gatekeepers may hinder timely delivery • Language and cultural differences
Job grade	• Involves all levels of organization • Follows a natural organizational hierarchy	• Need to ensure that leaders are sufficiently skilled to disseminate messages
Job type	• Allows for greater focusing of messages • Staff familiar with different job categories	• Different staff have different mindsets • Need to filter by channel as not all staff will have access to e-mail, intranet, etc.
Outcome	• Ensures right stakeholders are reached for programme success • Can disseminate key message according to who needs to know what	• No guarantee that stakeholders will buy in to the programme
Channel access	• Easy way to target key user groups • Good way to road test reactions with small groups of people	• Can limit access to information, eg controversial news • Most audiences are multi-channel users so can seem like duplication of messages
Attitude/ Disposition	• Addresses employees' concerns – can tailor different messages to people who are positive about a change and those who are negative • Gives IC a clear picture of what the mood is in an organization who can then road test the wisdom of planned proposals	• Can get over-obsessed with meeting the needs of those with a negative attitude rather than capturing enthusiasm of those with positive approach

The key learning points from this chapter

We have stressed a number of points in this chapter.

First, communicators can only function when we understand our audiences. Without understanding who employees are and what they think, it is just not possible to develop plans and tools to reach them.

A deep understanding of the audiences is one of the keys to our influence. Being able to reflect on how staff feel, what they might understand and how they might react to a message adds value to our advice and differentiates it from the guesswork and speculation of other senior people.

Importantly though, we should not see the workforce as a homogeneous mass. People respond differently to communications based on a wide range of factors including location, role, history or fundamental attitude to their employer. What works for one group may not work for another and a communicator should be ready to look at their audiences in a variety of different ways.

Notes and references

1 Quirke, B (2008) *Making the Connections: Using internal communication to turn strategy into action*, Gower Publishing Ltd, London

2 Barrow, S and Mosley, R (2011) *The Employer Brand: Bringing the best of brand management to people at work*, John Wiley and Sons, Chichester

3 See Berrier, R (2003) Using research to rebuild the internal communication strategy at Marconi, *Strategic Communication Management*, 4 (6), November 2003.

05
Messaging

What you will learn from this chapter

From the moment you get out of bed in the morning you are bombarded with information. The alarm clock tells you that you are late, the radio tells you the news, the weather and, if you are lucky, that your train to work is running on time. The avalanche of facts, figures and opinions continues through the day and only stops when you fall asleep.

No one can hope to process or act upon every communication they receive, which is why we actually ignore most of it. Only a few things grab our attention and make sense. It is often the individual who decides what this information means, why it is relevant and whether or not to take any action.

Throughout this book we have tried to stress that communication isn't about process, it is about results. A professional communicator doesn't just throw out information without concern for the impact it should have. She or he is interested in the outcomes and how they support specific business goals. The art of messaging is how we ensure that people notice, understand and act as we should like them to. It is a challenge simply because so much of the information in our world today is redundant. Professional communicators know this and develop the skills needed to cut through all the noise and make their point.

This chapter looks at some of the factors that decide what we listen to and provides a simple model for developing our messaging. We start with some general theory before moving into more detail about the questions we ask ourselves when planning our messages.

What is a message?

According to most dictionaries, a message is a communication left for someone who cannot be spoken to directly. However, in the world of professional communication it has come to mean a simple distillation of an idea.

At its most basic people think of communication as a process. One person says something and another person hears it. Classic communication theories attempt to explain why reality is not quite like this, why information is not the same as meaning. Writers like Shannon and Weaver[1] introduced the idea that background noise can drown out what we're trying to say and other people have developed explanations of what constitutes background noise; for example it might be personal history, other events happening at the same time or confusion about the motivations of the speaker.

However, into this world of theory has come the idea that a message needs to be encoded and decoded before it can be understood. To explain this idea some people have used the analogy of a broadcaster converting music into a radio signal and a radio in your home receiving that signal and converting it back into sound. If a communicator wants to share something they need to make sure it is expressed in language that the audience will understand and strip away things that might cause confusion or suggest an alternative interpretation. Anyone who has watched a family argument will immediately recognize the potential for misunderstanding based on ancient history, complex motivations and even generational differences in how language is used.

Later we will talk about the factors that distort a message, but given the infinite potential that exists for information to be misunderstood, communicators tend to think of a message as an uncomplicated expression of a thought or an idea. It is the kernel that binds together a package of information, giving it meaning and shaping the response we need for the receiver.

As a concept, the message is well understood in all walks of life. We hear preachers talk about the 'Christian message' or filmmakers talk about the 'message' in their latest movie (even if it is about flesh-eating zombies in a dystopian future). In effect, the idea that much of our daily interaction can only be meaningful if it can be distilled down into a short, pithy explanation is part of everyday conversation.

The experience of receiving information in short chunks is almost universal. Thirty-second TV advertisements force marketeers to be clear and direct and the shrinking attention spans of web users demand that we get straight to the point. Social media successes such as Twitter, WhatsApp and SnapChat are quite illustrative of how a growing part of the world prefers to send and receive information in small bits and pieces.

So at the bare minimum, a message is a brief expression of the information that is being shared. But for communicators it is a focused expression of the core idea that we want to share and connect our audience to.

It is not necessarily a slogan

Former UK Prime Minister Tony Blair said that he intended to be 'tough on crime and tough on the causes of crime' to summarize his policy on law and order. In a few words he explained a significant shift in attitudes within his left-leaning party. Politicians in the age of 24-hour news have learned the importance of feeding the media with short explanations of their positions. These short 'sound bites' or catchphrases can be considered messages, but messages are normally more complicated because they are more than words.

We draw inferences about the message from how it is delivered, when it is sent or who the intended audience is. Albert Mehrabian[2] has written extensively on the subject of non-verbal communication, suggesting that the words we use actually only account for about 7 per cent of the meaning we take from a communication. Although Mehrabian is talking about interpersonal communication, the lesson is the same: context, environment, personal preferences and channel are all significant factors which the professional communicator has to take into account.

It's our job to know why they won't get it

We all get frustrated when our message isn't understood. Everyone has had the experience of seeing a well-planned and considered communication get totally lost when it is unveiled and we've been left scratching our heads to understand why we seem to have created confusion rather than achieving harmony.

To a certain extent every communication professional needs to be a bit of a psychologist at heart. This is particularly relevant when thinking about messaging.

The first issue is to understand how people think about communication. Every internal communicator has had the experience of working with colleagues who have fundamentally different views of the purpose and mechanics of communication. We have all met the manager who always wants to lay down the law, or the colleague who wants to express their personal feelings about every issue. Many of us see communication as an opportunity to have a win/win situation that keeps everyone happy.

These fundamental approaches to communication are part of our individual personalities and are what psychologists would term 'message design logics'.[3] Essentially, how your organization or target group thinks about communication will define the approach you take to messaging.

If an organization thinks communication is about explaining rules and processes it will approach the style, tone and content of messages very differently from a workplace that sees communication as a vehicle for achieving emotional connections between people. As a starting point, the professional communicator needs to understand what the organization and the audience think is the role of communication.

The communication manager will also benefit by understanding a little of attribution theory.

Attribution theory holds that we draw conclusions about what are being told or seeing based on assumptions about the situation we are in, what we think of the speaker or what we would like to hear. We might, for example, assume that a poor performance by a CEO in a staff meeting might be due to her lack of respect for the audience rather than her dreading a trip to the dentist later that day. We might be frustrated by a boss who says they haven't developed a detailed plan for change because we expect the boss to be better prepared. A workforce might get angry when the external and unavoidable reasons for job losses are explained because they expect their managers to be in control even though there was nothing that could be done.

The communication manager can, in part, advise that the distorting effects of attribution can be anticipated by reviewing a communication for:

- Consensus – will people believe that the communication is what other people would say in the same position?

- Consistency – will people see a pattern to the messages and accept what is being said or will they look for a hidden motivation if the message seems out of keeping with what they expect from the sender?

- Control – is it plain that the message results from the choices made by the sender or is there something outside their power that is driving their behaviour? If an external factor is suspected, it will need explaining otherwise speculation will cause confusion.

Think about, for example, a staff meeting to discuss a reorganization. People are likely to hear the message clearly if they can immediately see that the plan is the sensible way forward, that the speaker is not saying anything they haven't said before and that the reasons for the change are clearly explained. The communicator needs to think through what unintended inferences will be placed on the message and see if they are likely to help people draw the wrong conclusions.

Naturally culture comes into the equation as well. How we view the world shapes what is expected from communication and will decide what sense we make of the cues we are getting.

National cultures will decide how we interpret a message. For example, in the United States a manager who raises their voice might be seen as expressing passion and emotion and demanding attention. In the Far East it might be seen as a sign of unprofessional weakness, calling into question the authority of the manager.[4]

A communication from head office might be welcomed in Asia if it is clear and precise about what is expected and required of the organization. In Europe, the same communication might be seen as aggressive, authoritarian and a sign of a lack of confidence in the local management team.

Senior leaders are of course also an audience. Relationship building with your senior executives so they trust you to help them communicate effectively is a vital part of your work (see Chapter 8 for more about senior leaders).

As if life were not complicated enough, a communication manager needs to understand that different divisions within the same organization might see things differently. In a university, academic staff might expect communications to be well argued and refer to lengthy thought processes and reflection, while the administrative team might just want simple explanations of what has been decided. Engineers might respond to detail and facts while salespeople might be buoyed by motivational encouragement.

In summary, a communication manager should make it a priority to have a detailed understanding of the different cultures within their organization, what people expect to hear from their leaders and how history will help them interpret things if they hope to develop messages with impact. There is much more in Chapter 4 on segmenting audiences.

Making it supportable

FIGURE 5.1   Making it supportable

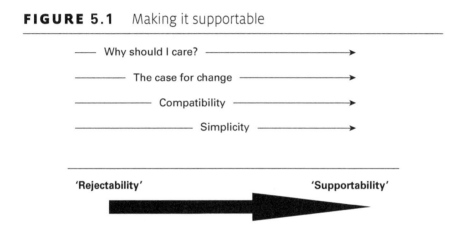

Making a communication supportable boils down to following a few basic principles.

Although not every message can contain all the following elements, the more you can include, the more powerful or attention-grabbing it will be.

For a start, if you can explain the personal connection you have a greater chance of being listened to. You also need to think about the case for change – the logical and emotional argument for doing things differently. Explaining it in the context of people's existing experience helps, as does finding simple ways of putting it over – finding the right language and examples to present something that is at its heart understandable by your audience is the core skill of the communicator.

Why should people care – it's always a personal thing

We said before that simple messages are desirable. But equally and importantly it has to be relevant or personal. There seems to be evidence that people's willingness to digest a complex message is directly related to the level of personal connection they have with the information.

For example, someone in their early twenties might find a communication about pensions impenetrable. When retirement seems so far off, it is hard to summon up the energy to wade through pages of information about annuities, 40 or 60th calculations and death in service rules. But someone in their fifties might find the same information much more accessible.

If you think about your own reading of the foreign pages of a newspaper you can see the same principles at work. You may skip or skim over stories about events in far off lands but then read a report in its entirety about a place you have visited or where you have friends. The personal connection is everything and why communicators need to think (sometimes quite creatively) about how messages can be localized while still serving the overall intention.

YSIC – how it can be more useful than WIIFM

In Chapter 3 about planning we talked about WIIFM ('What's In It For Me?') and YSIC ('Why Should I Care?'). In other words, what the message means to the audience, because communication is a human quality, not a tick box exercise. It is personal, or should be, so we, as communicators, need to see things from the audience's point of view. You want to build understanding and engagement, not resistance, to the direction in which the organization wants to move. You want communication to improve on performance and financial results, not have the reverse happen because the message is resisted.

We listed some questions and examples in Chapter 3 to help you think through what the employee benefits might be in a given situation. However, events inside organizations do not always deliver a benefit to the employee. It is dangerous to see every message as an opportunity to tell staff that they are well off or will benefit when, in fact, you are explaining something difficult like job losses, wage cuts or site closures. Looking for a positive message in everything is a shortcut to becoming a corporate confidence trickster.

We suggest you approach difficult issues from the standpoint of YSIC.

The communicator has to think of their audience and consider what will be their interest. Just because the CEO thinks something is a great idea doesn't mean the team on the production line will automatically get excited. Our role is to understand the concerns and mindsets of the wider organization and be ready to look at communication through the eyes of the people outside the executive meeting room.

Sometimes the YSIC is obvious. If you start talking about a site closure everyone is going to sit up and pay attention. But the vast majority of communications do not automatically answer the YSIC question.

IT might want to promote greater security awareness, for example. Clearly, suffering fewer cyber attacks or system failures from viruses is going to make the life of the IT team easier and save the organization money. But an ordinary employee may not be interested in new rules about password length or subtle changes to the policy on the acceptable use of computers. Communication experts have to find the connection that matters to the people working on PCs, perhaps by showing them what happens to their personal information when a hacker gets hold of it or teaching staff how to apply the same security rules at home to protect their children.

That connection has to feel credible and real. It is no use trying to tell employees that a change that excites only the finance department is of vital importance and worthy of immediate delight. If the message is not relevant to them personally it will just be ignored.

All this reinforces the point that we make throughout the book which is that the communicator has to keep asking what action or behaviour is needed and be the expert in what people think and care about. The communicator who does not understand the audience better than anyone else is not going to be terribly effective in the long term.

Making the case for a change – dilemmas, proof and emotion

When it comes to communication, people often talk about 'winning hearts and minds'. Sometimes you hear people talk about 'winning the argument' in the context of a workplace message. Our task as communicators is to ensure that there is a rational component to the message but not to lose sight of the fact that people are greatly influenced by more subjective factors. The relative importance of emotion and fact vary from place to place and from audience to audience, as we said earlier in this chapter. For example, in a university, academic staff may want to see the hard evidence for a proposed change before they embrace it, while blue-collar staff tending the grounds or maintaining buildings might be more influenced by emotional factors such as the chance to do a great job or be recognized for their craft.

Thinking in terms of dilemmas

When considering making the case for a change a communicator can be at a disadvantage from not understanding the detailed technicalities of an issue. The arguments behind a change of IT systems, HR rules or customer requirements may be highly specialized and outside our professional understanding. However, it is not our job to relay a perfectly detailed and technically complete explanation – we're employed to make sure other people understand at the level that is appropriate for them.

A simple technique is to explore what we call the 'message dilemmas'. Think through the basic question: 'What happens if we don't do whatever it is that is being proposed?'

Remember that some people are motivated by a need to change away from an undesirable situation while others are attracted by moving towards an opportunity. An 'away' person might be interested to hear how we can stop losing customers, while a 'towards' person might want to hear more about the new customers they could be working with. The communicator should then think through the dilemma question in two ways:

- If we don't do X what negative things will happen?
- If we do X what positive things will happen?

Having clarity on these two simple questions provides a shortcut to developing a simple case for change.

Where's the proof?

One of the defining characteristics of internal communication is that your audience knows what you are talking about. A press officer might try to get away with misleading or misdirecting a journalist now and again but that is not an option available to an IC professional, no matter how unethical they might be. And it could be illegal.

Employees know how things work in your organization. They know what didn't work in the past, they see the numbers of customers (increasing or decreasing), they are well aware if the marketing manager seems to have got a bigger car at the same time as there have been job cuts. You can't lie to employees and hope to get away with it for very long.

But while the communication manager may know that you can't bamboozle the workforce, sadly, plenty of people are willing to give it a try and would like your help in pulling it off.

There can be few communication professionals who have never had the experience of being told by a straight-faced manager that employees will absolutely love some initiative or another when we know they're being sold utter nonsense. Looking for solid proof points is your defence against the corporate propaganda-mongers. If you can't make the story stack up, you shouldn't be trying to weave it into your message.

For the sake of clarity, a communicator should not confuse honesty with total candour. There are times when the complete story cannot be told in one hit, perhaps for regulatory reasons or because personal confidentiality is involved. Sometimes it makes more sense to break down a message into chunks that can be understood, by perhaps explaining the need for new products and services before talking about retraining. Phasing information is not inherently dishonest unless the intention is to deliberately deceive.

In many countries it is in fact illegal to withhold information from employees and their representatives in situations such as restructuring and job losses.

The job of the communicator includes helping managers understand the best and fairest way to explain things to the organization without being deceitful. But the need for solid evidence is not just a negative requirement as part of your defensive strategy to protect the organization. Evidence is part of your positive selling approach. People are more likely to understand your message and see the value in your proposed action if they can see the logic behind it or see the detailed practicalities behind a high-level concept.

What constitutes evidence will vary in any organization and in each situation. The communication manager will look for things such as facts and figures, recommendations from external sources, stories about experiences elsewhere inside and outside the organization or testimonials from colleagues, peers or customers. Providing details of a practical plan is proof as well – it shows that your organization is serious and has thought through its ideas.

For example, the implementation of a new IT system may need proof points as follows:

TABLE 5.1 Where's the proof?

Message	Proof point
We need a new IT system	• We have had recommendations from the leading adviser in the field • Our customers have complained about our inefficiency • The staff survey says everyone is frustrated • The old system is 20 years old – the manufacturer recommended a life of just 10
It will be easy to introduce	• Here is our detailed 10-week implementation plan • Here are the 10 ways in which it is compatible with what you already do • We have already looked at other organizations that introduced the same system • Jo Bloggs from XYZ company has recorded this video explaining his experiences when his company introduced the system
You will be supported through the implementation	• There is a training course which begins on 1 October • You are being invited to a briefing meeting next Tuesday with the IT director • Here is a blog site where you can ask your questions

Don't be afraid to get emotional

We said above that a message is more than a bundle of information because it has to reflect what people expect and include a guide to the action or outcome the organization needs. There is another important reason why a message cannot be a collection of neutral facts: human beings just don't work like that.

It has become increasingly apparent in recent years that our emotions play a very large part in how we process and interpret information. It seems that the old joke – if you ask a question of five economists you will receive six opinions – has some foundation in reality. Human beings don't think in purely logical terms, unlike computers. When faced with a list of facts there is no guarantee that two people will reach the same conclusions.

The current thinking is that we use emotion to help us make sense of facts and information. We decide if we want to apply greater weight to one piece over another, using criteria that don't actually stack up when we challenge them objectively. Writers have coined phrases like 'emotional intelligence'[5] to explain this phenomenon and there is evidence that it is part of the physical functioning of our brain. Damage the bits of your brain associated with emotion and you are likely to experience problems taking decisions or evaluating data.[6]

What we have been building up to is that a message has to anticipate the *irrational* responses of the receiver. When developing messages, the communicator has to ask what sort of emotional response they are hoping for. This might lead them to choose some information to include or highlight and to discount other information.

For example, a safety campaign may need employees to feel that cutting corners in hazardous situations is generally undesirable. You might develop messages that show that doing tasks at a reckless speed doesn't save you more time or let you go home early. You might want to provide a table of statistics that show that people who complete a particular job faster are more prone to accidents. However, the audience may not care, perhaps believing that an accident won't happen to them, or that victims of accidents have been fools or unlucky.

To increase the possibility that the audience will believe an accident could happen to them, an emotional message perhaps showing someone they recognize talking about their experience might be useful. Or a message about the impact of accidents on a family might encourage people to reassess the scale of the risk they are currently ignoring.

In creating an emotional connection to the message, much depends, of course, on the channel you choose. Pictures combined with the right headline will make people stop and perhaps laugh, and films with the right people talking about personal experience combined with the right music will have the power to make people cry. The choice of channels is so important we have devoted Chapter 6 to it because the communication media you choose will depend on what you want to achieve from your communication and the audience you need to reach.

The point is that people might respond differently to rational or purely factual data when we trigger something in their subjective thinking. If we can connect with the things that people care about they are more likely to share our view of the world.

That's the central premise behind the bulk of advertisements, the church-filling rhetoric of preachers and 99 per cent of speeches by politicians. People do things because they feel or believe it is a good idea. They don't do things because they *know* it's a good idea: facts alone do not drive behaviour. We change our behaviour because we *feel* it is the correct thing to do, and if it works for politicians, priests and publicists why shouldn't it work inside organizations?

Therefore, messages need to resonate with both the rational and the emotional sides of your brain.

Thinking in terms of dilemmas, proof and emotion is also necessary when dealing with communicating major change in an organization. This is the subject of Chapter 9. Whether it is minor or major change it is always a good idea to prepare managers for answering difficult questions (see Chapter 8).

Compatibility – connecting to what they do today

A further reason for understanding the audience is the need to explain compatibility with current ways of working.

Imagine you are in a shop and a salesperson tries to sell you a new product that solves a problem you never knew you had. Perhaps it is a feature on a new mobile phone for finding pizza restaurants or a gadget for the kitchen that makes pasta. If you never eat Italian food or have a gluten intolerance you are unlikely to be interested.

Likewise, a communication in the workplace that talks to production staff about Excel spreadsheets is likely to be met with uncomprehending stares and vanish quickly from everyone's consciousness.

Every manager has had the experience of trying to explain a new practice and being confronted with what we call 'the difference question'. Staff will routinely ask questions such as: 'Didn't they do this last year?' or 'I thought we'd already done this – what needs to change?' People immediately trying to see what is likely to change is their way of reaching an understanding. Human beings naturally apply a compatibility test to everything we hear – is the message something I know already (and so can probably ignore) or is it potentially something that is big and possibly so scary I need to reject it?

The task therefore is to see how communication can relate to the patterns of work or lifestyles of the audience. For example, a safety message might need to be adjusted for office workers who have little call for hard hats or reinforced boots when sitting at their desks. An exhortation about selling a new product might have to be explained in the context of the existing bonus plan. Or the announcement of a new factory location might need to be accompanied with information about bus routes and the site of the new staff nursery.

A good discipline is to be ready to explain what has changed and what remains the same when sending out a communication. The closer your message is to existing experiences and practice, the greater the likelihood it is to be understood and acted upon.

Keeping it simple

So after thinking through YSIC, the case for change and the compatibility question, the communicator has already done much to simplify the message. The final step is to make sure that someone of average intelligence can actually understand what is being said without scratching their heads in complete confusion. This is where the lessons we have learnt through our technical skills as communicators come into play.

Cutting the bull

Our first challenge is about getting the language right. This is often no more complicated than applying the rules of sound writing such as keeping word length down, breaking up lengthy chunks of information, avoiding technical language that no one understands and selecting the right media that will get the message across (more about this in Chapter 6 about Channels).

This involves more than just cutting out long or obscure words and replacing them with everyday language. It also involves seeing the message in terms that are about the needs of the reader or audience and not of the writer.

Baffling readers with your command of the latest buzzwords from management textbooks doesn't impress many people – it just makes them suspicious. When you find yourself twisting words in order to satisfy the nice demands of the legal team or trying to keep the HR department happy with the text of the latest intranet article, you are sailing into dangerous waters. 'What is the simplest way of explaining something?' is the challenge that we should bring to every conversation with our colleagues who want something explained. If people don't want the audience to understand then they don't need our help and are quite capable of printing and sticking their own obscure notices on walls.

Can you explain the inexplicable?

Not everything can be explained away by the communication team, no matter how much our colleagues would like us to wave our magic wand and make miracles happen.

In one workplace, the authors of this book were asked to explain that a salary review had taken place and that some people would receive pay rises but only if their individual managers reduced other salaries by a corresponding amount. This strange model was euphemistically called 'self-financing'. As a result no one got a pay rise that year because few managers were willing to penalize their teams just to give a small boost to one or two individuals. In effect, the HR department had come up with a ruse for blaming line managers for the lack of a company pay rise and the communication team was expected to make sure staff would know that their line managers were responsible when no one felt the benefit of the salary review.

We refused because it couldn't be explained in terms that were reasonable. Instead we highlighted a different message: that there was a continued restraint on wages because of the economic conditions. This was not popular with the director of HR but was the only realistic thing to do. It wasn't a question of being honest, it was a question of explaining events in terms that people could understand.

Ensuring communicability doesn't only apply to big events in the life of an organization. It applies to the small things as well. There are occasions when something is so obscure or technical it is impossible to explain the detail to a lay person. Usually that is a sign that there isn't a message here that needs to be shared with a wider audience and in some cases maybe the better solution is actually not to share it at all (something which can go against the grain for a professional communicator!).

Take for example an IT department that has invested in a new type of server with some amazing new feature that has filled the pages of the computer trade press for months. Even though the technical people are delighted with it, do employees need to understand the system's full capabilities? The reality is that general employees might like to know that they can pick up their e-mail on their home computers or that everyone will be getting a shiny new laptop. There is no point or value in explaining how a new router works.

In our experience, if you can't explain something you either shouldn't be doing it or your audience won't be interested in the first place. It is wise not to confuse these.

Jargon – friend or foe?

Jargon – or technical language – has developed a bad reputation over the years. But that's not always its fault.

Every community or group has its own specialist language that insiders understand. There might be specific terms that help members of the group understand things quickly and clearly. Jargon is useful – if you are an insider.

The problem comes when you need to speak to people outside the closed community. Words that in one place aid understanding become, in another context, a barrier. Worse still, people tend to ascribe negative motives to groups from which they feel excluded.

Communicators shouldn't automatically be afraid of using language that is particular to their organization, but we should remember that within every organization there are multiple sub-groups – each with their own unique vocabulary or ways of describing things. HR people talk about compensation in very different ways to engineers for example! Finance colleagues might feel quite comfortable with terms like EBIT while salespeople just want to know how much money the company is earning. Strategy colleagues may use acronyms that lesser mortals can't decode.

The solution lies in understanding different audiences properly and asking if people will understand what everyone is talking about.

If in any doubt, revert to the 'pub test'. Imagine you are talking to a friend – with a short attention span – who doesn't work in your organization and try to explain your message. This soon helps you strip away any unhelpful jargon.

Planning your message – a standard template

We said before that a message has a few basic characteristics:

- it encapsulates a simple idea;
- it is more than a bundle of information;
- it reflects what the audience is ready to hear because, for example, it fits within their culture or experience;
- it is clearly focused on why the audience should be interested;
- it includes factual and emotional components;
- it relates to the experience of the audience;
- it can be explained.

In order to draw these elements together we use a simple template:

FIGURE 5.2 A message palette

	Why are we communicating – what business result do we want?
Our objective	
The master takeaway	What is the single compelling idea we want remembered?
The target audience	Who are they & what will shape reactions & attitudes?

Communications outcomes

DO	FEEL	KNOW
What specific behaviours or action do we need for this audience?	What beliefs or attitudes will help people do the actions we ask of them?	To shape the attitudes of this audience what information will they need?

What do we need for this audience?

Supporting messages

YSIC (why should I care?)	Rationale	What changes
The impact on individuals Supported by proof points	The case for change – factual and emotional Supported by proof points	Practically – and what stays the same Supported by proof points

Includes benefits, an argument, an appeal to emotion, practicalities and evidence.

| Find out more | Where and when will we know more? Include timelines. |

This reminds the communicator to set out a number of important factors:

- What the overall objective of communicating is – how what we do helps the organization or the programme we are supporting.
- A 'master takeaway' – the single compelling thought we need to share with our audience.
- Who the audience are, what we know about them and how they are likely to react when they hear the message?
- What we want the audience to:
  - do – the behaviour we are seeking;
  - feel – the attitude we need to encourage in order to promote the behaviour we need;
  - know – the base knowledge people need in order to form the attitudes we seek (the *KNOW – FEEL – DO* continuum more fully explained in Chapter 3 on planning).
- Our supporting message with proof points:
  - YSIC – the reasons why the audience should be interested, the personal benefits and the impact;
  - the rationale – the factual and emotional reasoning;
  - the change – the practicalities of what is changing, when and how.
- Where to learn more – where and when more information can be found or supplied.

FIGURE 5.3   An example: IT security campaign

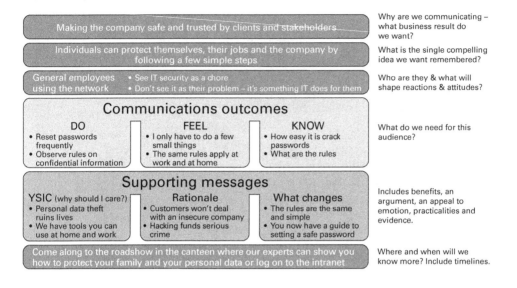

Making the company safe and trusted by clients and stakeholders

Why are we communicating – what business result do we want?

Individuals can protect themselves, their jobs and the company by following a few simple steps

What is the single compelling idea we want remembered?

General employees using the network
• See IT security as a chore
• Don't see it as their problem – it's something IT does for them

Who are they & what will shape reactions & attitudes?

Communications outcomes

DO	FEEL	KNOW
• Reset passwords frequently • Observe rules on confidential information	• I only have to do a few small things • The same rules apply at work and at home	• How easy it is crack passwords • What are the rules

What do we need for this audience?

Supporting messages

YSIC (why should I care?)	Rationale	What changes
• Personal data theft ruins lives • We have tools you can use at home and work	• Customers won't deal with an insecure company • Hacking funds serious crime	• The rules are the same and simple • You now have a guide to setting a safe password

Includes benefits, an argument, an appeal to emotion, practicalities and evidence.

Come along to the roadshow in the canteen where our experts can show you how to protect your family and your personal data or log on to the intranet

Where and when will we know more? Include timelines.

The master takeaway

Every message palette includes what is called the master takeaway. It can be as simple as the headline or the core phrase that you would like the audience to repeat back to you once they have received and accepted the idea that you are trying to convey.

Naturally, a message palette is not a script – it is a guide to what you want to talk about and include in your communications, so beware of crafting the exact words too finely – if they become a final expression the process of defining messages becomes inflexible and not very useful. Different media will call for the message to play out in different ways, which is impossible if you are stuck with a common slogan. It is easier to be intelligent about the best use of your channels if you concentrate at this stage on refining the thinking rather than the precise language you are going to use.

Figure 5.3 is a fictitious example for a small IT security campaign.

Channels and messages

How you tell the message is also a core consideration. As we have hinted earlier, people draw conclusions from multiple sources – not just from what you say. If you tell employees that you are concerned about colleagues who have lost their jobs and send redundancy notices by SMS it lacks credibility.

Refining your message palette intensively as we have suggested above will also pay dividends when you are considering the channels you want to use. Although this is the subject of Chapter 6, it is worth considering at this stage:

- What channels will add credibility and help build the right emotions into your message (or undermine the point you are trying to make)?
- Who in the organization is best placed to deliver the message to lend it impact and credence (remembering that the CEO should be saved for the really important things in life)?
- When is the best time to deliver the message (for example, people may not appreciate bad news the day before the Christmas holidays, or a message about cost cutting can be easily misunderstood on the day that the company profits are announced).

The key learning points from this chapter

In this chapter we have described how to make your messages resonate with your audiences so they connect with them rather than discarding the communication as irrelevant 'noise'.

As we say throughout the book, the core skill of the communicator is to act as the bridge between the leadership of an organization and the people with whom it wishes to communicate. The main tool we have is our ability to turn complex business requirements into something that is compelling, understandable and useful. We do this by crafting the right messages, using the right channels for delivery, and recognizing what might distort understanding for each individual audience.

Logic and emotion both play their part. Not all messages need to be given to all employees. Finally, timing. No matter how perfectly you have created the message it will fail if communicated at the wrong time.

The art of messaging is how we ensure that people notice, understand and act as we should like them to.

Notes and references

1 Weaver, W and Shannon, C (1949) *The Mathematical Theory of Communication*, University of Illinois, Chicago
2 Mehrabian, A (1977) *Nonverbal Communication*, Transaction Publishers, New Jersey
3 Dainton, M and Zelley, E D (2011) *Applying Communication Theory for Professional Life: A Practical Introduction*, 2nd edition, Sage Publications Inc, London
4 Trompenaars, F and Hampden-Turner, C (2012) *Riding the Waves of Culture: Understanding cultural diversity in business*, 3rd edition, Nicholas Brealey Publishing, London
5 Goleman, D (2009) *Emotional Intelligence: Why it can matter more than IQ*, Bloomsbury, London
6 Wang, S and Aamodt, S (2010) *Welcome to Your Brain: Why you lose your car keys but never forget how to drive and other puzzles of everyday life*, Bloomsbury, London

06
Channels

What you will learn from this chapter

Wouldn't life be fantastic if all communication at work could be handled with a single medium? Perhaps we could all install a soapbox in the canteen and have colleagues take turns to call out the news of the day?

The truth is that every workplace has a diverse population with different information needs. Shift workers may want to get their news at a different time from the office staff. It may not be possible to update people driving vans and trucks in the same way as their colleagues on the packing line.

We use the information in different ways. Some workers want information to entertain them in their coffee break, others want to be able to refer back to complex rules. A light news magazine may be just right for showing pictures of the annual staff party, but not have the shelf life needed for an official communication about safety procedures.

This chapter looks at channels – the media by which internal communication messages are carried to employees. These can be as diverse as magazines and interpretive dance, as varied as intranets and staff meetings. Our intention is to help you think about the channels you need from the standpoint of the results they can deliver for your organization.

The point about results is important. Throughout this book we've stressed that it is results and not process that matters the most in internal communication. We've suggested that a good internal communicator is interested in outputs rather than outcomes.

The aim is to provide you with a framework for delivering internal communication that looks beyond having an award-winning intranet or being concerned with trying out new channels just because you think more creativity is needed. This framework should equip you with the right tools and media to make a proper impact.

We will therefore explore some general models for choosing the right channels and help you understand the respective uses and weaknesses of each one.

It's all about results

Almost every useful book on employee or internal communication written in the last 20 years has started from the position that we're not in the business just to look good. There is little point in a beautifully designed magazine or a brilliantly produced video if it does not add value to the organization.

Our starting point for everything in internal communication has to be the thinking we explored in the early part of this book. The IC manager has to begin by asking:

What do we want people to DO?

And then:

How can internal communication help my organization get the results it needs?

Or, perhaps more aggressively:

Why should the CEO fund my job and activities?

You may recall that in Chapter 1 we suggested five broad areas where internal communication can contribute:

- it is the law (the law requires employers to talk to their staff);
- holding on to good people;
- working harder and on the right things;
- helping people say the right things;
- supporting major change.

Any conversation about internal media or channels has to start with clarity about the overall role of the IC function and then move onto the tools it needs to do that job, as we explained in Chapter 1.

Bill Quirke[1] introduced us to the idea of the now famous 'channels escalator' in the 1990s. His idea, at its most basic, is that you should match the tool to the task. If you want people simply to be aware of something, a notice board or an e-mail might be sufficient. If you need people to fundamentally change their attitudes and behaviours, a more personal approach may be needed.

Every communication manager will, at some stage, have a conversation with a colleague asking for video, or a series of posters or a website. Rather than simply acquiescing and asking for a cost code, the communication professional should start by exploring the purpose with which the channel is expected to serve.

It is our job to point out that a well-crafted note from the CEO will not, on its own, deliver a culture change or that a 15-minute animated video might be a heavy-handed way of announcing the new opening times for the canteen.

FIGURE 6.1   Choosing your media

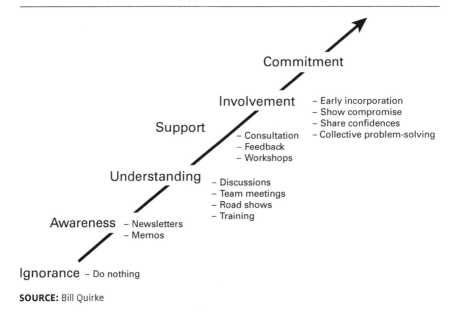

SOURCE: Bill Quirke

The medium is the message

In Marshall McLuhan's famous phrase, channels are not neutral. *How* you say something is often as important as *what* you say. Think about companies that have been lambasted for sacking employees by e-mail, or have baffled people by putting trivial news on the front page of the intranet or made it the subject of an e-mail from the CEO and you'll see the point.

Humans read as much into *how* we say something as they read into the words we use.

At work, people will draw conclusions about a message based on where they see it. For example, if it's an e-mail coming from the CEO it should be important. If it's on a noticeboard where employees rarely look they would expect it to be of minor significance. Using a new channel signals that something new is happening. Use an old channel and accept the associations with the messages that have been delivered by that route in the past.

Different channels are received with different expectations and we should understand them and know how to use them to the benefit of the messages we want to deliver. We should guide our colleagues to understand which channels are going to work best for their message and we should also act to protect the value of the channels from inappropriate messages. If people come to expect rubbish from an intranet they will stop using it, if they stop thinking the CEO ever says anything important they will delete his or her e-mails unread and if managers are asked to recite a script you can wave goodbye to your cascade system.

FIGURE 6.2   Your repertoire

PUSH	• Putting information out there – whether they want it or not	E-mails, pop ups, web ads, print magazines, posters, leaflets, line managers, TV screens, Intranet news
PULL	• A place to find it – at the moment they're ready	Intranet/SharePoint, online news, videos, blogs, mobile apps, employee annual reports, DVDs
TALK	• Where we can debate – and test understanding	F2F events, webcasts, TV channels, *Ask the CEO*, working groups meetings, discussion boards
COMMUNITY	• Where they feel part of something	Social networks, online team spaces, team events
ENGAGE	• Where we talk about the things that make us want to commit	Print, awards, online discussion, blogging around issues
INTELLIGENCE	• Where I see how I make a difference – to my team and the whole company	Surveys, online polls, focus groups, pulse surveys, feedback to board/ staff, regular team meetings

Think about a repertoire

Every organization needs a mix of channels for communicating.

We need multiple media for a variety of reasons. First, we should remember that once is rarely enough. There is a tendency in organizations to assume that everyone is reading every word that appears on the intranet or is in a constant frenzy of excitement awaiting the next posting on the noticeboard. Experienced communicators know that people need to hear something several times before it registers with them. For a message to get our attention we might need to see it on a poster, hear it in a team meeting, read it on the intranet – or have it shouted at us by a security guard!

Second, people expect to hear certain things in certain ways. They don't expect the CEO to be e-mailing them about the issue of car park passes and they wouldn't expect the safety newsletter to talk about the next social event. If you only have one channel, communications becomes an undifferentiated wall of noise that is likely to be ignored.

Third, different audiences will want to receive things in different ways as Chapter 4 on audiences and Chapter 5 on messaging make clear. The teacher will respond to one type of message, the engineer to another, and their responses will, in part, be conditioned by the channels chosen.

So as we said earlier when we talked about Bill Quirke's ideas, different channels have different impacts. Some are useful just for telling people things while others offer the opportunity for interaction and debate. When you want to give people a chance to understand something, a poster that simply raises awareness isn't enough. When you want to translate a corporate message into a local action plan a team discussion might be more effective than an all-staff meeting.

Channels don't have fixed uses: how you use them matters. For example, posters can be a simple channel of awareness raising or, as we know from the advertising or political worlds, images can be unsettling or challenging. The intranet can be an online library or it can be a hub of debate. A team meeting can be the quickest way to induce sleep or an opportunity to excite and enthuse people about quite complicated subjects.

The important thing is to understand what you need your channels to do for you and then develop approaches that will do the job that needs doing.

To help you think about the media you need at your disposal, you may find it useful to consider general uses that you need to fulfil with your communications. Broadly, these might fall into the categories of Push, Pull, Talk, Community, Engage and Intelligence. We will explore these now, while stressing that channels can fulfil different purposes and the purpose a channel serves is not fixed: it will depend in part on how you choose to use it.

Push channels

Every organization needs the facility to broadcast information to employees. At its most basic we need a system for warning people that there is a fire, alerting colleagues to changes of rules or announcing events. Channels that deliver a one-way flow of information are often called 'push' channels because they send information out. The recipient is a passive actor, doing nothing on the receiving end.

Typical push channels might include posters, leaflets left on desks or e-mail.

Internal communicators will need at least one push channel in their repertoire if only to meet the legal obligation to tell employees certain things. If you operate in a fast-moving situation you also need a reliable mechanism to deliver information to people, for example, telling sales staff about particular offers or letting operations staff know about changes to services.

Push channels also matter during crises. Employees may need to be told about safety issues or have information to help them explain things to customers. Having experienced crises covering everything from business failure, piracy and corruption to hostile takeovers we can't stress strongly enough the need to have a reliable push channel in place well in advance. When things go wrong, you don't want that to be the first time you've thought about how you put a piece of paper in everyone's hand within two hours!

The crucial thing to remember is that people rarely ask for push channels and so you cannot guarantee their efficiency. If we're honest, we have all deleted e-mails from the CEO without reading them or dropped a memo left on our desks straight in the waste bin. As communicators we should be wary of the delusion that push communications work in creating awareness. If we subscribe to the philosophy that good communication is about having an impact and making a difference we will need to be careful and think of back-up approaches. In short, pushed messages will need to be repeated often in multiple places if we really hope that they will get through.

Pull channels

In life, we rarely receive information at the moment when we need it. How often have you found yourself at home wondering where you put that important letter from the bank or where you left the instruction manual for the coffee maker? As consumers of information we want to be able to 'pull' information when it is relevant or of interest to us.

At work we need to provide pull channels that help our colleagues find the information they need and in recent years we have been fortunate to see the development of great intranet tools. Writer Gerry McGovern[2] has talked a lot about the fact that most people have a very functional approach to many digital tools – they go to the intranet to find things – highlighting the fact that people are selective about the information that they consume at work. Most communicators will report that the most visited pages on their intranet include the staff directory, the canteen menu or information about benefits. Corporate news is rarely at the top of employees' daily search routine.

Pull channels therefore present an opportunity and a challenge. The opportunity is in the fact that if someone has sought out information they are more likely to be interested in its content and likely to be engaged in it. The challenge lies in the fact that a communicator has to match messages to the subjects that interest employees. If you want people to come looking for your story, you have to present it in a place and in a format that can be found.

As a result, communicators need to understand their audiences well enough to present the information in a way that will capture their attention. For example, when connecting with teenage staff in a chain of fast-food restaurants you might adopt a different tone of voice to one you might use with bank staff in a head office. And presenting the information in an engaging way means understanding the 'What's In It For Me?' and 'Why Should I Care?' mantras explained in Chapter 5.

You will also want to match communications with the routines of different groups of employees. For example, airline staff may not have time when travelling to connect with company information, but might be receptive when visiting head office for training. Staff working in a customer service centre might only have time to look at an intranet when they are relaxing so your pages are competing with other fun media.

An IC manager therefore needs to ask if there is a suitable place or person an employee can refer to when they are ready to engage with communications. It might be an intranet or an information manager, but the aim should be to maintain the reliability of the channel. Employees should believe that when they go to their trusted point of reference, the information they can access will be relevant, up to date and useful.

Talk channels

Communication managers believe that their role entails managing some form of dialogue. Later on we discuss the role of channels in drawing together a community or in promoting engagement. Even if community and engagement do not matter to your organization, it is likely that you will want to promote discussion as a way of building understanding.

Most of us develop our understanding of information or ideas by asking questions or by taking part in some form of conversation. We need a place where we can ask how something is new, what we have to do about an instruction or explore practicalities.

Digital media has considerable promise inside organizations to help colleagues talk and react to information. Microblogging tools like Twitter, Yammer, Socialtext and even larger platforms such as SharePoint give employees a place to comment or to check if they have heard something correctly.

Face to face remains one of the main mechanisms for conversation – either through line management (the subject of Chapter 7) or through fora such as town hall meetings or opportunities to sit down with senior executives over lunch. A good starting point for a communication manager is to ask whether every employee has a space where they could take part in a debate or a discussion if they so chose.

Community channels

Sociologists have long known that being part of a community or a team is one of the reasons many of us go to work. When we feel part of something we work harder and are more committed, which has a positive effect on staff turnover and absenteeism.

Strong communities at work are more collaborative and, experience shows, generally achieve better results. Therefore promoting a strong internal sense of belonging is naturally an important function for an internal communicator.

People approach the challenge in different ways.

Traditional approaches such as events, parties or get-togethers will continue being part of the IC repertoire for many years. Apart from marking the normal celebrations such as Christmas or Eid that people expect at work, organizations also place great value on giving employees a collective experience. For example, some companies ask all staff to become involved in a common activity on a particular day – such as working on an environmental project or fundraising for a charity.

Larger organizations often sponsor sports and social clubs as a way of building a sense of membership. In the UK, the employee-owned retailer John Lewis places great emphasis on staff participation in its internal community as one of the drivers of its strong brand and business success.

The role of the IC function at such times varies. However, a communication professional differs from a party planner in that our focus is not just on ensuring that everyone has a good time. Our job is to ensure that defined business objectives are met and that any event has a place within a wider communication plan.

Increasingly, digital channels offer the communicator a wide range of options. In the earlier days of online communications, organizations commonly provided their employees with a place for sharing experiences and ideas. These still exist and vary from internal buy/sell boards, information boards for people with a common interest or need (such as networks of Christians or gay staff or people with a sporting interest) or places for chat and gossip.

Modern digital tools also have significant potential to support community membership. Platforms like Jive are specifically designed to promote collaboration and allow colleagues to share ideas and identify peers with common interests. However, experienced IC managers will know that groups without a clear focus can quickly degenerate and lose any business value. At their worst, online fora can become dominated by a very small handful of employees and their existence becomes difficult to defend to senior managers who see them as a waste of time. Effective online communities tend to have a defined purpose, an identified and committed community manager and, possibly, a finite lifespan. Clear rules of engagement are also needed as a way of re-assuring leaders that the community is not a waste of time and to protect the organization in the (unlikely) event that unacceptable behaviour takes place.

Engage

In the chapter on messaging we talked about the need to inject some emotion into communications. People are more likely to respond to an idea when there is both a rational and an emotional component to the message and every workplace needs the ability to excite and inspire people.

You can excite and inspire people through a range of channels and generating an emotional response is likely to need more than one approach. The essential point is that you need the capability to create a stir from time to time: something which is difficult if you rely exclusively on a single channel. It is a challenge if you don't have a history of trying it in the first place.

Remember that people respond most powerfully to other people. Bringing peers, colleagues, customers, suppliers, friends and wider society to life means great writing, images and events. Any media that allows you to tell stories is going to help you grab attention and excite people.

If your staff can interact with your communications so much the better. If you really want to engage people, your tools should have the scope to be questioned, to provide discussion or solicit ideas. Build these characteristics in and you could be about to start a revolution!

Intelligence

Finally, people at work need to know that they are listened to and a communicator should have a range of formal and informal channels where they can share their views and attitudes. There is a fuller chapter in this book about research and evaluation (Chapter 10) and one of our golden rules of communications is that for it to work you need a way to understand what the audience is thinking and hearing.

Some of this intelligence will reach you as you travel about, but you will need to stimulate the flow as well.

Naturally you will put in place tools such as surveys and regular focus groups but you might want to create a space for colleagues to share their views whether you have asked them directly or not. Providing such a space demonstrates the value the organization places on individual ideas and contributions and can give you an early warning of other issues or communications problems.

One of the oldest tools for seeking formal feedback is the suggestion box, whereby employees are invited to make observations about processes or aspects of work that could be improved. Traditionally organizations with a staff newspaper would reserve the letters page for employee comment and in more recent times organizations have introduced services like a 'Tell the CEO' webpage where comments or issues can be raised.

Good communicators make sure that comments and feedback received are acknowledged by the organization. This can be as simple as the CEO remarking upon the views of employees in their regular e-mails, or it can be more sophisticated in the form of formal events such as open discussions in a town hall meeting.

The international bank HSBC runs employee-led meetings globally. These are a simple way to collect feedback and uncover issues. The idea is essentially that managers host a quarterly meeting for their teams, but the agenda is open, the manager can't talk and is only there to take notes. Themes from the discussion are fed into an online system and then an analysis happens to establish themes. The tool is so powerful that the senior executive team spends a couple of hours on it every quarter and the CEO goes online to respond via video.

What channels do audiences value?

An IC manager knows that different audiences may need different channels. What connects with a worker in an office may not work for a colleague driving around meeting customers. What might amuse staff in a contact centre might seem patronizing to researchers in the R&D department. We explored this more fully in Chapter 4, but here are the three questions you should ask yourself when deciding which channels to use:

- What access do they have to digital media?
- What are they exposed to in the rest of their lives?
- What is their work pattern?

Armed with these answers you are unlikely to make the mistake of attempting to reach employees permanently on the road with a poster campaign, or scheduling daytime meetings for night workers.

Social media – misunderstandings and opportunities

In recent years there has been much published on the subject of social media and internal communications. A great many commentators are excited by the possibilities offered by new technologies and applications to promote greater interaction at work and promote even higher levels of employee commitment. The level of anticipation around the potential of social media is enormous.

It is hard to deny the enthusiasm that surrounds the potential of social media, but until many of the prophesies have come to pass the communication manager should exercise caution about the uses of social media internally.

When considering the discussion around new tools you should be aware of the confusion that exists around the language: many people conflate terms like 'digital', 'social' and 'online'. Tracy Playle makes the point that a medium only becomes 'social' when it allows for interaction. She gives the example of a blog, which can hardly be considered social unless readers are able to comment and interact – otherwise it is just another form of one-way communication.

The lack of clarity in the language should not obscure the potential for change in our working lives that social media could bring.

While the vast majority of companies use social technologies in some way, very few are anywhere near to achieving the potential benefit. Bodies such as the McKinsey Global Institute (MGI) claim that internal application of social tools could represent double the potential value that could come from their use in marketing. MGI's estimates suggest that by fully implementing social technologies, companies have an opportunity to raise the productivity of interaction workers (high-skill knowledge workers, including managers and professionals) by 20 to 25 per cent.[3]

We should not underestimate the difficulty in getting organizations to invite employees to engage in debate. Conversations with managers about internal social media quickly become dominated by fears of uncontrollable bad behaviour and references to some of the worst practices of the wider internet, including hacking and cyber-bullying. Thankfully this is changing as tools like Jive and Salesforce.com are marketing themselves on the basis of the business value they bring and case studies are published highlighting how good practice is making a difference.

Finally, we should be aware that there is debate about the real potential for social media inside organizations, based on the fact that many organizations are too small to make it work.

The issue is sometimes referred to as the '1 per cent principle',[4] an idea that has existed for several years. In crude terms, web users are said to fall into three broad categories – browsers who just look and don't get involved (thought to be around 90 per cent of us), occasional participants who mostly browse but from time to time participate, perhaps by commenting or posting material (estimated to be 9 per cent of web users) and activists who spend time creating content and getting involved in discussions. This last group is said to be around 1 per cent of all web users.

If social media depends on 1 per cent of the global population to drive things along and make interesting things happen, what does that mean in the workplace?

When translating this inside organizations, the maths make it very difficult for social media to catch fire. If your organization is only 10,000 strong, you might expect only 100 or so people to be activists. Anyone who has ever had to close down a discussion board dominated by a small clique of bores will recognize the truth of this! Given that the bulk of organizations number a few hundred people, this principle would suggest that promoting high levels of online participation internally is going to be tough.

The opportunity

It seems that there is unlikely to be a large-scale transformation in internal communication practice as a result of social media alone. However, we are already seeing social approaches being used to enhance other activities such as:

- short-lived activities, perhaps to support a conference, product launch or campaign;
- gathering ideas for process improvements or intense sessions involving people to solve a specific problem;
- supporting cost and process efficiencies;
- celebrating peers;
- making the intranet interesting or interactive.

Getting started with social media internally

Writer and consultant Tracy Playle[5] suggests the following basic planning steps when thinking about social media:

- Remind yourself what the purpose of internal communication in your organization is – what are you trying to achieve?

- Remember who you are trying to reach and ask:
  - What is their current use of social technology?
  - What is their attitude towards privacy?
  - What sort of technology can they access?
  - Do they think there is an open culture that will appreciate them sharing their thoughts?

- Check that your culture is ready... is it open or is it risk averse and controlling?

- Ask what other tools are available?
  - And how will our social tools integrate with them?

- Get your business case clear:
  - What is the business need?
  - What are the risks and how will we manage them?
  - What is the benefit you are going to offer leaders and individuals – is it compelling?

- Look for the pilot projects and take baby steps.

- Monitor, measure and revise.

More from Tracy Playle can be found on her website: **www.picklejarcommunications.com**

Conducting a basic channels audit

Sooner or later everyone needs to conduct a basic audit of the communication channels and tools that they have in their organization. It is actually quite a simple activity and can often be done as a desk exercise.

The following questions are a good starting point:

- What is the role of internal communication in our organization and what is our strategic mission?
- Do we have channels that Push/Pull/Talk/Engage/Build commitment or provide intelligence?
- For each channel, are we clear on its purpose?

- Is there a sustainable plan for the use of the channel for the next 12 months?
- Who are our audiences and what do they like?
- What data do we have to tell us what actually reaches people?
- What do we know what they think about it?
- How does it compare with the best in other organizations?
- How much does it cost to run each channel and does this seem reasonable on a cost-per-employee basis?
- Who would notice if we closed the channel down?
- How are we going to track and follow up?

This exercise can be conducted in the following steps:

1 Initial workshop to identify the channels in use:
   - Remember that the IC department will often not actually know all of the channels in use around the organization, so it is sometimes worth asking contacts around the business to keep hold of any relevant e-mails, newsletters or general communications they are sent for a month or so.

2 Data-gathering phase:
   - Collecting data on things like intranet usage, budgets, distribution, employee attitudes.

3 Field research:
   - Interviews with a limited number of senior managers asking what they like and value.
   - Focus groups with employees, asking them what they like and value (prepare to hear some uncomfortable news!).

4 Benchmarking externally:
   - Sometimes you might want to conduct a simple survey, but think carefully about the information you want to gather. Are you interested in perceived usefulness, expectations of what information to find where or perceived communication gaps? Furthermore, getting a strong response to surveys about channels can be very difficult so before committing to a questionnaire it is worth conducting some qualitative research. You may get all the information you need from some focus groups.

5 Review and planning workshop.

Discovering what good looks like

We all need inspiration from time to time, and IC people tend to be particularly interested in seeing the tools used by their peers.

There are a number of ways in which this can be done:

- **Just pay a visit.** Usually the only way to see someone else's intranet is to actually visit their offices and sit down and compare notes. Making time to compare notes in this way is rarely wasted.

- **Set up your own benchmarking club.** If you think that other people in your sector have experiences to share, why not set up your own benchmarking club? It isn't difficult to contact a few colleagues from a similar organization or business to your own to come together for a conversation.

- **Join a commercial benchmarking club.** There are commercial organizations like the Corporate Executive Council, Melcrum's Strategic Communications Forum or the Intranet Benchmarking Forum that exist to facilitate the sharing of best practice.

- **Join a professional association.**

- **Understand what is published on Ragan, Simply-Communicate and Melcrum and see if any of the named best-practice organizations would like to meet you.**

Of course it is always worth looking at the winners of awards such as those promoted by the CIPR's Internal Communications Group, the Institute of Internal Communications and the International Association of Business Communicators.

A channels matrix

The communication media you choose will depend on what you want to achieve from your communication and the audience you need to reach. The right channels for raising awareness may possibly be the wrong ones for gaining ownership and commitment. Similarly, the needs of a manager working in head office will be very different from an engineer working in the field. Assuming you're already thinking about both these things, Table 6.1, overleaf, is a simple summary of the key channels to choose from (produced in collaboration with Sue Dewhurst).

Your channels matrix

A useful tactic for the internal communication manager is to write up their basic channel repertoire onto a single page. It helps provide clarity to the communication team and colleagues. Importantly, it provides a useful starting point for discussing with colleagues why you think their issue isn't suitable for the intranet but might work well for the CEO's e-mails.

Table 6.2 on pages 112–13 is a simple example from one company.

TABLE 6.1 What media?

Channel	At its best	Potential downsides	Think about
Team meetings	• Can make communication personal and relevant to the team involved • Opportunity for discussion, feedback, questioning and ideas • Good line manager can facilitate a lively and interactive session • Can help build understanding, involvement and ownership	• Success depends on skill of leader • Time commitment for both manager and audience • Beware of content overload: other channels are more effective for simple information delivery	• Making the best possible use of this time – it's valuable • Training line managers • Making sure you uphold meeting discipline if you want them to happen • Clever ways of engaging and two-way communication
E-mail	• Can reach mass audiences fast • Cost effective and simple to use • Consistent and controlled message • Reaches the recipient directly • Good for information/awareness/ instruction	• Not everyone may have access • Impersonal and open to misinterpretation • Can result quickly in information overload, eg through poor conduct • Can't tell if messages have been read • Doesn't prioritize messages • Can't generate dialogue/ discussion • Can be forwarded to audiences outside the organization	• Controlling access to mass distribution lists • Using the subject box to get across your key message • Keeping it short and simple • Using headings and bullet points for key messages and to break up the text • Establishing a Code of Conduct • E-mail-free Fridays

TABLE 6.1 *continued*

Channel	At its best	Potential downsides	Think about
Intranet	• Fast and consistent • Possibilities are endless: can be entertaining, visually snappy and very engaging • Good for information store, reference and awareness raising • Info shares and bulletin boards good for involvement and discussion • Webstats show who is reading	• Not everyone may have access • Relies on people seeking out information • People may not have time to read it • Difficult to police • Can become unwieldy, hard to navigate and full of outdated information • Can quickly become redundant if not kept relevant, interesting, compelling and trustworthy	• Including 'killer content' to draw people in (expenses forms, classified ads, processes people need to do their jobs) • Making it as compelling as the external website • Making it a news hub, the No. 1 trusted information channel • Making it accessible on mobile devices
Internal social platforms and social media	• Can build strong communities that enable sharing across functions and geographies • Can provide feedback • Social media an accepted way of sharing for many	• Can be dominated by a little group of vocal people • Needs to be monitored and curated to foster dialogue and activity	• Why you're doing it (really needed?) • Getting help to build and facilitate the networks • Embracing micro-blogging sites like Yammer/Twitter/Chatter • And collaborative platforms like Jive

TABLE 6.1 *continued*

Channel	At its best	Potential downsides	Think about
Video	• Consistent, controlled message • Creative and entertaining • Can show real people talking about their experiences • Appeals to emotions • Can show proof of/track progress • Makes people and places accessible for a mass audience • Cost efficient way of getting eg CEO messages to global audiences	• Not interactive on its own • Can be seen as glossy corporate propaganda • Talking heads alone rarely engaging! • Can be difficult to arrange for mobile workforces to see	• Using as part of a briefing session to stimulate debate • How the video is to be staged and utilized • Using 'real people' to talk about their experiences, not just senior execs • Using customers, can be very powerful • Playing to people's emotions for understanding and commitment
Podcasts	• Can provide more information than a newspaper or magazine article • Provides the personal and emotional element missing from text	• Not a popular choice of channel so should not be used alone	• Acquiring proper audio editing computer software: podcasting a relatively simple software option with a microphone or standalone audio recorder with a USB cord • Buying an adapter that plugs audio recorders into phones to record interviews or conversations over the phone • Making a podcast hub and promoting it through your other channels

TABLE 6.1 *continued*

Channel	At its best	Potential downsides	Think about
Internal TV	• Establishes alignment across global communities • Adds credibility to strategic messages with the right host and journalist • Can be engaging and deliver several messages in short amount of time • Great for training your execs	• Potentially expensive • Not everyone may have access to watch it • Poor communicators shown up • Best communicator to talk about a subject may not be the most senior person, causing grief to IC people	• The right equipment including for reports outside the studio • Choosing the right host and journalists • Airtime choice/shows on demand. Don't overload and think you are going to be the new 24 hour CNN.
Print magazine	• Reaches the entire company with a consistent message • Even time-pressured staff can read in coffee breaks/on trains • Can address/reflect staff feedback and respond • Can show how everything fits together & reinforce company brand • Still the no. 1 preferred channel for remote workers • Utilizes offline/online conversion possibilities like QR Code and Blipper	• Can be seen as biased and not credible • Information dates quickly • Challenging to make it relevant to all audiences • No opportunity for discussion/checking understanding • Distribution can be costly	• What will hook people to open it? Eg a competition. • Using great pictures and interesting infographics • Using a staff editorial board to test content & make sure articles address the real issues • Being ambitious about your magazine content, getting famous people on your cover

TABLE 6.1 *continued*

Channel	At its best	Potential downsides	Think about
Notice boards	• Visible and may catch people's eye when too time pressured to read anything else • Good for instructions & information • Utilizes offline/online conversion possibilities like QR Code and Blipper	• May not be read • Usually no owner – how often do you see out of date posters? • Lose their impact if over-used by every project in the company	• Putting a 'display until' date on posters • Posting in prominent places such as in the lift or by the coffee machine
Text messaging	• Good for reaching remote workers • Good for crisis communication • Can be used to direct people to further sources of information • Can update senior managers on important news whilst on leave	• Will annoy people very quickly if overused! • Poor language and abbreviations not understood by all	• Making sure you have mobile contact details for all your senior team in case of crisis • With the possibilities offered by smart phones, opportunities to engage with rich content and dialogue tools
Events/road shows	• Opportunity for key people to reach mass audiences face to face • Flexible and responsive • Can include Q&A sessions, break out groups & involve people • Can build team spirit and motivate • Good communicators can use it to address controversial issues	• Can be one way 'tell' sessions • Agenda set by centre may not be what the audience wants • May be expensive • Time consuming for organisers, presenters and audience	• Involving staff in setting the agenda and format • Involving staff in event itself, as hosts or facilitators • Using interactive voting technology to maximize audience involvement

TABLE 6.1 *continued*

Channel	At its best	Potential downsides	Think about
Open forum	• Gives opportunity to raise and discuss the real issues • Genuine open dialogue • Helps leaders to understand how things really are • Enables people to feel heard	• Dismissive or aggressive response to questions can close down dialogue • Line managers can feel disempowered if their decisions are over-ruled or contradicted • Can be hijacked by a disaffected employee	• Issuing a summary of discussion for everyone to see • Proactively raising difficult issues or asking for questions in advance to prompt the real debate
Site visits	• Shows leaders are listening & want to see what the real issues are • Keeps leaders in touch with the real issues • Promotes dialogue & understanding	• Leaders won't experience the real issues if treated as 'royal visits' • May do more harm than good if leaders show by what they say that they are out of touch • Time-consuming for senior leaders to visit multiple sites	• Including a spell of work shadowing/call listening alongside organized forums • Giving leaders a good brief on site issues before they visit • Tracking issues raised and reporting back on actions
Voicemail	• Helpful for remote workers • Opportunity to hear about issues from senior leaders	• People will hang up if the message is too long	• Using a text message to alert remote workers to an urgent voice mail announcement

TABLE 6.1 continued

Channel	At its best	Potential downsides	Think about
Web-casting and similar	• Opportunity for senior leaders to reach mass audiences with consistent message in real time • Can involve Q&A sessions	• May be expensive • Needs the right technology in place • Noise levels may be inappropriate in some offices • May be difficult for all staff to be available at the same time (eg call centres)	• Finding out about new technology continually emerging in this area
Teleconferencing	• Live and two way, good for debate and discussion • Connects people across distances in a cost-effective way • Some companies will provide managed conference call facilities, particularly helpful for large groups	• Managed calls can be costly • People can be reluctant to ask questions	• Inviting questions in advance
Consultation forums	• Opportunity to involve and engage staff in key issues • Can help shape development of projects and communication to make sure it hits the mark	• May be challenging to convince leaders to involve staff early rather than tell them later... • May need to allow more time for implementation to allow for consultation	• Establishing a group to reach quickly and easily to test ideas • Making sure you understand when you must legally involve your consultation forum or union (very important) • Breaking down silos by involving people from different departments

TABLE 6.1 *continued*

Channel	At its best	Potential downsides	Think about
The rumour mill	• Great for understanding what are the hot topics and concerns	• Not the way you really want people to be getting their information	• Making sure you have a few informal routes of tapping into what rumours are doing the rounds (eg ask smoker who meets others to smoke)
Workplace accessories (eg mouse mats, PC surrounds)	• Puts key information visibly right in front of people • Particularly good for job-related information or instructions	• Need to be used sparingly to be effective	• Trying an innovative channel for job-related information eg printed sleeves for coffee mugs
Gimmicks and incentives	• Captures people's attention • May entice them to become involved or look at key information • Can add a light-hearted and humorous dimension	• May be seen as an unnecessary waste of money – environment needs to be right	• Reading about some of the things other companies have done to spark your imagination (Sky used chocolate pennies to raise awareness of pensions!)
Policies and actions	• Actions speak louder than words and will send a strong signal about the company's intentions	• Actions speak louder than words and will send a strong signal about the company's intentions!!	• Whether there are key policies or actions that will undermine your communication message

SOURCE: Produced in collaboration with Sue Dewhurst

TABLE 6.2 A sample channels catalogue

	It's for	It's not for	For whom	Notes
Update	Monthly operational and forward-marketing bible	Quick bites More enduring updates	For everyone but mostly operational managers	To be supported by monthly briefing
The monthly briefing	Highlighting important actions and laying out the big picture	General news Detailed instructions	Everyone but focused mainly on junior and customer-facing staff	Remember – our managers are not animated notice-boards – focus content on discussion
NOW!	Our magazine for celebrating teams and successes. It's where we talk about the brand	Lengthy instructions Sensitive material Management 'guff' or propaganda	For everyone with emphasis on team members	We aim at a positive and light style – it's about our family and reflects the voice of employees
Espresso	Newsflashes – short and sharp and directing managers to more detailed content on Intent	Lengthy items Items that can wait for Update Items that are not critical to safety, security or operational performance	For managers	Only the head of IC can issue Espresso notices. The channel is for urgent items only

TABLE 6.2 *continued*

	It's for	It's not for	For whom	Notes
Intent	Our intranet has two functions – news and as a repository for information. News has to be interesting and reflect the needs of readers	Internal propaganda or vanity updates (the needs of the reader are what helps us shape content)	All staff – with selected areas of additional information	We aim at a positive and informative style. People look at items in split seconds so relevance is key
Exec news bite	Ad-hoc communications by the exec team addressing urgent issues, performance or areas of celebration	Frequent use Matters that don't deserve the CEO's voice Long expositions	All staff – with facility to send limited release editions to top 100 or operations managers only	Copy is always drafted by IC – CEO will expect to edit himself – often considerably. Rarely stand-alone – supporting with Intent/In briefing notes

The key learning points from this chapter

The success or failure of a communication can depend on something as simple as choosing the right channel for delivery. Is it a push channel where you send the communication, or a pull one where people have to find it themselves?

You will need channels for communicating information fast, whether to update sales staff or communicate what is happening in a crisis. You will need channels that enhance inspiration and motivation among employees: one size does not fit all.

Don't be seduced by the social media sirens. While social media in the workplace can be useful, remember that only about 1 per cent of social media enthusiasts take an active part in it.

Notes and references

1 Quirke, B (1996) *Communicating Corporate Change: A practical guide to communication and corporate strategy*, McGraw-Hill, Maidenhead

2 McGovern, G (2010) *The Stranger's Long Neck: How to deliver what your customers really want online*, A&C Black, Edinburgh

3 Chui, M, Manyika, Bughin, J, Dobbs, R, Roxburgh, C, Sarrazin, H, Sands, G and Westergren, M (2012) *The Social Economy: Unlocking value and productivity through social technologies*, McKinsey Global Institute

4 McConnell, B and Huba, J (2006) The 1% Rule: Charting citizen participation, *Church of the Customer Blog* [Online] http://web.archive.org/web/20100511081141/ http:/www.churchofthecustomer.com/blog/2006/05/charting_wiki_p.html

5 Playle, T (2012) *Exploring Internal Communication*, PR Academy

07
Why line managers matter and how to support them

What you will learn from this chapter

Line managers are often the poor relations in the communication hierarchy of an organization. They get the blame for poor communication. They may have been promoted because they were good at their previous work, not because they were good people managers and communicators, yet they also have the job of connecting the grand strategy formulated by the board with its delivery by the employees on the shop floor.

Line managers do not always receive formal training on how to deliver a message in a compelling way or how to deliver difficult news, for example what to say when making people redundant. There are executives and leadership teams that consider communication a tick box exercise, part of an overall project plan to meet a deadline, but it's the local leaders and supervisors who have to make sense of the direction of the organization and make grand plans actually work.

However, with employee engagement becoming vital for successful organizations, executives are increasingly keen to establish frameworks and build capabilities to promote better internal communication through middle and frontline managers. Leaders of today understand that it requires skill to create buy-in. They are turning to their team of communication professionals to support and coach line managers to make this vital part of the communication chain work.

As one manager told us, 'Communication is not rocket science – it's more difficult than that.'

For a communication professional, helping your organization's leaders become better communicators is one of the most valuable legacies you can leave. This chapter will tell you how to do it. We look at why communication competence for line managers is essential, the answers to the five key questions that must be asked of them in relation to that competence, and give tried and tested ways of supporting them to communicate and engage more effectively.

The line manager as the make-or-break factor

"People don't leave companies, they leave managers."

We're not sure who said it first, but the truth behind this statement seems to be universally accepted. It was the message in Roger D'Aprix's 1982 book *Communicating for Productivity:*[1] the line manager is the key to engagement and motivation. It's a point we've returned to time and again in this book because every communicator discovers fairly quickly that if you truly want to engage audiences, you need to recognize that it is never going to be about articles, materials or PowerPoint presentations.

Employees have a human relationship with a manager. It is through human relationships that we get answers to the core questions that D'Aprix says are at the front of every employee's mind:

- What is my job?
- How am I doing?
- Does anyone care?
- How is my unit doing?
- Where are we heading?
- How can I help?

It is your local manager who is the expert in you and your job and, when s/he has dealt with your specific needs, is able to explain the bigger issues in a context that you will understand.

The evidence has been building around this point for many years. The work of Buckingham and Coffman looking at the relationships between high-performing teams and line manager behaviours highlights the importance of communication.[2] Drawing on data from 80,000 interviews with managers collected by the Gallup Organisation over 25 years, they found that high performance seems to be linked to relatively few factors. In fact, they argued that just 12 questions in a survey can tell you all you need to know about employee engagement and its impact on business success.[3]

Of interest to us is the fact that 8 of the 12 questions suggested by Buckingham and Coffman touch directly on communication issues. Furthermore, as we said in Chapter 2 on organizing internal communication, the work of Kathryn Yates also highlights a connection between business performance and communicative managers.

Underlying this is the role of the manager as the conduit of trust. Trust is the essential lubricant in an organization:[4] without it things don't get done, performance falls and engagement suffers. As any journalist will tell you, 'people trust people', so a strong set of local relationships is key to the success of any organization.[5] In short, if I trust my manager I probably trust my employer.

What then do we need managers to do?

D'Aprix put his finger on six specific questions that managers need to answer and highlighted that after dealing with the immediate challenge of defining someone's job they become translators. Larkin and Larkin,[6] wrote about the need for managers to put things into a context that regular employees understand. While head office might produce grand themes and messages, the line manager has to explain what it means on the ground and help people understand what they have to do differently.

Explaining change

Describing the role as a translator risks understating its importance. Make no mistake, if local leaders do not support a change or new message it will die. This is highlighted most strongly in the work of veteran consultant and writer Thomas J Lee[7] who consistently argues that change communication is most powerfully delivered by leaders (a term we use interchangeably with 'line managers').

Lee argues that regular communications such as those generated in the central communication team actually had a tiny impact on people's willingness to change their behaviours. He said that 'infrastructure' such as prescribed procedures or an IT system that ask people to follow set processes were only slightly more effective. We've all seen the truth in this point, witnessing people subvert official ways of working when they believe their old ways are better.

It is leaders who have the most impact on driving change, says Lee. Get them role-modelling and talking about change, he argues, and you'll see real results.

But what stops them doing it?

There are a large number of reasons why managers are not always successful at fulfilling their role in communication and driving engagement.

Communicators generally experience weak communication behaviour among managers, according to research from organizations such as Melcrum. They consistently point to issues such as:

- context: managers themselves not understanding how initiatives and plans fit within an overall vision;
- not buying the message: managers being expected to communicate messages with which they do not agree;

- responsibility for communication: 'it's not my job, it's the communication department's job';
- lack of personal confidence: not feeling that they have the skills or feeling they only have a limited repertoire of skills;
- not making time for communication to take place: communication seen as an added burden in an already heavy workload;
- nobody cares: knowing that no one would notice if they didn't bother to communicate or if they did, whether anyone would be interested in their feedback.

Are they walking the talk?

Finally, we should add a word of warning. A manager who communicates well is only useful when their actions match their words.

We said before that managers are the essential conduit of trust between an employee and their organization. Roger D'Aprix introduced us to the idea that there needs to be alignment between rhetoric and behaviour. As Figure 7.1 suggests, the impact of a lack of authenticity or honesty undermines the overall communication culture in an organization.

FIGURE 7.1   Just saying it doesn't make it so

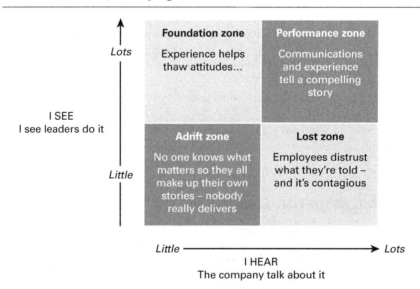

SOURCE: Based on work by Roger D'Aprix and Bill Quirke

Getting managers to do a great job of communicating therefore helps build commitment and engagement, drive performance and support change. But get it wrong and the damage to trust can be devastating.

It's not what you do but the way that you do it: the five key questions

How a manager communicates with his employees impacts the profitability, productivity and efficiency of an organization. We know from experience that real communication is very much more than an award-winning staff magazine, a best-practice intranet and a CEO who is willing to talk to his employees. These are all simply outputs. By themselves they will do little to produce the outcomes – the changes in employee behaviour – needed.

So where do you start to improve the effectiveness of your leaders at every level in their communication?

There are essentially five key questions that a communication manager can use to address the challenge. We believe that very few people have the perfect answer to all five questions, but it is our experience that concentrated effort on one or two of the questions will see real results in your organization's communication.[8]

FIGURE 7.2 The five questions

Do they know it's their job?	Who's talking to them?	Are they trained?	Have they got the right tools?	Is anyone listening?
Have they been told to do it? – in general – on specific topics	They can't add value if it is dumped on them without briefing	Are they getting more than presentation skills training?	Do they get materials that actually work with their teams?	Who cares if they don't do it or gather feedback?

1. Do they know it's their job?

A survey some years ago designed to kick-start better IC asked managers in a major oil company how they understood their responsibilities as communicators. Their answers ranged from: 'I haven't got time' to 'There's a house journal' to 'Don't they read the newspapers?'

These managers hadn't appreciated it was their job to communicate, possibly because no one previously had told them or showed them the connection between running a business and communication. There were few structures in place to reinforce the requirement. They were not trained for it, they were not assessed on it, and there were no performance bonuses for doing well at it. While there were team-briefing processes for both general and specific announcements they were not always followed. As one manager said: 'When I get those little pieces of paper from head office I put them in a drawer until they are dead.'

In fact, our experience in major organizations is that communication skills actually rarely feature in formal competency models for managers. Where they do, the detail of that competency tends not to be defined very much. Therefore, a communication manager might consider the following tactics to get the message across:

- Tell them it is part of their job:
  - either yourself or via the CEO;
  - make the point in general and repeat it with regular updates, perhaps stressing different day-by-day requirements.
- Define specific communication competencies together.
  - Go beyond talking about presentation skills, but talk about standards (how often) and what 'good' looks like (discussion, debate as well as awareness and understanding).
- Gather feedback from employees on how well their managers are communicating (and share it).
- Encourage the senior leadership team to set communication as a KPI.
- Make sure your data is robust enough so that communication effectiveness can be a consideration in pay and bonuses.

Crucially, ask upper managers to lead from the front, because mimicking the boss is almost universally seen as career enhancing!

2. Who's talking to them?

While managers are assumed to know more than the people reporting to them, that is not always true. Yet their teams expect them to know what is going on and how any changes will affect them. This only works if managers can bring rational information to life and make it meaningful. They cannot do this if the information has simply been dumped on them, with no chance to discuss it themselves.

Communication is a two-way process. Managers who simply repeat, parrot fashion, the information they have been given to pass on are not convincing. Simply stating the company line without putting it into context does not win hearts and minds.

If they feel that they have no value to add to the communications process you risk them blithely forwarding on e-mails and PowerPoint slides without comment. No manager wants to stand up in front of their teams and act like an animated noticeboard or look stupid when asked questions that assume he or she knows more than is in the official *communiqué*. In reality, most managers just won't do it – they would rather stay silent than risk being made a fool out of.

The question the communicator has to keep asking is 'How do I ensure the manager can add value to the communication?'

Bill Quirke and Dominic Walters[9] talk about communication as 'an unbroken chain of shared meaning'. They stress that 'leaders can only sell what they own, and ownership comes out of discussion and understanding – which takes time at all levels'. They argue for giving managers time to digest what is being shared and the space to extract the meaning that would make sense to their teams.

In short, managers need to understand the context themselves if they are to put information in context for their employees. That means:

- giving them the chance to discuss information before they relay it;
- getting to grips with its significance;
- challenging the rationale for themselves so that they can feel some ownership.

Broadly speaking there is a range of approaches you might need for keeping managers up to speed. Some are outlined in Figure 7.3 below.

FIGURE 7.3   What are your choices?

	Total immersion	Detailed briefing	Some sharing	Osmosis
Good for:	Where dramatic or sudden change is likely	When the situation is evolving quickly	When understanding is high	Stable situations
	• Major conference or senior briefing	• CEO conference call • Detailed or specific briefing packs • 'Key communicator' sessions	• Managers' newsletter • Cascaded 'core brief' • Localized briefings – focus on operational matters	• E-mail cascade • Day-to-day contact between supervisors • Informal feedback from events

At one extreme you might want to invite all managers to a conference or specific training where they get a deep immersion in the background issues. This might typically work for really significant events such as new strategy, unveiling the next year's targets or a major initiative.

The value is to demonstrate to managers that the business expects them to develop a deep understanding of the subject. It's a chance to reinforce the message that they should be communicating. A useful tactic for the communicator is to make sure that all speakers at a conference include in their content: 'What you need to discuss with your teams...'

So while managers are being briefed, encourage them to consider the questions that they should expect from their own teams. In one example we supported, managers were not even given copies of the materials to take away – all they had was a blank form prompting them to make their own notes and consider how they would handle the issues they would expect to come up. That ensured that issues were debated during the initial briefing.

If you are supplying follow-up materials, don't wait three weeks to send them out – ideally people should leave the event with them or at least have them waiting in their inbox overnight.

Naturally no organizations can afford to have their managers attending a continual round of internal conferences, but a more regular rhythm of communication can be achieved with a regular event such as a CEO WebEx or a monthly briefing. The aim should not be to hand out a pack of slides and hope that managers will be happy to parrot the contents unthinkingly. Instead, these sessions should have the flavour of a collaboration where managers get to debate the information being shared, raise questions and get the sense that they can shape the story before it goes on general release.

Remember, if you don't want managers to think they are being used as animated noticeboards they will need a chance to get comfortable with the issues being communicated. A lively discussion has the benefit of reinforcing to the managers that their peers are also communicating and giving them confidence that everyone at their level will be delivering a common message.

A rather old-fashioned approach is to send out a monthly core brief with some instructions about the issues to be discussed. It is our experience that this approach, without a detailed briefing conversation, is fast disappearing. It is tending to be replaced by more flexible processes such as a briefing conversation supported by some interactive tools.

Finally, the default briefing process of choice is osmosis – senior leaders commonly just assume that their managers know what is going on. Strangely enough, promoting someone or elevating their job title does not confer powers of clairvoyance. If this is the natural assumption in your organization, a communicator can add considerable value by staying close to the senior leadership and challenging them by asking: 'How will our managers know?'

The point we need to underline here is that a manager cannot be expected to translate messages and make them relevant for their team unless they have a depth of knowledge and insight that is greater than what can be shared in an e-mail. If you want a working line manager communications channel, senior leaders have to invest consistently in sharing and supporting their management cadre.

3. Have you trained them?

Let's start by stating what this is *not* about. It is *not* about turning managers into slick PowerPoint presenters. It is *not* about turning them into orators. It is *not* about giving them the jargon-filled vocabulary of business speak, teaching them how to 'put a positive spin on...' And it is not just about finding the right words for e-mails and team briefings.

Great managers who are brilliant communicators need to learn how to:

- focus on the team and what they need;
- translate ideas and information into something relevant for the team;
- listen;
- understand different points of view;
- be authentic, meaning what they say.

Positioning any training is vitally important. Telling managers they are poor communicators is probably going to be counterproductive as it won't ring true to anyone who can read, write and talk and so believes they can communicate perfectly well.

It is far wiser to encourage managers to take time out in a workshop to think about what they are doing, share ideas with colleagues and change their mindset from simply telling to listening and engaging.

Organizing training for managers in team communication skills can be problematic. Managers tend to be short of time and, as they progress in their careers, may not feel a personal need to learn more about a subject they have already mastered.

Think about starting with a simple toolkit full of tips and hints that might 'remind' them of things they have 'forgotten'.

Consider developing communication training that fits within another subject, for example we have seen very effective communication components built into training on leading safety, quality management and ethics. Wrapping skills development around an issue that is a pressing concern always works well and is often welcome because it comes at a moment when the manager is worrying about explaining a particular issue.

Where you have a large network of communicators it is worth considering developing a standard one or two-hour module that the communication team can facilitate around the organization.

Your training should not just be about formal team meetings. It should also be about managers' everyday behaviours and interactions with others, whether by the coffee machine, in a canteen or being asked for a one-to-one session. When they have understood that genuine communication is not about polished perfection but about taking care and being authentic (or personally credible) then it is time to move on to the next steps.

Well-planned training and coaching will help them think about:

- **Why am I communicating?** Leadership communication has a purpose. There is a desired outcome that means the manager must anticipate what they want people to think, feel and do to produce that outcome.
- **What will my team think?** They will not think anything unless the communication is made relevant or meaningful for them. The manager therefore needs to explain the context of the communication and think of answers to anticipated questions.

- **What do I want people to remember?** This is about focus on the key messages. It is wise to limit them to three or four – too many messages and people do not remember any of them – or only remember the least relevant ones. Sometimes it is useful to promote a model of talking about the same three things, for example CUSTOMERS–PERFORMANCE–PLANS, as a handy rubric for structuring their thoughts.

- **What type of message do I want to deliver?** Is it about a practice fire drill, explaining that the IT system will be down for a couple of hours, or the start of a change management programme? Is it an e-mail, a one-to-one or a team discussion?

- **What is the best way to say the messages?** With this, as with the preceding questions, the internal communicator can work with the manager to make the messages interesting, acting as a sounding board for how they will land.

- **Is there a practical example that I can give?** Many of us respond better when we can hear a story that illustrates the point being made rather than when poring over endless spreadsheets and tables. Help managers to think about gathering genuine examples that bring an issue to life (we include some advice on coaching story-telling in Chapter 8 on working with senior leaders).

- **How will I know it worked?** Getting feedback is an essential part of the communication process, not least because it will tell the manager if anything else needs to be done (we will discuss more on feedback later in the chapter).

To recap, a manager's communication is about credibility, context and translating 'strategy' into 'to do'. It is about making time for debate. It is not about repeating facts, company propaganda or information better conveyed by other departments such as pensions information. The most convenient channel, for example e-mail, may not be the best one. For a leader, communication is part of the day job. It is not something to be left to the communication department. It is about taking responsibility for engaging people. It is about being clear with regard to what you want people to *know*, *feel* and *do*.

What should you cover in manager training?

Every organization has different needs but here is a checklist of topics to cover in training for line managers:

- what is expected of them as line managers in your organization;

- understanding their role as translators and facilitators and that communication is about more than telling;

- planning their communications, starting with the desired business outcome;
- seeing things from the audience's point of view;
- deciding on simple messages;
- starting a discussion;
- making it interesting – tips and tools to vary the pace;
- using stories to bring it to life and make it authentic;
- keeping a discussion going;
- gathering feedback and reactions;
- handling common challenges in a discussion;
- keeping the momentum up – making a regular commitment.

4. Are you giving them the tools and materials they need?

There are few things worse than a line manager feeling that they cannot add value to a communication and so simply hitting 'forward' on the e-mail containing the briefing package. A communicator needs to understand what tools managers need to help them translate messages into something valuable for their teams.

Start by actually asking managers what they like and value. This can be done in a number of ways:

- As part of your regular contact with managers ask what tools they are finding useful and what less so.
- Ask managers occasionally what they actually do – they often have their own tools that they are happy to share or can be developed for wider use.
- Ask new joiners how manager communications worked in their last organization – they often have experience that can be directly translated into your workplace.
- Actively get feedback on everything you send out – what works? How could it be improved?

Remember, as we keep saying, that your ambition is that managers should be more than animated noticeboards. They have the most impact when it comes to helping people understand and get excited – which are reactions that are most likely to come when there is some form of interaction and conversation. However, not everyone is naturally adept at starting a conversation – many of us are terrified enough just standing in front of an audience, so facilitating a discussion represents a whole new level of fear!

A communicator should therefore think about supplying tools that help make the task of getting the conversation started easier and developing it into practical ideas. There are a number of approaches which we have found useful over the years.

- **If you really have to use PowerPoint...** at least tailor it! Avoid the temptation to cannibalize information from the presentation used for financial analysts and think about making it visually appealing. If possible consider replacing the slides with images and inserting explanatory text in the notes pages.

  Make sure they know where you expect them to customize the material. A simple trick is to include blank pages headed in bright red with 'INSERT LOCAL EXAMPLE HERE'.

- **Suggest activities.** Provide a simple activity that they can use in a team meeting. This might be a fresh format for a brainstorming session or instructions on how to get everyone out of their chairs to take part in a problem-solving task. A conversation with the training team in HR can often come up with some inspiring ideas, as can looking online for training games.

- **Video packages can work – if they are short.** Provide a short video to explain a complex idea or a subject that the team leader cannot be expected to be an expert in. Assuming that the manager has the ability to actually show a film, try to keep it short – cost and limited attention spans suggest that under three minutes normally works (although we know one animator who believes 70 seconds is the optimum length for a film in a team meeting).

  Accompany a video with a one-page set of talking points to make sure the team manager is able to follow up on the film.

- **Supply a page of talking points.** On a single sheet of paper, list the key messages that the manager might want to deliver and a set of suggested open questions that they can throw out to get the conversation going.

- **Questions and answers... use with care.** There is often a temptation to supply a set of standard Q and As and very often no one ever looks at them! Q and A sheets get used in our experience when they are short, factual and not written for the benefit of the legal department. The communicator's skill lies in anticipating the questions that real people will ask and suggesting simple ways in which they can be answered.

  Consider being clear about where and when more information will be forthcoming. Most importantly, remember that your organization employs line managers who are not idiots and who won't want to sound like they are the unthinking mouthpiece of the senior management.

Finally, anticipate that the written Q and A sheet may well find itself in circulation – a patronizing or evasively political answer is best dropped before you turn your organization into a laughing stock!

If you are working with a global population, managers will have different approaches around the world. Crudely put, European managers may see the need to discuss and debate issues with their teams while in other parts of the world staff will expect their leader to issue clear instructions: here a discussion might be confusing and uncomfortable. In such cases you may need to produce different tools to support different groups of managers. Perhaps one group might want discussion guides and materials to chew over, perhaps another wants a lively but clear video saying what has to be done in detail.

Simple tips and advice

Many organizations provide their managers with simple guides or *aide memoires* to help them handle common communication issues. If you have not already produced one, consider developing a toolkit – it's also a handy way of reminding managers that communication is their responsibility.

Below we suggest some possible subject areas.

Tips for communicating bad news may include:

- Do not necessarily wait until you have all the information.

- Aim to reduce lag time between telling employees and the event, so build in regular update sessions.

- Craft the message, because the potential for misunderstanding is highest in emotional situations.

- Give the full information: do not start talking about something and then stop and withhold information.

- Handle questions honestly with this simple formula:

  - ACKNOWLEDGE and listen carefully to the emotion and sentiment behind the question;

  - RESPOND with the facts as you know them;

  - BRIDGE to your core message.

Tips for dealing with permanent sceptics include:

- finding ways to involve them;

- taking time to cover all aspects of communication, tying up loose ends;

- setting up channels for feedback and upward communication;

- being firm, repeating the message/s;

- above all, not waiting for consensus before acting.

What process are you using for them? Options for team briefings

Here are some examples of different types of team briefing templates that need little adaptation, but which work well.

Example 1: quick huddle or 'toolbox talk'

When faced with rapid change, managing a project or when there is a daily need to remind people of business or perhaps safety issues, consider developing a format for a daily huddle or 'toolbox talk': a system where you could run a team briefing in a very short period, as little as 10–15 minutes. Break down the meeting into a standard set of 'air time' minutes:

- four minutes to open;
- four minutes to clarify topics;
- up to one minute to close.

You can simplify the format even further by standardizing the topics into a memorable list such as CUSTOMERS–SERVICES–PEOPLE (which also lends itself to a format for noticeboards or other communications).

Provide a guide that spells out what to talk about in the first four minutes, the next four minutes and so on. You can enhance the experience for managers by giving them blank documents to use themselves to run team briefings on their own if they have a topic to discuss.

The idea is that this is so quick and so sharp that it gets to issues quickly. You can do it at the beginning or at the end of a shift without cutting into work time too much, or you can make it part of the daily timetable by naming it '10 at 10'!

Example 2: team conversation template

Where a team has a regular meeting, provide a blank template such as the one opposite, with a number of standard headings. The standard headings underline what is important in the organization and should help a manager translate larger messages into local actions.

The subject boxes can be as basic or creative as you like. It is more memorable if you can find an approach that perhaps covers PRIDE–PERFORMANCE–PEOPLE or CUSTOMERS–COSTS–CARE–PEOPLE. These are examples from organizations we have worked with but the approach works well in most places with a little imagination.

How a template might work is illustrated in Figure 7.4.

FIGURE 7.4 Team conversation template

ISSUE	MY NOTES
SAFETY • We need to know about all near miss incidents • If we don't know we can't spot trends and prevent something nastier happening • It might seem trivial at the time but there could be a pattern • We can only achieve Target Zero if we get smart	• Remind about ladder issue last week • What is stopping us reporting near misses? • Has anyone reported a near miss lately – how did they find the process? • Tell Solihull story
CUSTOMER NEWS • We won the XYZ contract last week – details online at CONNECT • This win secures work in South West region for two years • It shows we can break into new customers • We have helped XYZ customer secure funding for their bid to run XYZ project	• What do people know about XYZ? • XYZ contract means a number of us will be busy on set-up in August • Feedback from ABC – what are we doing right there?
TRAINING AND TOOLS	• New craft courses taking bookings – will be putting in next week • What skills are we missing after Helen? How can we replace?
PEOPLE	• Birthdays this month (Peter, Sukhjit) • Holidays – who off? Are all dates on planner? • Congrats to Crew 1 on XYZ completion • Linda and summer barbecue

Preparing the template is also a task that can be done in a briefing with a more senior leader. Managers can use the blank sheets as an *aide memoire* for their own messages and take the opportunity to debate with their peers the best way to discuss a particular issue or problem.

Where a standardized approach is not appropriate, you might offer more detailed advice about the structure of a team meeting along the following lines:

1 Open the meeting (5%).

  – Briefly but clearly outline the purpose.

2 Paint the overall picture of change (20%).

  – Be honest and clear.

  – Establish 'line of sight' (ie the connection between the information for the team and how it fits into the big picture)

  – Establish 'what's in it for them' – how the change will benefit them.

3 Have an open discussion on the implications of the announcement (60%).

  – Draw out concerns.

  – For each concern, reiterate it first to get clarity and show understanding. Then either provide an answer or be honest that you don't have an answer, but promise to have one by a specified date.

4 Agree on actions/next steps (10%).

  – Get clarity on what will happen as a result.

  – Capture these ideas and be sure to follow them up.

5 Close (5%).

  – Reiterate the two or three key action points to come out of the meeting and be sure there is agreement.

  – Be positive and confident about where this will go.

  – Encourage employees to come to you with any further concerns they may have.

  – Thank them for their time and input.

Consider providing a simple guide to briefing dos and don'ts:

TABLE 7.1   Dos and don'ts: advice for managers

DO	DON'T
Give them time Remember employees are trying to process all this information for the first time. Be understanding if they do not get everything in one go. (Beginning the reply, 'Well, as I explained only a minute ago...' will cause resentment and other legitimate concerns will get buried.)	**Be defensive...** impatient or antagonistic: 'I hear what you're saying, but you're not focusing on the things you should be.' 'I think that's a very pessimistic attitude to take.' 'Well, I hope you don't all feel like that.'
Give them respect Show understanding and, where appropriate, concern and sympathy.	**Be evasive...** by brushing aside challenges without answering them: 'Look, I understand you have concerns, but we just need you to get behind this right now...' 'Let's focus on one thing at a time...' 'We haven't got time to go into that now...' (if you really do not have the time, name a time when you will, preferably as soon as possible)
Give them answers And keep them honest, relevant and precise. Be open if you cannot answer a question and either: a promise to follow it up – but then you must follow it up, or b engage the audience by throwing it back onto them and asking them to suggest solutions or answers, where appropriate.	**Be destructive...** by passing the buck: 'I know, I know, it's head office again, they've got no idea...' **And the cardinal sin: NEVER promise to come back with an answer, then fail to do so.**
Give them a voice Take their feedback back up the organization. Let them know you have done so, and what is being done as a result. If nothing can be done, say why: it is legitimate for an organization to say 'no' on grounds of, for example, cost, timing or competitiveness.	

5. Is anyone listening/watching?

Earlier we said that communicating is not something that every manager thinks is his or her natural responsibility. If they think no one cares or is interested in their contribution to the communications mix, they will soon become disheartened. If you ask them to gather feedback that goes nowhere, you'll just alienate them and they'll be less inclined to make an effort if they think their team does not believe they have a line to the top!

In planning your line manager communications you need to think about two elements of tracking:

- acknowledging feedback;
- monitoring that they are actually doing it.

Acknowledging feedback

When managers send you feedback, not unreasonably they expect something to happen with it. The communication team should think carefully about ensuring the feedback reaches the person who should act on it.

This may be as simple as providing the CEO with a regular printout of the feedback received and encouraging them to refer to it when they speak to the organization. Imagine how potent it is when the CEO talks about an issue your manager promised to raise with him or her!

Perhaps you can make a space for the feedback to be discussed at the next leaders' briefing or maybe there is an article you can publish on the intranet highlighting concerns raised in team discussions.

Monitoring that they are actually doing it

People approach this challenge in a number of ways, ranging from adding questions to the staff survey like: 'Have you had a regular meeting with your team manager to discuss change?' to simply asking to sit in on a few sessions.

Chapter 10 on evaluation should give you some inspiration in this area but make sure it is done with sensitivity. Managers work best when they do things their own way and many will be uncomfortable with the whole process. Micromanagement rarely gets positive results in the long term!

It is best to focus on the outcomes rather than the process, as we keep repeating in this book. If you are going to use a survey, consider what outcome measures you need, such as testing whether people understand how change applies to them or whether they feel supported during change.

Coaching tip – it's not about the words

Communication coaching is not just about helping managers frame
the right messages to deliver in the right places at the right time.
How they deliver those messages is at least as, if not more, important.
If a manager delivers a statement looking hunched up and defensive,
even if it is good news it will not be believed.

The value of a line manager communicating lies in the human contact: employees want to look them in the eye and make a personal judgement based on their gut instinct. While they don't expect Nelson Mandela or Barack Obama, they want to feel that the person talking with them is comfortable with the message and has the confidence to lead them. So the communication professional needs to explain to their managers how their style is perceived, work with them to play to their strengths and learn how to perform in a way that is not second nature to them. Those comfortable with facts may not be comfortable with feelings and vice versa, but both are needed for effective line manager communication.

Mehrabian[10] suggested that the words we use when we communicate actually account for a relatively small proportion of the impact. What we take away from a conversation can be dictated by the body language or the tone of voice of the presenter. But most of us spend ages on the text that we want to deliver and forget to think about the other factors that will shape the audience's perception.

While you may not be able to get a manager to undergo a fundamental transformation in their personality, you can coach them to make life easier for themselves. Suggest that they make themselves familiar with the room where they are to present rather than rushing in at the last minute. Encourage them to think about clearing their diary so they don't have to worry about the next meeting and ensure they have enough time to manage a conversation in an unhurried way.

Explain the core principles they must work with:

- seeing the communication from the point of view of employees;

- setting clear expectations of what is going to happen next;

- setting the context before diving into the detail;

- anticipating potential interpretations (and misinterpretations) of messages, events and symbols;

- avoiding thinking that one person speaks for all;

- remembering that the credibility of a source shapes everything;

- repeating yourself is necessary – not boring!

Contracting to be effective

When you study line manager communications practice in your organization, you will most likely come across, time and again, the same problems. You'll hear of managers who frequently cancel team meetings or of employees frustrated that there is never any follow up on important issues. Helping managers to inject a degree of discipline into their arrangements makes a world of difference.

You can help by creating the idea of a team communication contract.

Start by interviewing the team either individually or as a group and exploring their communication likes and dislikes. Remember that people often use 'poor communication' as a way of talking about wider issues, so a conversation needs to be facilitated carefully. Be sure to ask for specific examples and suggestions and challenge people to tell you what benefit they would see in adopting a particular course of action.

If possible, get the team to categorize their views into four categories:

- things we'd like to STOP altogether;
- things we'd like to see LESS of;
- things we'd like to see MORE of;
- things we'd like to START doing.

Armed with this feedback you can discuss with the manager of the team what might go into a contract that they would be able to discuss with their teams. Typically you might find that the contract will cover issues such as:

- timing;
- content;
- participation;
- sharing information.

Discussion with the team will enable you to come up with a small number of routines that everyone can pledge to follow. After six months ask the teams to review the contracts and discuss what has worked and what is no longer relevant.

This exercise will also help you develop the syllabus for any general line manager training that you might want to develop.

The key learning points from this chapter

We have attempted to underline some key points in this chapter.

Line managers can be one of the most powerful channels of communication in your organization because people like to hear from and discuss issues with someone they know and, crucially, who knows them. A line manager is an effective communicator when they can translate messages into a local context.

However, line managers are not always naturally active in fulfilling their role and the communication team can see dramatic improvements when they address five issues:

- Make sure they know what is expected of them.
- Make sure managers are properly briefed – they need love and attention and not just to be treated as animated noticeboards.
- Think about developing skills and capabilities.
- Give them tools and materials that they want to use.
- Make sure they know someone is listening to the feedback that they gather for you.

Notes and references

1 D'Aprix, R (1982) *Communicating for Productivity*, Harper and Row, New York

2 Buckingham, M and Coffman, C (1999) *First, Break All the Rules: What the world's greatest managers do differently*, Simon & Schuster, New York

3 For an interesting discussion of the usefulness of standard models such as the Gallup Q12 look at Walker, S (2012) *Employee Engagement and Communication Research: Measurement, strategy and action*, Kogan Page, London.

4 To explore more around this issue, it is worth looking at the work of David Guest, including Guest, D E (2004) The psychology of the employment relationship: an analysis based on the psychological contract, *Applied Psychology*, 53 (4), pp 541–55.

5 An important case study that dates back to 2002, looking at the behaviour of staff in a chain of hotels and how trust in managers shaped it, is in Simons, T (2002) The high cost of lost trust, *Harvard Business Review*, 80 (9), pp 18–19.

6 TJ and Sandra Larkin's landmark thinking on this subject is laid out in Larkin TJ and Larkin, S (1996) Reaching and changing frontline employees, *Harvard Business Review*, 74 (3), pp 95–104. Although quite old it is useful reading for anyone wanting to understand the evolution of the idea that good leaders are great communicators.

7 Thomas J Lee blogs at MindingGaps.com and has been published widely in *Strategic Communications Management* and *Communication World*, among other places.

8 This work was first outlined by Sue Dewhurst and Liam FitzPatrick in *Strategic Communication Management*, in the article 'Bring out the excellent communicator in managers' in the Aug/Sept 2007 issue.

9 Quirke, B and Walters, D (2003) What every manager should know about communication, *Strategic Communication Management*, 7 (5), pp 26–29

10 Mehrabian, A (1977) *Nonverbal Communication*, Transaction Publishers, New Jersey

08
Working with senior leaders

What you will learn from this chapter

In the past, a chief executive was a mysterious and remote force in most organizations. They arrived in a chauffeur-driven car, parked in their dedicated space outside the front door of the executive block and disappeared into their offices. The provision of executive dining rooms and toilets ensured that no ordinary mortal ever needed to see them. If a regular employee did hear from them it was through the staff magazine once or twice a year. Communication was something that the personnel department worried about: the idea that the big boss needed to motivate and talk to staff was probably seen as a strange idea, something quaintly military or even an impertinence.

Now you will struggle to find a leader who doesn't say that communication is a high priority. In his book on the subject, Kevin Murray was able to quote dozens of leaders from the public and private sectors who claimed that good communication was the central challenge of the executive floor.[1]

The recognition of the need for great communication from the top is one of the reasons why internal communication has become a serious profession. If it matters to the CEO then it needs to be properly resourced.

This chapter looks at why and how the internal communicator should support their senior leaders and argues that fulfilling the role of trusted adviser opens the door to achieving many of the other things we believe are the rightful role of the IC team. If you can help the CEO deliver, you win the licence to do all the other things that you need to do.

We also talk about our concept of 'executiveness' – remembering that the boss is the boss and not spreading them too thinly. Sometimes it seems that every project manager is convinced that their initiative is doomed unless they have the public endorsement of the CEO. We talk about the role of the internal communicator in not squandering the ability of the CEO to make an impact.

We'll talk about not just how to work with the CEO, but how these thoughts are equally applicable to any senior manager such as divisional director, site manager or programme leader. In this chapter we will use the terms 'CEO', 'senior leader' and 'boss' to refer to anyone who should be performing a role as a figurehead and to whom local supervisors or managers look up.

Why should anyone care about making the CEO look good?

In 2012, the IABC published a study looking at what CEOs thought about communication as a discipline.[2] It highlighted that top leaders care about communication – in the modern era there cannot be a CEO who thinks communication or reputation are unimportant. When, according to management consultants Booz & Co (now Strategy&), CEOs in large companies have a shorter and shorter period of time in office when they can make an impact, it is hardly surprising that getting communication right is high on their list of priorities.

The IABC study said that the men and women who run our companies and enterprises worry about being always visible, aligning competing interests and diverse stakeholders, talking to everyone, being flexible in their styles to reach different audiences and knowing that the personality of the top person is often taken to be the personality of the organization. 'Get your communications wrong and it could be fatal' is the message that has been drummed into them at countless business schools and over long careers.

There's a truism that can be seen at work in most organizations: what the CEO does gets copied. If the boss wears a tailored suit every day so will most of their subordinates. If the boss starts turning up in jeans and getting excited about sports cars, guess what the upper levels of management will start doing. If they act like communication is unimportant then managers lower down the organization will deprioritize talking with their teams.

Get the boss doing the right thing around communication and you are halfway towards persuading line managers to make an effort to engage and connect with the people they manage. This is because senior executives understand that there is a difference between management – the process of seeing things done properly – and leadership – the process of getting people to follow a vision and be inspired to commit to the success of the organization.

However, most top leaders do not get the job because they are communicators. It is estimated that over half of CEOs begin their careers in accountancy or finance. Being an expert at how to manage communication is not a core competence on the way up, so they need help. That's not to say that CEOs are all high-functioning sociopaths, just that communication management is not a skill they tend to develop on the journey to the boardroom.

Leaders need help to get it right and the rise of internal communication as a professional function is surely linked to the realization in boardrooms that what we do is important. Being blunt, supporting the most senior leader in our organization is perhaps one of the most important parts of our role. If the boss fails at communication, we have failed.

The boss and engagement

Your CEO or top leaders should care about communication because it is perhaps the single biggest driver in employee engagement, and they know it.

Above we mentioned the IABC study into what CEOs think about communication. The study found leaders saw the importance of good communication and there is good reason for that view. When leaders are visible, communicative and interesting, people work harder. They produce better results than in organizations that are less well engaged. Communicators need to understand the evidence for this.

Consistently, commentators and analysts such as Thomas J Lee,[3] David MacLeod and Nita Clarke,[4] Melcrum and consultants Towers Watson[5] highlight that the actions of senior leadership are one of the top drivers of employee engagement. Indeed, this is the central theme of John Smythe's landmark book *The Chief Engagement Officer*.[6] This is borne out by findings from employee research companies such as International Survey Research (ISR).[7] Based on a statistical analysis of over 350,000 workers in their worldwide database, they concluded that the drivers of engagement (in order of potency) are:

- leadership;
- development;
- empowerment;
- supervision.

Emma Soane[8] talks about four key areas where strong leadership supports engagement:

- Idealized leadership – the extent to which leaders create a sense of pride and discuss how people are all working for the same purpose.
- Inspiration motivation – how far the leader excites people about a set of goals and the route to achieving them.
- Intellectual stimulation – encouraging followers to look at issues and problems in a different way, promoting individual responsibility and creativity.
- Individualized consideration – taking time to understand what people need from their jobs and making space for them to be supported in their development.

In other words, we are most likely to be connected and committed at work when we have good leaders, both locally and at the top of our organization. We make judgements about issues such as the rightness of the organization purpose, the validity of our goals, the achievability of the processes and how we fit in as individuals as much on emotional criteria as on rational factors. Our attitude to the top leadership of our organization is key: we'll follow if we think the individuals at the front are worth following.

Why should the IC team care?

We said above that when the boss fails at communication, we have failed in our job. In our experience, the most effective communication teams work in organizations where the top leadership communicate well. The relationship is not coincidental: it is symbiotic.

Somebody has to help – but it's a privilege, not a right

Our leaders have many pressures on their time and energies. They certainly don't have time to worry about the mechanics of communications and will delegate logistics and planning work to someone. That someone should be us.

Our experience is that helping with the most routine logistical issues makes a difference. A leader might want someone to fix the audiovisual equipment for a town hall meeting, but would someone without our professional background understand the impact that the wrong choices of microphone might have? And would a non-professional working on a PowerPoint deck spot the dangers of over-wordy slides?

Surely if the CEO needs help it is best that she or he comes to someone who can be more than a technician. Our professionalism is about more than the delivery of tools or collateral. We're at our best when we advise, when we bring insight and when we coach. When we can be treated as a trusted adviser we bring so much more to our work.

Senior communication managers consistently talk about their role supporting the CEO or the key leaders in their organization. They will tell you that their role involves making sure that things work when the boss needs to communicate but also talking about ideas and issues beyond the immediate remit of how a particular event should be managed or the words to use in the next leadership e-mail.

This is possible when we bring two things to the conversation: dependability and insight.

The CEO has to have someone who will always make things work. When they need help they will always turn to the person on whom they can depend to give them what they need, be it a working microphone, a speech they can deliver or a web chat that is efficient and well attended. Getting communication right for a CEO is commonly highly stressful and someone who can remove that stress is likely to be appreciated and trusted. The person who adds to the stress, who lets the boss stumble or who lets them look lost will find themselves quickly replaced.

When we are dependable we are indispensable.

Additionally, a smart CEO knows that they are surrounded by people who they cannot always trust to tell them the whole truth. The moment you are promoted, your friends stop telling you things and by the time you are running the business, your colleagues invest time in managing what you know about their areas of responsibility. If you are a senior director are you going to proactively tell the boss about problems in your area of responsibility that you should be fixing?

Who is going to tell the CEO what people in the business are really thinking or saying?

The role of communication management puts us in the ideal position to make sure that the people who run our organizations know what is going on. Because we have to argue in favour of a particular tone of voice or tactic, we have to be able to demonstrate that we are connected with the internal audiences. As we have suggested in Chapter 4 on audiences, once you have established that you have a reliable ear to the ground you will find that your advice is not only accepted but sought out time and again.

'Executiveness': using the resource wisely

Sooner or later, a project team decides that their initiative is doomed unless the CEO records a personal video supporting it. If that doesn't work, perhaps an all-staff e-mail from the CEO's account is exactly the thing to assure the success of the scheme on which they are working.

There are occasions when this makes sense: when the project is of sufficient importance or significance that the boss's stamp is clear for all to see. However, most of the time, it won't make much difference and for most projects the endorsement from the top won't be the make-or-break factor.

From an employee's perspective, it is a real turn-off when they get endless exhortations to support one trivial initiative after the next. As it is, you will probably find that a large proportion of your workforce automatically ignore messages from the very top. Start spamming them breathlessly with news of the canteen reupholstering project or the roll-out of the latest Windows product and you'll turn them off even further.

The boss is the boss and should talk about boss-type issues. We call this quality *executiveness* – in other words, people want to know that someone senior is running the place and that they are concerned with the things that matter. When people receive multiple messages from the same source it becomes hard to tell what is really important. Executiveness is a mindset about having clarity over your message, focusing on strategic rather than trivial issues and letting middle managers manage the areas where they have responsibility.

It's someone's job to make sure that this quality is protected and used when it can have the right impact.

Every CEO or senior leader is different in their style and how they like to communicate. Some prefer to be highly visible or hands-on while others feel more comfortable being reserved. Regardless of personal style they have to be the voice of something important: what the boss talks about is what matters. It sets the tone for the whole organization and it is the business of the IC team to make sure it doesn't become diluted or squandered.

This isn't just about limiting the subjects on which the boss makes pronouncements. It is also about considering how best to use the limited time they have. If people see more of the boss than the security guard at the entrance gate you may be watering down the impact that a message from the top can deliver.

Our role is to work with the most senior managers to plan the cycle of their communications. This might involve deciding a cycle around key business events such as quarterly results, the findings of the employee engagement survey and the setting of annual objectives. Setting out some core dates and events around which communications happens will lessen the risk of over-familiarity and give local managers the space to communicate.

Finally, having someone worry about the messages coming from the CEO or most senior leaders helps promote consistency. If messages are mixed, if promises to follow up are not honoured or the story seems to change from week to week, your boss is going to lose credibility. If we can keep them on track, remind them of what was said last week or point out our potential inconsistencies we can help them maintain engagement and drive the organization in the direction they want.

What does it mean to be a 'trusted adviser'?

The role of the IC team in supporting the most senior managers is vital to the health and well-being of the organization. They need support and that support should cover practicalities, providing honest feedback, keeping their message clear and ensuring people hear what is really important. No one else is better placed to bring together all the skills needed to fulfil this role. If we are not offering all these types of support, where else is it going to come from?

Being present at the moment of practical need is an opportunity for internal communication. How often do we hear talk about getting a 'seat at the table' because having the ear of senior leaders enables a professional to do so? When we are trusted we get the space to try out new ideas, to challenge when we see how our messages are undermined by business practice and to build a team that can do all the things we know need doing.

How this works is explored in detail in Maister, Green and Galford's book *The Trusted Advisor*,[9] which should be essential reading for anyone in an internal communication role. Originally written for providers of professional services such as accountants and lawyers, much of its advice can be applied to internal communicators.

The authors' key point is that over time, an adviser progressively offers information, then solutions, then ideas and finally a 'safe haven for hard issues'. In order to deepen the relationship with the client, the adviser starts by providing specific technical support or answers, then focusing on wider business problems before becoming progressively more concerned with the individual needs of the client.

In essence, the challenge is to come to the relationship with an interest in what matters to the boss and how to provide it. This is the exact opposite of sitting with the CEO and discussing why you need a bigger intranet or what best practice in our field suggests he or she should be doing. You get results and build a relationship by asking yourself what it is that the boss needs from a business and from a personal perspective. And by taking every opportunity you can to deliver it to them.

This means seeing yourself as part of the CEO's outer office. Often people are advised to 'make friends with the CEO's PA' because you and the team supporting the boss should have the same objectives. Spending time with that team holds the key to developing a relationship based on your ability to anticipate and deliver for the uppermost leaders and if you are delivering for them you will be delivering for the organization.

Getting alongside the boss – some core relationship principles

- See yourself as part of the CEO's home team.
- Know the business and industry as well as them.
- Know agendas and calendars.
- Never let them down.
- Never let her or him go out unbriefed.
- No one should have better information about your audiences, their likes and issues than you.
- Fiercely protect their executiveness.
- Use your interactions properly:
  - come with data but use it to tell a story;
  - it's always about them – if your agenda doesn't match theirs don't waste everyone's time;
  - be ready to grab the chances when they come.

Keep it brief – or keep a summary version handy!

Starting out by counting the 'Cs'

It can be a challenge to know where to begin when it comes to supporting senior leaders. You can sit back and wait for them to call you for advice, but the call may never come. Or you can think through where they could be improving their impact and how you can help in anticipation of the day when you meet in the lift or you are summoned to help draft the New Year Message!

There is a bewildering amount of advice on the subject of leadership communication. However, knowing where to begin can be a challenge so we use a simple checklist called the 'four Cs of the C-Suite' as a shorthand for identifying where there are opportunities for improvement. The closely interrelated principles are that the leader needs to be:

- clear and compelling;
- connected;
- consistent;
- committed.

FIGURE 8.1 The four Cs of C-suite communication

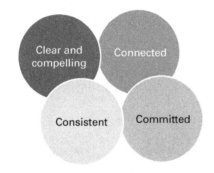

Clear and compelling

Almost every book that you read on the subject of leadership talks about the need for leaders to set out a clear vision. People talk about 'setting a dot on the horizon': showing people where the organization is headed.

Unfortunately, the communication challenge is more difficult than sending an e-mail containing the target budget for next year. Talking money alone rarely does it for most employees – especially when they cannot see the link between the success of their organization and the size of their pay packet.

Rather, people want to know that their organization has a clear reason for being: one that they can discuss with their family and friends with pride. They want to know that their leaders share their vision and that there is a plan for taking the organization forward. In fact, Mercer Communication

Consulting[10] found that 40 per cent of employees they surveyed in the United States and United Kingdom said they would consider leaving if their leadership failed to communicate a clear vision of the future. Nearly as many said the failure would make them dissatisfied with the organization.

In his book on leadership communication, Kevin Murray says that employees want:

- to be inspired;
- an enduring purpose – something they should get out of bed for – something more than profits;
- not to hear about numeric goals that make no difference to them;
- a reminder of why the organization exists and how individuals within it contribute;
- a sense that they are making a difference to humankind;
- not to be patronized by slogans like 'Thinking About Tomorrow'
- simple, grab-able ideas like NASA's aim in 1961 to land a man on the moon within a decade.

In other words, we should ask whether our leaders are articulating a destination or direction of travel that makes sense and excites the rest of the organization. Great companies keep it simple, such as Nike's aim 'to bring inspiration and innovation to every athlete in the world'.

In our experience, people will make judgements about the validity of the mission or the plan based on the personality of the leaders, rather than on the quality of the data being shared. People trust people and every communication manager will experience the disproportionate impact that meeting a CEO will have on a workforce.[11]

This applies every bit as much to a divisional director as it does to the most senior leader in your organization. The only difference is that the director has to take the overall vision and show how their plans for their realm will support it.

It can be tempting to get caught up in the semantics of what a vision, or core purpose, or mission is and the differences between these. It is not our intention to explore this issue here. Rather, the essential challenge is to see if you can be as clear as Anita Roddick, human rights activist and founder of The Body Shop (a natural skin care producer and retailer) who simply and engagingly said: 'I just want The Body Shop to be the best, most breathlessly exciting company – and one that changes the way business is carried out. That is my vision.'

This also implies that the message is expressed in terms that the employee understands and is relevant to them. We have all had the experience of listening in total confusion to a leader talking about the place where we work in terms that make no sense to us. In their very funny 2005 book *Why Business People Speak Like Idiots*, Fugere, Hardaway and Warshawsky[12] suggest there is a direct correlation between the lack of clarity in a CEO's communications and the likelihood of scandal! This should come as no surprise, because we naturally assume anyone using complex jargon is probably trying to hide something.

So what's the job of the communicator?

Looking at the mission story we have to ask:

- Is it clear where we are going?
- Is it explained in ways that people understand and can get excited about?

Over time we should be working with our leaders to help them be clear about the direction or vision for the organization. Because we understand the way employees see things, we should be able to help leaders make the connection between what they need to say and how the workforce will understand it.

Practically this will involve helping your leader define a few focused messages. In Chapter 5 we explained how to do this. It will entail discussing ways to illustrate the narrative.

Research also suggests that managers who paint a broader picture of the context facing the organization tend to be more successful.[13] Messages about the core purpose of the organization and adaptation to wider pressures and challenges are more compelling than announcements about strategic decisions and how programmes are to be implemented.

Are there set stories that the CEO can use? Perhaps there was a conversation with a customer or maybe an observation of the work on the production line that can be used to bring colour to the messages?

Once the message is agreed, we might look for new vehicles or opportunities to share the vision and that should include finding ways of introducing emotion. Perhaps a video of the CEO with a customer could make the story more compelling than a town hall meeting? Maybe asking some friends to read the CEO's e-mail before it goes out can strip away language that confuses. If people associate the annual webcast with bad news you might want to use local meetings to deliver a positive picture of the way forward.

Connected

Consistently we have argued that the key to great communication is understanding the audience. As soon as we learn to speak we learn to adapt what we say to the needs of our listener and a professional communicator is concerned with how to make a bridge between the speaker and the people that they are addressing. That can only be achieved when you really understand the audience. If a senior leader wants to make an impact they need to understand how their people think and be ready to listen as part of a dialogue.

Without a sense of the audience, the senior leader can at best seem remote and at worst appear uncaring or even untrustworthy.

Showing that they are connected and interested in the well-being of the audience matters, according to research by Mercer Delta quantifying the impact of senior leadership communication on business performance. Working with a major European high-street retailer, the consultancy found a link between the individual profitability of 190 stores and their levels of staff engagement. Crucially, their analysis showed that 35 per cent of the variation between scores was connected to senior management communication.

In particular, they identified a compelling statistical relationship between profitability and (in descending order):

- the extent to which senior leaders are in touch with the way people feel;
- whether the top leaders encouraged or supported people in the business;
- the extent to which senior leaders encouraged feedback;
- how approachable the senior leaders were;
- how visible the senior leaders were.

In other words, there is a direct relationship between business success and the sense that the top boss knows what is going on, understands how people see things and is seen as willing to listen.

This isn't just about what employees are saying. Staff want to know that the boss is on top of external factors and can explain things such as customer attitudes or what the media is saying about the organization. The task is to show the workforce that the people at the top are not remote from the day-to-day realities that regular employees deal with.

Naturally, senior leaders have a million and one things to worry about and can easily become trapped in their offices. Staying in touch is a major challenge where the communication manager can be a real help. There are a number of things that we can do:

- **Be the intelligence operation.** Elsewhere we talk about the need to provide informal feedback to senior leaders. We talk in some detail about small ways to ensure that the upper managers are getting a clear view of the situation. Remember that many senior leaders have a real interest in giving the CEO a biased picture of employee sentiment, so a trusted communicator has real value to add.

  Fulfilling this role might be as simple as providing the results of your monthly call-around on a single sheet of paper to the CEO or asking your panel of contacts around the business to answer a specific question that is on the CEO's mind.

  Importantly, providing the feedback is not enough. You need to be ready to suggest to the CEO how they should respond. Ideally, employees should see that their CEO is aware of what people are saying and is ready to comment on it.

Remember to be the first with the news. After an event such as a new blog post or a town hall, the CEO should be used to hearing from the communication team how things have been received. There are plenty of people around the overall leader who will share their personal version of events, so don't make the CEO rely on them because you are too slow to gather the real feedback.

- **Weave feedback into communication.** However you gather feedback, be sure to reflect it in statements from the CEO. Perhaps their blog can comment on current issues or refer to conversations that they have been having. Maybe their presentation at the town hall can include a story about a situation that will be familiar to staff? Be careful not to limit it to a formal response to the annual employee survey, but find ways of doing it throughout the year.

- **Get them out and about.** Familiarity breeds consent in our business. Below we talk about a number of tactics to get the leaders out and about. These need not be elaborate or highly produced: perhaps just get the CEO's PA to book meetings away from his or her office so there is a natural reason to wander around the site.

- **Give them the chance to be involved.** The boss is often no different to everyone else at work – they like a bit of fun. Depending on their tastes make sure that they know well in advance about the charity cycle ride, the fundraising day or the five-a-side soccer league. This doesn't have to seem like a contrived opportunity to mingle with the lower orders: just a regular person getting involved.

Storytelling

There's a lot of talk about storytelling in business communication these days, says organizational storytelling consultant, writer and lecturer Ezri Carlebach. That's hardly surprising, since storytelling is a universally shared experience, part of what makes us human. It's rooted in the fact that our brains are wired to respond to stories. Given the choice between a complex, accurate explanation and a reduced but internally consistent story, we prefer the story because it requires less effort to take in.

Leaders will always want data, but data only gives us the *what*, and sometimes the *how*. Stories give us the *why*. We naturally seek meaning in what's going on around us and that's why stories can have a big impact in business, particularly at times of change.

So how do you get your leaders to tell a compelling story?

Everyone tells stories: it's not like asking your leaders to become concert pianists or portrait artists. But everyone tells stories differently and, naturally, some are better at it than others. Investing a little time in planning will help you to get it right. A great start would be reading anything by Steve Denning, particularly *The Leader's Guide to Storytelling*.[14]

Prepare your leaders to tell *authentic, compelling* stories. The *authenticity* will come from a story that is true to the person telling it, the audience it's being told to and the moment of its telling. Hollywood producer Peter Guber outlined the 'four truths' of the storyteller in a classic 2007 *Harvard Business Review* article.[15] The *compelling* part comes from understanding the structure that underpins all good stories. Ask your leader to think about a story under these three simple headings:

- **Substance.** What is the issue they're seeking to address? Do they need to raise their profile, change employee behaviours or communicate a change? Are they certain of the story's purpose?

- **Structure.** Suggest a structure that follows these steps:

    - Where are we now/what does the status quo look like?

    - What was the moment of realization that change has to come?

    - What trials will we face along the way?

    - What will the future be like?

    Ask them to talk about a person they met: a colleague, customer or supplier. Where did the meeting take place? What sort of day was it? What sights, sounds or smells can they include? Adding some descriptive detail will help to bring it to life. It's important to keep stories simple and not over-complicate them with lots of data or jargon. Connecting stories back to personal experience will help strike the right balance.

- **Style.** Leaders should then rehearse their story, either alone or with a trusted coach, but encourage them to *know* the story rather than to memorize it. Telling it slightly differently for different audiences and settings is a good thing. Stress the importance of delivering it in person, *not* by e-mail or in a presentation. Video can work, but nothing beats a live experience!

    If they absolutely must use slides, try to make sure that they finish their presentation by reverting to their story. Drawing people back to the emotional connection with the story is a powerful way of keeping them onside.

Consistent

Strangely enough, while we all personally reserve the right in our private lives to be inconsistent from time to time, we expect our senior leaders to be as constant as the Rock of Gibraltar! However unreasonable this might be, the job of the communicator is to make sure that the CEO is consistent in their message and that employees can see the unifying thread running through all senior leadership communications.

This matters for a number of reasons. We know that a message has to be repeated multiple times before it registers. That is the core idea behind placing advertisements in multiple places: we may have to hear something on many occasions before we become conscious of it. Sometimes senior leaders think that because they have said something once in a staff blog or at a town hall meeting it has been transmitted perfectly through the hive to the majority of the workforce. Sadly employees are not actually all that interested in today's thoughts from the executive suite, so will only notice them when we have delivered them in multiple ways.

But consistency is not just about repeating our statements. Roger D'Aprix[16] introduces us to the idea of the 'say/do conflict'. Our colleagues are very quick to identify when an organization does not practise what it preaches. When people see a discrepancy between statements and deeds they rapidly lose interest and commitment.

The communicator's job is to highlight the impact that a particular policy or action might have and how people will see those impacts in the light of what the CEO has been saying. For example, when a CEO talks about growing the business, how will employees interpret site closures and consolidations at the same time? If your leader is the focus of a film about safety, what will people think when a divisional manager is not disciplined for allowing dangerous working practices to be followed?

The role is not to be a continual voice of dissent, but rather advise about the style or force of the message being portrayed. If we know that the organization cannot live up to a bold statement about excellent customer service for example, perhaps we can help the CEO find the right way to express himself or herself.

We need to make sure that we think ahead. Commonly, change programmes start with grand statements of ambition but lose the attention of the senior management team when immediate cost savings have been achieved or the CEO moves on. A communicator knows to teach leaders to be cautious about the breadth of their statements and not create problems for themselves in the future when promises fail to materialize.

Again this reinforces the importance of the communication manager both having a deep understanding of how the audience will understand statements and an awareness of the realities of corporate decision making. By asking continually of any statement, 'What will staff understand from what is being said and how will they react if promises fail to be delivered or even be contradicted?' the communicator can start to anticipate the advice that they need to deliver.

Finally, the communicator should be mindful of the need to project an authentic impression of the CEO. Staff will spot fakery very quickly and will probably not react to it in a positive way. Many senior leaders feel that they have to communicate or present themselves in a particular light because of some received wisdom about leadership communication. They will force themselves to do things like hold town hall meetings when the idea of speaking to large groups of employees actually fills them with dread.

If they hate the communications experience it will show and employees cannot be expected to understand why their highly-paid CEO looks terrified and is mumbling and over-compensating by acting like a TV evangelist.

Equally, be mindful of what the audience will see as authentic. A group of marketers may be more receptive to aspirational statements, while police officers might want a more grounded approach.

The communication manager helps by matching the personality of the senior leader to the communications process. An extrovert CEO may be very happy performing in front of a packed stadium while an introvert might prefer smaller gatherings. A detailed discussion about figures might suit an accountant, a back-to-the-floor exercise might allow an engineer to play to her or his strengths.

Coaching them around conversation starters can help. One CEO we know who felt he had little to say to staff found great success by simply asking employees to tell him what customers were saying. Another who was prone to dominating large meetings learnt to build a coffee break into town hall sessions before taking questions, thereby allowing people to discuss the issues they wanted clarified.

At the heart of all this is making sure that employees hear and experience the same message over and over and they get it from a leader who is comfortable with a personal style that can be sustained.

Getting in the diary

Here is a practice tip from Katharina Auer, from when she was Global Head of Internal Communication at AstraZeneca. She had tried in the past to put together a formal face-to-face communication programme for her senior leaders with a PowerPoint presentation and message in a set format, to an agreed timetable. But like many she found it almost impossible to make it fly: too many leaders with too many accountabilities and too many different styles of communication (and, in different locations, different needs from the audience).

So she based one on flexibility. Having got her Senior Executive Team (SET) to agree to having more face-to-face dialogue sessions with employees for 2005–06, she set about making this happen, in the following way.

The executive PA agreed to put her on the e-mail list for a weekly timetable of SET movements. Each Friday, she received an Excel spreadsheet detailing where each SET member would be the following week. As soon as she received it and it said, for example, that the Vice President of Marketing was going to Shanghai the following Tuesday, she contacted her internal communication person in Shanghai to alert them, 'SET member coming to your facility; set up a Dialogue F2F session!' At the same time, she reminded the SET member of their previous promise and asked them to set aside some time to meet with employees.

Committed

Every communicator dreams of working with a CEO like Steve Jobs: life is so easy when the boss takes communication seriously. Events don't get moved around in calendars, there is space for proper rehearsals before conferences and they push and challenge us to do better, be more creative or just do more.

And, if we're honest, most senior leaders probably think that they are committed to good communication. When we get frustrated with these leaders who don't bend to our will, perhaps we need to ask what we can do to help them be as good as they can be at communication.

The first step is to keep things as simple as possible so that the CEO can actually make commitments about communication that their PA can defend. Demanding large chunks of their time to travel or overloading the programme of CEO blogs is asking for trouble.

As we said above, you need to defend their executiveness: not exposing them to the risk of diary chaos is central to this. Come up with a programme that is appropriate and that is achievable if you want to help.

But commitment goes beyond showing up. We said earlier that engagement is heavily influenced by the belief that the CEO is interested in feedback and cares how people see things. This is demonstrated not just by the sentences we sneak into their blog but by how they behave. The questions they ask in meetings, whether or not they walk round the company, the telephone calls they take, what they reward, the appointments they make all are read as signs about the communication priority of the CEO.

A leader whose calendar is dominated by administrative minutiae will be seen as an administrative leader. A leader whose calendar is full with customer and employee meetings will be seen as a communicator. This is a simple exercise but very powerful: if you have leaders who believe they are communicating but do not, go through their calendar with them and see what it is saying about their style of leadership.

Getting your plan sorted

Earlier we said that the communication manager needs to develop a clear plan for executive-led communications. Without one we run the risk of being at the mercy of the ad hoc whims of senior leaders and could miss the opportunity for structured conversations with the key people in the business.

When pulling together the plan there are a few basic steps you need to take:

- auditing the internal reputation of your leaders;
- matching the rhythm of the organization;
- identifying your tactics;
- establishing your intelligence operation.

Auditing the internal reputation

Every plan should begin with some data gathering. Without evidence you are flying in the dark and, in all probability, your initial credibility as a high-level adviser will depend on bringing data (no matter how sketchy).

Elsewhere we have talked about the need to be continually gathering information about understanding and sentiment. When you have the opportunity to advise the CEO you should do a little additional preparation.

This need be no more complicated than adding a few additional questions to your rolling survey, holding a few focus groups and digging out data on how many people are viewing the CEO's blog or attending his or her town hall meetings. Your aim is to understand how conscious people are of the boss, how well they respond to his or her messages and what they think is actually being said.

Your aim should not be to find evidence that the top team lack visibility (virtually every senior leadership team gets accused of invisibility at some stage or another), rather you need to understand the impact that your senior team could make and the approaches or channels that will work best.

Specifically you will want to know the answer to:

- How often do people hear from the CEO? (Not how often he or she speaks.)
- What do people perceive to be the CEO's main concerns?
- What do staff expect to hear from their CEO?
- What do people think about the issues that you know matter to the CEO?

Your aim should be to collect useful subjective and, if possible, objective data about the internal reputation of the CEO and how it bears on the needs of the business. When you get a chance to talk to the boss you want to be ready to talk about their problems and how communications can help. You do not want to turn up with a litany of disconnected grumbles and criticisms which have neither relevance to the business nor are solvable by internal communication.

Matching the rhythm

Earlier we talked about saving your boss for things that really matter. Does it seem right that your most senior boss is commenting on everything from the long-term vision to the new canteen menu? We argue that the communicator's job is to manage the CEO's executiveness as a scarce resource.

Your planning should therefore consider the following questions:

- What is the appropriate curriculum of communications for the boss?
- What activities will provide your boss with a platform where he or she can be authentic?
- Is there a natural rhythm to the communications from the boss?

The appropriate curriculum, or the list of issues that are suitable for the boss to discuss, will be obvious in many ways but will also reflect the personal tastes of the CEO. You would probably avoid issues that are plainly trivial or for which there is another clearly identified senior leader with accountability. For example, day-to-day HR issues like training will be owned by HR, talking about the IT strategy might normally be the domain of the CIO.

The important thing is not to disempower the people who report to the CEO and to protect the most senior boss from the operational problems for which they cannot be blamed. However, the list needs clarifying over time with your CEO. They might like to show that they have their finger on the pulse and so will expect to be the face of every internal communication. Ideally though, our mission will be to protect their status, and having some clear ground rules agreed will help their team (which includes the communicators and the people who control their diary) manage their reputation.

We also spoke earlier about finding the right vehicle for the CEO. This is partly about matching their personal style to communications formats that allow their personality to shine. If your CEO is a massive introvert, perhaps a series of informal coffee meetings might be unsuitable. If your senior leader is deeply interested in people maybe you need to give them opportunities to spend time with colleagues on the front line. Perhaps a more informal video platform where an employee starts by asking 'What's on your mind...?' could be suitable.

Once you have decided the format of events that suit your leader and the topics that they wish to address, you will want to create a timetable.

There may be an obvious routine across the year. Perhaps you can build a cycle around the business results – each quarter having a town hall event discussing the results and priorities for the next three months, followed by a rolling series of meetings where the CEO discusses the challenges in the business and listens to how staff feel about things. There will be the traditional moments in the life of an organization – Christmas, New Year or Eid, when people expect to hear a message from the top. When you have added in annually recurring events such as the major trade show that is always a focus of activity, the safety awards or the graduation of the apprentices, you will find that you have a pretty full agenda.

The point of drawing up the calendar is that it enables you to see how a core set of messages can be developed over the course of a year. It prevents trivial things from creeping in through the back door and highlights dead spots in the year when there is space for other campaigns.

For each moment in the cycle you will want to look at a cluster of activities, not just one-off events. For example, at the quarterly results you will want to do more than just hold a town hall meeting. Apart from coordinating messages with external and investor relations, you will want to build in detailed briefing activities for senior managers, message packs for local managers and perhaps a Q and A session. Maybe there is scope for a CEO blog on the intranet or you might want to find a more interesting way of landing your messages – perhaps during a visit to a manufacturing site.

Getting them ready

Surprising as it may seem in the modern age of media awareness, relatively few senior managers are naturally great communicators. An internal communicator who is lucky enough to work with a great performer will be loath to change jobs and there are countless cases where IC managers have followed a CEO as they change from job to job just because working with them is such a delight!

An internal communication manager will therefore have the job of helping their senior managers become better communicators: a job that is both challenging and highly rewarding. Providing simple and valued advice on small issues of presentation can be a powerful stepping stone to advising on more fundamental issues like engagement. Taking your opportunity when it comes is therefore very helpful.

Many CEOs will have already been taught how to manage conversations with the media. They will be well versed in the soundbite and in getting a key message over. But being a good communicator inside an organization is about rather more! Leaders need to know how to listen, how to draw out questions and how to bridge between the boardroom and the shop floor. These are skills that require coaching and development and take more than half a day with an ex-broadcaster to acquire.

A number of communication managers work with presentation coaches in order to give a CEO advice and insight on their physical presence. Often bringing experience from the world of theatre, these coaches can provide very practical suggestions for making a leader more impactful when they present and interact. But our role is to make sure that the right message and content is plain. An actor might highlight weaknesses in the script and we need to be on hand to help the CEO think through what they need to say.

There is a raft of writing on the subject of coaching, some of which is tailored to the relationship between the CEO and their supporters. We mentioned Maister *et al*'s work before and most business schools offer programmes to develop the skills of a coach.

There is an important difference between a coach and an adviser. Classically a coach is someone who helps the CEO find the right answer, an adviser will be more directive and suggest practical steps that the CEO might wish to follow. In our roles as communication advisers we have to combine elements of both, but the core principle is that we cannot hope to issue instructions to our masters, especially on the subject of something as personal as communication.

The internal communication manager therefore has to own their technical expertise and be ready to be acknowledged for it. They have to be ready to discuss with their senior leaders what results those leaders would like to see and explore ways in which they can be achieved. This mix allows us to be both recognized as experts who present ideas and options and also optimizes the likelihood that a CEO will support an idea that they feel will help them achieve their objectives.

Becoming proficient in this area of communication management is a matter of experience, but there are a few general principles that are immediately useful. This is a major topic in its own right so we limit ourselves to a few practical thoughts.

Be invited

One of the first rules of giving advice is to be invited to do so. When you are about to touch on someone's performance as a communicator it is a sensitive area that should be handled carefully.

If the advice is invited it is more likely to be listened to, when you at least know the boss is curious. If the CEO thinks they are brilliant you are unlikely to be appreciated delivering cold news that they neither expected nor wanted.

This doesn't mean you should be passive. Providing data, comments from the audience or observations from other situations might provoke the question, 'What do you think?' and it is acceptable for you to ask the direct question at the right moment along the lines of, 'Do you want my thoughts?' Be careful to offer the advice in a way that can be declined. Just because the boss has said yes to your offer of advice, don't assume that they are actually interested!

Listen – it's about them not you

Good coaching begins with the subject, not the coach. A CEO is not going to do something because their communication adviser orders them to do it: they have to believe that whatever action is being proposed matches their own agenda and needs. Telling a CEO that they simply must have a blog or Yammer feed is bound to fail unless they can see how it will solve a problem they have identified or a goal they have set.

A smart communication manager starts by understanding what the boss really wants to achieve and as we have said elsewhere, knows how communications will help. Our mission is not to arrive with the boss hot with excitement about the latest communications fad we just heard about at a conference.

The CEO isn't there to make our jobs easier or more fun. It's the other way around.

In discussions, make a point of asking open questions about what the CEO wants to achieve, what they think this would look like for them, what they are comfortable doing and what they dislike or don't believe will work. Over time we can influence and change how they see things but our aim is always to be there to listen and understand.

Come with data... that's relevant

We cannot repeat the point often enough. In most organizations the boss likes to see evidence and data. In communication our subjective opinion often carries no more weight than that of the PA, the engineering manager or the guy in the canteen.

Establish the principle that on a frequent basis the CEO – or your most senior leader – will require some facts from you. But make sure that it's data that they care about.

The length of time people spend looking at stories on the intranet from month to month may not excite the CEO, but they might sit up when you show the feedback after their last town hall meeting. Attitude data about the canteen menu may not be dear to their heart, but evidence about the levels of understanding of safety or customer messages may grab their attention.

If you do venture an opinion off the cuff, always be ready to back it up. You will find it easier to do so if the boss accepts that you have an ear close to the ground or, over time, has experienced the usefulness of your advice. But until then, facts are your friends so gather them where you can.

Do be careful about quoting industry norms or received wisdom from the wider communication profession. Not all the data that gets shared is actually reliable and data from inside your own organization is always going to be much more persuasive.

Be ready

Never go to a meeting with a senior stakeholder unprepared.

No matter how familiar you are with the boss, their time is valuable and your access is a privilege. Your time with them should be treated with the respect it deserves.

That means having a clear idea of what the boss needs to achieve when they see you, being on top of the data and the events that are happening around the organization and knowing what is working or not.

Sometimes your encounters with the CEO might not be scheduled. You might be called upstairs suddenly or simply meet them in the corridor. Performing in these situations is a matter of being aware of what happens next in the communication plan, the status of current feedback and the big issues that are likely to be in the CEO's mind.

Be practical

Wherever possible make sure your advice is practical and achievable. You might want to suggest a different way to ask for questions, share some thoughts on body language or propose a change to the timing of events – but make sure that when you raise an issue you have a possible solution that will work.

Be careful

If you have direct access to the most senior leaders you have a highly privileged position. What you witness, hear and discuss are of acute interest to other people in the organization. Anything you share can spread rapidly, become distorted easily and actually damage the people you are trying to help.

Therefore your working assumption and that of the team with whom you work should be that any conversation with senior leaders deserves the discretion of the confessional.

Channels and tools that work

In Chapter 6 on channels we discussed a range of activities, however there are a number of special approaches that you may need to master when working with senior leaders.

As with all channels, it is always valuable to speak to friends and contacts in other organizations to understand their experiences and to gather advice. Given that your credibility and the reputation of your boss are at stake it is better to see something working before you try it yourself, rather than simply trusting the enthusiasm of posters to online fora or a supplier.

The leadership conference – essentials

Senior leader conferences are a key moment in the internal communication cycle and an internal communication manager should do everything in their power to take a leading role. In the run up to the event core messages for the rest of the year are agreed, senior leaders are receptive to advice on their style and after the meeting managers expect to take a message and develop it in the wider organization. These are not events at which the voice of the IC team should be absent.

Planning

- Clarify the exact objectives for the conference – who is the audience? What are the aims and the benefits for both delegates and your wider organization? What feeling do you want people to leave with after the conference?

- Clarify the budget – setting limits in advance allows you to manage expectations about what is possible and get the most from suppliers.

- Break down the conference into key chunks to help organize delivery, eg project management, logistics, themes and content, audiovisuals and photography, merchandising, design and print, web, etc.

- Create a 'conference project team' based on the above and be clear on the exact roles and responsibilities. Which internal and external resources will you require? Who will be your key decision makers? Who will manage suppliers? Do internal staff have the time to commit to the additional workload?

- Devise a schedule with regular weekly meetings for the project team to update progress and resolve issues.

Preparation

- How will you manage suppliers – individually or through a single organizer? An organizer will cost more but will save you time and stress in the long run – if they do events all the time they will anticipate problems and know solutions that you may miss.

- Craft your vision – devise the conference theme, story and key messages. Try to avoid banal slogans – it is always better if the theme is linked to a specific action or task that you want people to take away afterwards.

- Create the agenda and break it down into 15-minute units so you know what is meant to happen moment by moment – it helps ensure that things keep moving and lessens the risk of endless PowerPoint decks. The idea is to keep mixing things up to maintain interest and fight off tedium. You should keep a running tally of how long in a session delegates are expected to sit passively – your aim is to keep changing the pace.

- Against each element list out who is presenting or facilitating, the intended outcome of that moment for delegates, the materials needed and any technical instructions. This will continually evolve but this running sheet will become your bible.

- Who is going to facilitate or act as compère? Consider an external helper for this as they can ask questions and keep things moving.

- Give people clear deadlines for their content and build in enough time to coach them on their style or ideas to make their sessions more interesting.

- Make sure that logistics for the venue and delegates are watertight – nothing distracts from the impact of an event like a delegate who doesn't know when they are supposed to arrive or a venue with unreliable wifi!

Delivery

- Build in rehearsal time – as a rule of thumb every session will need twice its allocated time for preparation and rehearsal. If the presenters turn up the night before the conference (expect to be sitting up all night!) build in a dry-run session with the host well before the event – it will highlight what is missing and whether the story is coherent.

- It is often only when speakers see the venue or the size of the screen that they start focusing on their materials. Schedule more rehearsals on the eve of the event, but not the night before. You want the venue for a day at least and the CEO will always want to express an opinion on the materials being used by the other speakers and their individual performances. If someone is not cooperating with your final delivery work, ask the host or sponsor for help – they are the ones who are going to look foolish at the end of this.

- During the dry run and later rehearsals, be on hand to provide advice about how slides might be improved, how questions could be phrased and the issues that the audience might throw back. Naturally you have to be sensitive and build the speakers' confidence, but don't let anyone make a fool of your boss by performing badly!

- Aim to have all content in a final draft at least two weeks before the event – you won't get it but at least the presenters will get the point!

- Make sure the key people – including the host – have a copy of your final running plan.

- Make sure that you have sufficient backroom staff – without allocated roles – to step in when you need unexpected help holding microphones or putting up emergency signage.

- The final dry run at the venue is your opportunity to make sure the technical staff know things like which microphones will be needed, which pieces of film to cue and when activities are happening.

- During the event, does the host know how to find you at all times?

- At the end of each day, do the senior team know where the wash-up session is being held and have you got notes for everyone on how the day went?

- Before the final session, how will you discuss with your CEO or senior leader what they are going to say and what reflections they are going to share?

Cascade and feedback

- Ensure delegates get conference materials as they leave the venue – a week later is no use. Perhaps create a closed online site where they can also download conference photos and the cascade package you have prepared.

- How will delegates tell you what they thought of the conference? Naturally you want to know if they had fun and slept well, but your CEO will want to know that their objectives were met. You should consider a quick online survey but also make sure you are walking around during the breaks at the event to capture the mood and be aware of issues.

Conduct a full debrief with the project team – collate and review feedback forms from delegates and take lessons learned into future conference planning.

Video

A film is one of the most useful ways of spreading your CEO a bit more widely when they cannot do a visit to every site or if there is a message that needs to reach everyone.

Just because they are your CEO, they are not naturally so interesting that your colleagues will watch them for hours on end – people are used to getting information from the news or politicians in a matter of seconds and rarely for over a minute and half.

The questions you need to ask when planning a video for the CEO are:

- How will people view this video? In a meeting when their attention is fully engaged, or on a PC where your video will need to compete with other distractions?
- With which format is my boss most comfortable? Talking straight to camera, explaining things to an unseen interviewer or chatting to a member of the team?
- Can we reinforce the key points with captions?
- Where should people go for more information?
- What is the 'call to action'?

Experienced and wise heads will warn you about the usual presentational pitfalls of standing next to the expensive Ferrari when job losses are being planned or remembering the need to look through the camera viewfinder yourself to check that the final picture will be what you want. If you have never done a CEO video before, choose your camera team carefully: if they have done corporate work before they will be able to guide you.

Before filming starts, be very clear about the message and the examples that the boss wants to talk about. Take a note as they speak of the sections where they maybe miss that point, trip over their tongues or when you need to ask them to reshoot. Your film-maker or editor will welcome your guidance on the pieces where you felt the message was delivered most strongly.

Business TV

Increasingly, well-dispersed organizations are finding that it's easier than ever to create their own internal TV service. Typically this will be a regular magazine programme, often modelled on a variation of a breakfast TV show with a professional presenter sitting on a sofa or at a desk and introducing various packages and asking invited guests to contribute thoughts.

Done well these programmes can be very impactful as long as there is follow-through into other communications activity and channels. Done badly they can be a painful waste of time and effort, attracting only viewers who want to laugh at the clumsiness of the presentation.

In order to make your leaders look their best, consider:

- giving the same level of briefing as they would receive before an external TV appearance;

- briefing the presenter with questions that don't appear soft or sycophantic to the audience;
- avoiding a commitment to doing these shows on a regular basis – save them for special occasions when the difference of style enhances the importance of the message that you want to relay;
- be tough-minded about the number of people who really will be viewing and the cost of reaching them.

Live audio or web chats

Simple technology now makes it possible for a CEO to address large numbers of their staff through either text-based web chats or audio over the telephone system or the IT network. Understanding how these might be possible in your organization is a great idea and if you are not already doing them run a few small-scale pilots to get you familiar with the technology before unleashing it on either the CEO or the whole workforce.

For a live audio call don't let the session last too long and consider a radio-style format to make it easier to listen to. A few prepared questions will show listeners that you are willing to talk about hard issues and a mix of voices will make the session more interesting.

Preparation around no-go areas, bringing questions back to key messages and where people can find more information will make the session run more smoothly.

Live online chats are a quick way of getting a point of view expressed, as long as you are willing to be quick in your responses and not obsessed with drafting every comment by committee!

As with any interaction the CEO has with a workforce, be sure that you can give them some feedback later on how the message was received. Encourage the people around the CEO to wait and hear feedback before expressing opinions about how things went – it is natural to make reassuring comments to the boss but save them until you can put them in the context of improvements or next steps.

The CEO letter or blog

Possibly the most common activity for a CEO is the CEO letter or blog. These take a variety of forms, ranging from a regular self-authored column on the intranet to a more formalized e-mail. It might happen ad hoc or around set events such as the year end or the launch of targets for the coming year.

A communicator needs to be realistic about these communications. Any simple analysis will show that most of the time they will get a very small readership – even among senior managers and even when you keep the message short and focused. Unless you are lucky enough to have a witty, interesting or exciting boss, you should not think that people are stopping whatever they are doing to read an e-mail from them when it comes in.

The CEO's communication adviser should therefore always be ready to suggest activities that will complement the reach of the message. This task is made much easier if you have agreed a regular cycle of messages that you will deploy over the course of a quarter or half year.

There is sometimes debate in communication circles about the permissibility of ghost writing the CEO's blog. We see no harm in someone drafting a message for the boss and indeed it can save time and guarantee that something actually gets published when a good writer is involved. For the communication manager, discussing the potential content of the blog or letter is a great opportunity to understand the mind and pressures of the senior boss.

And, of course, maintain your CEO's 'executiveness' by not having too many letters or blogs.

Set piece face-to-face events

Work by bodies such as the International Association of Business Communicators suggests that leaders place great store in running face-to-face events. As we have said before, staff make choices about engagement based on personal experience of their senior leaders, so most people commonly welcome an opportunity for some live interaction.

However, we are not all naturally good performers at large events and the communication manager needs to develop a number of different formats that will suit the personality of the leaders and the challenges that internal communication is supposed to be helping with.

The town hall

A town hall event is commonly a meeting for a significant proportion of staff where an address is made and questions are taken. It might happen in front of several hundred people in the local concert hall or in smaller offices in a meeting room.

A successful town hall event requires preparation. The communication manager should ensure that some sort of briefing is supplied on local issues and a conversation with the local managers is held beforehand as part of the briefing process. Likely questions should be discussed and lines to take defined in consultation with local management.

If you are planning a series of meetings, perhaps using the same material, you will get enormous value from a dry run involving an invited audience of regular employees who you can trust to give you their reaction. We have seen whole campaigns rewritten because of useful input from people in this way.

We have found that questions are more forthcoming when the audience members are given a moment to discuss their thoughts with each other before questions are thrown out. If the audience thinks they are going to get a straight answer they may be more amenable to joining in a discussion.

Naturally the level of interaction also depends on the culture – expect audiences in Europe to be very different to those in the East. You will need to tailor your approach accordingly.

Do make sure that you have developed specific content for the audience. Resist the temptation to recycle material that worked well for other groups such as the financial analysts. Invest in making it look professional: make sure slides are well laid out.

Finally, discuss in advance the examples and the stories that the presenter is going to bring as a way of connecting with their audience.

Don't forget the evaluation! Some people ask staff to fill in comments forms which can get you a fair degree of information and are useful if you have time to digest the data and want to track the feedback over time or across locations. However, remember that within 10 minutes of the meeting ending your CEO will have been offered opinions on how well the meeting went by a range of other senior managers: you need to be quick if you want to be helpful.

The easiest thing to do is position yourself outside the meeting and catch a few people as they come out. You might need a bit of help from one or two local contacts if this is not your normal site. When you have gathered one or two useful thoughts be ready to suggest to the CEO how they might act on them.

The travel pack

Often a formalized town hall or set-piece meeting might be hard to plan: the travel schedules of senior leaders are erratic and changeable. In which case you should consider providing a 'travel pack': a standard set of materials and meeting formats that the boss can use when they find a useful gap in their timetable at a site somewhere.

A good travel pack is updated around three or four times a year – possibly to reflect a quarterly cycle of messages. It will contain a selection of slides or other materials that touch on things like customer wins, market conditions, internal successes and challenges. It would be suitable to include additional material supplied by the local management team.

The aim is that whenever an opportunity arises, the senior leaders have a ready-made 'stump speech' that they can pull out. Because it is produced infrequently, you have greater opportunity to ensure that the materials are well designed and you are less likely to be forced to cannibalize other presentations such as those for the financial markets which no one understands!

Back to the floor

Some leaders will get a massive amount of value from spending time on the front line in the organization and, in some businesses, particularly in retailing and fast food, there is a formal expectation that all managers will block out time to work away from their desks.

Creating a programme where the boss works alongside regular colleagues is extremely useful in internal communication. Rather than setting up a formalized meeting where people feel inhibited or uncomfortable, arrange for the CEO to work a shift on the production line, take calls in the contact centre or go out on the road with mobile staff.

Over the course of the shift people relax and there is space for a frank exchange of views. It keeps the CEO in touch with how people see things and helps them understand the importance of tailoring messages. For the employee it is an opportunity to explain how they see things.

In planning these sessions you will want to consider what kind of work the CEO can usefully do, whether you want to talk about the exercise afterwards (sometimes you may want the word to spread organically rather than posting a write-up on the intranet) and what feedback the staff who worked alongside the boss should get.

'Tell the boss' pages

You may want to create a page online or an e-mail account where people can post their questions to be answered by the CEO. This can be a powerful way of understanding what issues are being discussed across the organization without having to rely on the interpretation of middle managers! Assuming you can answer questions quickly and openly, this is a great way to demonstrate the willingness of the leadership to take feedback.

If you have such a space you should be ready for a range of quite parochial questions – we've had to deal with people asking why sauté potatoes cost more than chips in the canteen – and you can expect a few regular correspondents who are on a personal mission to tell the boss how the company should really be run. However, clear rules of engagement, knowing the identity of questioners (even if their posts appear anonymously) and not trying to be too clever or political with your replies, will ensure you have a focused and useful discussion.

Such platforms often work best for short periods or around a single issue. When interest dries up or the forum has outlived its usefulness it can be replaced without looking as if the CEO is running scared from the weight of employee opinion. An internal communication manager should also be aware that getting answers to questions that some managers consider impertinent can ruffle feathers and needs managing carefully.

The key learning points from this chapter

Employees are influenced above all by how they perceive communication from the senior leadership. If they can buy in to the way top management communicates the organization's vision, if they can trust and feel a personal connection with what senior leaders are saying and if they can believe in the personal authenticity of their leaders, they will respond positively. Conversely, poor communication leads to poor employee engagement and poor performance. As communication specialists, IC people have a key role in advising and supporting senior leadership, but first they have to win the trust of their senior leaders.

Communication managers are often heard complaining about not being a trusted part of the decision-making process. But unlike other professions in support roles we have an open ticket to influence the people at the top of our organizations if we just learn how to use it.

Our view is that the key to being invited into a conversation is a mix of making ourselves reliable and indispensable and of accepting that our role is to help the CEO succeed. When we bring our own agendas to meetings with the leaders we wish to help, we are asking to be frustrated and probably ignored.

This means understanding where we can be of most use to our leaders and how their communications can help the organization achieve its goals. Preserving their executiveness, making it easy for them to meet people and developing a programme that fits with the other demands on their time is key.

Especially when it comes to CEOs, it is important that you help establish a rhythm to their communication internally, for instance quarterly, to protect them but also to get your organization used to when they can expect to hear from their leader.

Finally, remember, everyone who walks into the CEO's office brings data and insight. Why should communication be any different?

Notes and references

1 Murray, K (2012) *The Language of Leaders: How top CEOs communicate to inspire, influence and achieve results*, Kogan Page, London

2 IABC Research Foundation (2012) *A View from the Top: Corporate communication from the perspective of senior executives* http://discovery.iabc.com/view.php?pid=2094

3 Thomas J Lee writes extensively on the subject of leadership and communications and his blog at www.mindinggaps.com is a useful resource for communicators interested in this subject.

4 MacLeod, D and Clarke, N (2009) *Engaging for Success: Enhancing performance through employee engagement* – a report to Government, Department for Business, Innovation and Skills, London

5 Writing in the May 2012 edition of *Communication World*, Towers Watsons' Kathryn Yates outlined data on the relationship between strong leadership communications and business performance.

6 Smythe, J (2007) *The CEO: The chief engagement officer – turning hierarchy upside down to drive performance*, Gower Publishing Ltd, London

7 Markos, S and Sandhya Sridevi, M (2010) Employee Engagement: the key to improving performance, *International Journal of Business & Management*, 5 (12)

8 Emma Soane in Truss, C, Alfes K, Delbridge, R, Shantz, A, Soane, E (2013) *Employee Engagement in Theory and Practice*, Routledge, London

9 Maister, D H, Green, C H and Galford, R M (2000) *The Trusted Advisor*, Simon and Schuster, New York

10 Mercer Communications (2011) One in two US employees looking to leave or checked out on the job, says What's Working research, *Mercer Press Releases* [Online] http://www.mercer.com/press-releases/1418665

11 For an interesting study that touches on the impact of senior leaders on employee sentiment, see Using research to rebuild the internal communication strategy at Marconi, *Strategic Communication Management*, 4 (6), November 2003.

12 Fugere, B, Hardaway, C and Warshawsky, J (2005) *Why Business People Speak Like Idiots: A bullfighter's guide*, Simon and Schuster, New York

13 Conger, J A and Nadler, D A (2012) When CEOs step up to fail, *MIT Sloan Management Review*, 45 (3)

14 Denning, S (2006) *The Leader's Guide to Storytelling*, John Wiley & Sons, Chichester

15 Guber, P (2007) The four truths of the storyteller, *Harvard Business Review*, 85 (12), p 52

16 D'Aprix, R (2010) The challenges of employee engagement, *The IABC Handbook of Organizational Communication*, pp 257–69

09
Change

What you will learn from this chapter

The vast majority of internal communication is about change in one form or another. You could also argue that most change management is actually related to the skills and competencies of the communication discipline. Communicators are often asked to help talk about change in all shapes and sizes – from the new canteen menu to the complete transformation of an organization.

This chapter highlights some important issues in the discussion of change that concern communicators, looks at the role of communicators during change and explores some approaches to developing plans to support change programmes.

We also talk about the importance of intelligence gathering during change – the subject of Chapter 10.

What is change? Getting the terms right

When people talk about change in organizations they tend to cover a very broad range of things. If the communicator is not clear at the outset of the conversation, they face the prospect of a good deal of frustration and they run the risk of creating more confusion than clarity.

A useful starting point is the distinction made by Bridges and Mitchell[1] between change and transitions or transformations. Essentially, things change and people transition. So a project can involve practical change or personal transformation – or both.

For example, a company introducing a new IT platform will be managing practical change as new equipment and programmes are installed. The company will want people to know that new equipment or software is coming and how to make use of it. It will also want some form of personal transition or transformation as it asks staff to adopt new ways of working.

A communicator in this example would perhaps help support the change by explaining when the new system is arriving and outlining what it will do and the benefits it will bring. The transformation part might need internal communication to explain how people will work differently, highlight the training that is to be provided, talk about overcoming challenges and the incentives for employees to change and celebrate when individuals or teams have successfully adopted the new platform.

Alternatively, think of a company moving offices. There may be practical changes that need to be implemented such as handling the logistics of getting everyone into the new accommodation. But the company may also want to transform behaviours through hot-desking or the creation of a more collaborative mindset. In this example, change is about the move, transformation is about the attitudes and behaviours of employees.

Having this distinction is helpful because it enables the communicator to show the colleagues driving change why some communications activity will not be enough to bring about change. If an organization wants, for example, to completely shift behaviours around safety, then the communicator should be able to point out the need for more than just a newsletter talking about new safety rules. If we keep asking the question 'What do you want people to *do*?' we can develop plans that demonstrate practical change and personal transformation, which will make a real difference.

A word of warning

Change and transformation is one of the areas of consulting that never seems to stop growing. Google will throw up hundreds of millions of hits for terms like 'change consulting' or 'change model' and every practitioner tends to have their own approach to the subject.

A degree of caution is necessary around change methodologies as they are often little more than the wisdom or condensed experience of an individual practitioner, or an academic study based on very small case studies. Postings on specialist websites and fora also deserve a sceptical eye for all the usual reasons connected to internet ramblings.

Some theory

Kotter

The work of John Kotter on change is some of the most commonly mentioned and was the product of many years of research and consulting.[2] First published in 1996, his book *Managing Change* was the source of an eight-step model that is still now widely used.

FIGURE 9.1   Communicator's checklist based on Kotter's model

Sense of urgency	• Have we explained the market or external environment? • Is there a positive reason for change? • Is it something employees will care about?
Guiding coalition	• Have we said who is driving the change? • How will we keep reminding people of who is involved?
Create the vision	• How can we link the vision to what excites employees? • Have we touched on the emotional reasons for change as much as the rational ones? • How will we keep repeating the message? • How can we make it personal and relevant on the front line?
Empower others	• How can we show people what they can do? • Where do we celebrate their successes? • Are we gathering intelligence to make sure the change team are realistic about the barriers facing staff?
Short-term wins	• What is our mechanism for communicating immediate successes? • How will we know what is happening day to day?
Consolidating	• Can we maintain enthusiasm? • Are we listening to what employees are saying? • Can we spot where people are tiring or losing momentum?
Institutionalizing	• Can we remind people of how things were before this all started? • What do employees want to celebrate? • Can we stop leaders claiming success before regular employees see it?

At each stage of the model there is a clear role for the communication professional, perhaps as the technician delivering media to explain the 'sense of urgency' or laying out the vision of the future direction.

Alternatively, the communication specialist might become a coach for senior leaders as they try to explain their message. Maybe we could help by injecting a note of reality to conversations about change based on an understanding of the audiences?

Kotter's model provides a useful checklist for the communicator who has been asked to help with a change or transformation.

Kübler-Ross's change curve

Sooner or later every communicator will come across the change curve – a model based on the work of psychiatrist Elisabeth Kübler-Ross.[3] The ideas behind this model have become so widespread that they have slipped into

FIGURE 9.2   The change curve for communications

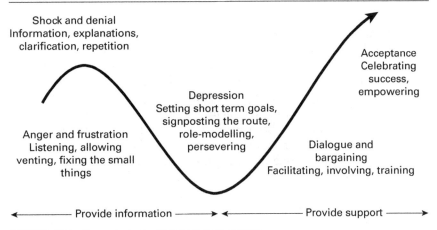

Shock and denial
Information, explanations,
clarification, repetition

Acceptance
Celebrating
success,
empowering

Depression
Setting short term goals,
signposting the route,
role-modelling,
persevering

Anger and frustration
Listening, allowing
venting, fixing the small
things

Dialogue and
bargaining
Facilitating, involving, training

← ——————— Provide information ———→ ← —————— Provide support ———→

SOURCE: Kübler-Ross, adapted by FitzPatrick and Dewhurst

everyday language: we have all heard about people being in the 'denial' stage when facing a personal transition.

Kübler-Ross's idea that when faced with change, we personally go through a cycle of emotions, was first outlined in her book *On Death and Dying* and was based on her work with people coping with terminal illness. The core idea has been adapted by a great number of writers – sometimes rather clumsily, so many of our colleagues are a little suspicious of it.

The relevance to communicators is that the change curve explains that people react to news of change in different ways at different times and their attitude will evolve over time.

It helps explain why leaders who have had a long time to debate a change will feel differently from regular staff who are hearing about a change for the first time. While leaders may have moved to the point where they are working out practical solutions, their teams could be struggling at the initial stages to understand what has just been revealed to them.

John Smythe uses the metaphor of a train in a tunnel. He describes leaders as sitting in the driving seat where they can see daylight in the distance and can control the speed of the train, while employees are like passengers with no idea how long the tunnel is and no influence on the speed at which they are being carried.[4]

It is useful to keep the two dimensions of the curve in mind when thinking through a change process. The X-axis is time and the Y-axis is engagement level (or what others would call motivation or energy). Ideally an organization would want to move people quickly through the curve in order to minimize impact and protect engagement, and communication plans should support this as far as possible. Naturally communicators are aware that the psychological process of adapting to change is complex, but our focus should be on maintaining performance during a period of uncertainty, which means providing information and support in a timely manner.

Writers suggest that communication can help people move through the curve by initially providing information. The idea is that in order to pass through the initial stages of the curve people need to understand what they are being told and so have a high demand for facts and data.

To pass through the later stages of the curve, the role of communication moves from an information source to that of providing support and encouragement. It is at this point that the role of local leaders becomes particularly important and the professional communicator should shift their focus to equipping line managers to coach their teams.

A change communications plan starts with identifying the impact this change will have on different audiences as well as tools for delivering news and progressively delivering materials and advice for line managers to use. The plan will acknowledge the need to move at the pace of regular employees who are only just learning about the impending change and not be driven by the impatience of senior leaders who have had many months to digest the need and shape of change.

While this model is particularly useful when describing difficult change such as job losses or site closures, we should be careful of applying it everywhere. Change is actually commonly a positive experience – imagine moving to a beautiful new office or waving goodbye to the awful IT system that has been driving everyone mad for years. People do not always make a psychological transition that rigidly follows the change curve and some of your stakeholders might be puzzled if you start using the language of loss and grieving in a situation that is genuinely positive.

Five principles for announcing change[5]

1 **Leave nothing to chance.** The initial announcement of change is crucial – done well, it leaves a lasting positive impression, do it badly and you'll spend months unpicking the mess. To paraphrase the Duke of Wellington: time spent on planning is seldom wasted.

2 **There are no prizes for coming second.** The person who tells the news first normally has the most credibility and if you delay communication you risk being overtaken by rumours and leaks. When you are left to react to misunderstandings or gossip it is hard not to appear untrustworthy or reluctant to come clean.

3 **Face to face.** Face-to-face communication is nearly always best, especially when the news is difficult. People like people and like to see a human face rather than an anonymous e-mail. Can you gather everyone together or is it clear what managers are expected to do?

Do make sure that people have a further written communication to which they can refer later or share back at home.

4 **This is no time for amateurs.** There are few things worse than being told you are losing your job by someone who lacks any skill at communicating. In your planning, think about how you will prepare or coach the leaders who are to deliver the news.

5 **Why should they care?** At the heart of everything, come back to the question 'Why should they care?' Asking this question continually ensures that you see the announcement through the eyes of the audience and not just through the haze of excitement from the executive team.

Quirke's escalator

In Chapter 6 we introduced Bill Quirke's idea that different communications channels play different roles in driving change. Crudely put, Quirke explained that some tools like memos, e-mails or posters will only at best achieve awareness. He argued that transformation will commonly require some form of involvement on the part of staff.

His essential point is that humans are more likely to understand what is happening if they have an opportunity to discuss and question what they are being told. If we have a say in what is to happen, the chances of us supporting and embracing the necessary transformation are greatly increased, he argues.

For communicators this has a couple of important implications. First, the scale of communication effort needed is directly proportional to the scale of effort needed from employees. A voicemail alone will not achieve significant transformation: a concept that communicators continually find themselves repeating to colleagues!

Second, communications from head office are useful in establishing awareness, but the role of local relationships becomes increasingly important as the change begins to focus more on the personal transformation.

A planning template

Over time we have found it useful to apply a simple five-step model for thinking through the communications needed around change and transformation. The journey planner (overleaf) has evolved from working on a large number of international change projects. It is the product of a very wide

FIGURE 9.3 Your journey planner

Basic awareness	Do they get it?	Do they believe?	Can they actually do it?	Is it business as usual?
CORPORATE IMPACT				**LOCAL IMPACT**
Have we explained what we are all about?	**Do we know if they understand?**	**Have we excited them about it?**	**Are they able to deliver?**	**Does it feel like the right thing?**
• Much workplace communication is just about telling people things – eg the canteen menu, changes to HR policy or downtime of the IT system	• There are many issues where we need to know that employees have understood – eg you need to be certain that employees understand safety messages or that they have got a message about change	• Think about linking the message to something they care about – eg customers, issues like food security, the environment or personal achievement	• Crucially, communication alone cannot drive behaviours. People need the tools, skills and resources to do their jobs	• How can we celebrate successes – large and small?
• The channels used are normally one-way and much effort goes into making them eye-catching and interesting	• Employees will want to check their understanding at their own pace – perhaps on an intranet	• One of the most compelling steps at this stage to overcome any resistance and bring staff along with you is to involve them in some way – either in developing the direction of the change or getting them to translate the overall vision into local and personal tasks	• Hold workshops to look at tools and processes	• Make time to celebrate achievements
• Awareness alone rarely leads directly to action	• And they will want to ask questions – ideally of someone who understands their situation… this is where local leaders start making the difference		• Provide links to training	• Be sure to remind people of how far things have changed
			• Invite colleagues from other departments to talk about their experiences	• Get colleagues or customers to talk about the difference they are noticing
				• How are you tracking all this?

range of influences including insights from students on courses we have taught and the advice of strategy consultants we have worked with. In other words, we are not claiming that the work is wholly original, but what we have found is that it provides a simple structure to complex challenges – and it gives you an idea of where to start from.

Step 1: have we explained what we are all about?

Every change communication programme begins by creating some basic awareness.

What do we want people to know as a basic minimum? Do we need them to know about the market? Perhaps we have to tell them about the essential background for our change? We certainly need to tell them that change and transformation is coming, what it will cover, when and for whom.

The old journalistic rubric of *who*, *what*, *when*, *where*, *why* and *how* applies here.

It is also worth remembering the importance of context in all communications. Much has been written over the years about the role of the communicator as a 'sense maker', a person who ensures that news and events are understandable. Our role is to ensure that colleagues receive both factual information and the broader context. Basic awareness should therefore include the background to events and change as well as the initial detail of what is being proposed.

If you think back to Kotter's model earlier, it highlights the importance of creating a sense of urgency. Some people call this 'the burning platform', ie the reason why change is unavoidable. So during the awareness stage of change communications you will want to provide data and facts that explain why a transformation is being contemplated.

The communicator will therefore want to ask the following questions of the team planning change (as a minimum) at the start of the change communication journey:

- What are the basic facts of our situation?
- What are the issues that necessitate the change being proposed?
- What is happening in our wider environment (eg the marketplace, among competitors or in government) that could shape our situation?
- What is the aim for change – where do we want to get to?
- What, objectively, might happen if we do not change?
- Who has decided to drive this change?
- Who will be affected by this change?
- When will the change happen?
- When will people know how they are affected?

Typically at this stage, no matter the size of your company, one-way or broadcast channels are at their most effective. Often some kind of official announcement like a CEO town hall works as a launch pad for sharing the news and for larger companies the town hall could be streamed live to the rest of the world. Sometimes senior leader 'stand ups' taking place simultaneously in various locations are also used. The announcement is then commonly backed by intranet postings, social media posts, background data, film, posters or newsletters. If your aim is simply to raise awareness, 'tell' tactics will generally work.

However, in our experience, simply shouting about an impending change is often not enough. At work, people are often happy to ignore the vast bulk of centrally-generated communication. They pay attention when someone close to them tells them to do so. Just posting material on an intranet does not constitute effective communication. You will often need local managers or use a network of advocates to follow up on a global announcement to help translate what this means in a local context.

You should help people read and digest the news in their own time, either via a handout or on an intranet. People will not understand the full rationale or detail on the first time of hearing news of change.

There is an old saying in communication that people need to hear a message at least eight times before it registers. Make the message frightening or challenging and the number of times it has to be said multiplies even further!

At this stage of your communications you need to be ready to repeat yourself beyond the point when you think you are getting boring. Remember also that senior leaders will have had many months to get comfortable with a message and so may need help to understand that regular staff might need many weeks or even months to even realize that something is happening.

Step 2: do we know if they understand?

There is a world of difference between knowing something and actually understanding it. When communicating change or transformation you want to give people an opportunity to check their understanding and, as this is usually a personal process, local leaders have a significant role to play.

Commonly, change is announced at a high level and sometimes it is actually quite conceptual in its early stages. Leaders will often want to share an intention or a general outline long before the specifics of transformation are known. Indeed, labour legislation in many countries requires that organizations announce a potential or a suggested change at the moment when they first think of it.

The result of sharing early for regulatory or other reasons is that some employees may struggle to see how change will affect them or translate the high-level intent into specific actions that they will be expected to follow. A communication manager has to manage the potential vacuum and the resulting impact on performance when everyone stops working while they wait for the full facts to be shared. This is often one of the most difficult situations to manage for communication professionals.

In the context of the change curve we talked about earlier, this is all about the first half of the process, as people work to make sense of what they are being told.

It is good practice to be clear to everyone about dates when things can be shared and to keep repeating the reasons for change in as many innovative or interesting ways as possible. Your role as a communicator is to support leaders with sound advice to navigate and manage engagement levels – and to keep them out of legal hot water.

When the time comes to be more specific, the communication challenge turns towards equipping local leaders to provide the explanation that people need. Making the connection between the high-level intent and the role of individual employees is most effectively done by someone who has an insight into their world, their work and their concerns. People are more likely to understand if someone close to them is on hand to show them how the transformation will play out for them. Also, employees like to have a real person to question. Often this will be their manager or a local leader.

However, beware of the assumption that people always want to hear from their line manager. Work by data expert Angela Sinickas[6] suggests that employees want to discuss change with whoever is the most knowledgeable. On many occasions, this might be the local manager but on others it could be an expert perhaps in HR, IT or an altogether different function.

Importantly we should be wary of placing all of our communication faith in the hands of other people. If you have managers who do not value communication, are not confident enough to deliver the right messages or think they do not have the time for it, you risk leaving clusters of employees in the dark. Whatever the reason, not all managers fulfil the role you need them to, so you have to provide disconnected employees with ways of finding out more or asking questions.

This might be a website where they can ask questions, or a series of face-to-face open meetings – perhaps conducted by a roll-out team that travels to various locations – where the issue can be discussed and people can take on board the news that their managers might be unable to share with them.

You should also consider the value of having colleagues talking to each other about their experiences. Maybe you have bought a solution, like an IT platform, that has been used elsewhere – and some staff could visit their peers in another organization and report back on the intranet. Or perhaps some of the change has been piloted in another office and maybe staff there could be filmed. One of the authors of this book once had colleagues in Sweden doing video diaries where they talked frankly about their personal emotional journey during a change that would later hit 50 other offices around the world. The value of involving employees is that it took away rumours and helped establish better understanding of what was coming.

The communication manager should therefore ask a number of questions at this stage:

- What information do I need to provide managers with in order to help them discuss the issues with their teams? (Chapter 7 on line manager communications should give you some inspiration here.)
- What tools will leaders find useful (eg videos, talking packs)?
- Who is briefing the managers? Are we offering more than an e-mail from the CEO? Where do they get to ask questions?
- Have we fully explained the case for change to leaders – is there a simple statement that all top management will sign up to and which can be shared with local leaders?
- How do we make sure managers are comfortable handling tricky questions? What coaching can we provide?
- If managers get questions they can't answer, who will they turn to for a rapid response?
- What direct route are we providing to staff? Is there a very clear intranet area where they can interact? Have we planned a roadshow to which staff can come?
- What opportunities exist for people to sample or experience the change or transformation? Can you show it working elsewhere and is there a chance for people to talk with their peers about the transformation and the lessons?

TABLE 9.1   Advice to managers about telling it straight

Dos	Don'ts
Acknowledge that it is difficult news to convey. Express regret. Be clear and straightforward.	Sugar-coat or downplay the message, or try to put a gloss on it.
Be specific about details (time, place, impact, those affected).	Make promises you can't keep or assurances that may not come to pass.
Explain **why** the action is being taken and the business rationale.	Be unsympathetic to personal distress.
Tell people where they can go for more information, and what resources are available. Offer your support.	Fail to deliver on the promise, and ignore/avoid it after the meeting because it is too difficult.

Step 3: have we excited them about it?

Change and transformation programmes often falter simply because of a lack of faith in the initiatives.

Anyone who has worked for more than a few years will have tales to tell about multiple change initiatives that were never delivered, or were always heralded as the last chance for the company. You do not have to be around that long to witness change programmes where management have lost interest as soon as the initial cost savings were delivered or were replaced by the next great idea along with the new CEO.

In short, there are plenty of reasons why employees should be suspicious of the latest smart idea from the executive team/strategy consultants/anyone wanting to impress the boss. The communicator has to think long and hard about making the change exciting and compelling, as well as thinking about how they can influence leaders to follow through on their plans and explain the change with integrity.

However, even if the organization is not cynical and jaded, getting people excited about change is not always easy even when everyone agrees the change is for the better. We all have many other pressures in our jobs already and very often we feel that we are doing alright as it is.

The communication manager has a number of specific challenges on the road to making transformation exciting.

Saving the world – data vs emotion

Everyone likes data, but it is emotion that gets us up in the morning when it comes to communication. Clearly we have to have a well-argued reason for change, but we also have to suggest ways of really motivating people.

Writer Tony Quinlan suggests that the most potent motivator is the opportunity to 'change the world' – not literally, but to appeal to people's sense of personal impact. The argument goes that few people go to work just to earn a wage – most of us attach social significance or some form of importance to what we do. Anyone who doubts this should spend time talking to frontline staff: they will very quickly realize that pride in a job well done is a significant motivator.

A communicator should look for the emotional triggers that matter in their organization and ensure that the change story reflects them. Perhaps people care about customers or service users, or being part of a strong team or beating the competition. Whatever it is that gets people excited, the communicator should understand it and be able to explain how the change will support what matters to people.

Essentially, remember that few people feel their pulse racing because of things like gross margin improvements, EBITDA or the operational profitability growth of 'top quartile world-class operations'. But show us how we can make a difference in someone else's life or somehow break the mould and you might just get our attention.

The case for change – from and to

When it comes to personal transformation, people need to have both something to move away from and a destination to move towards. Kotter talked about the idea of a burning platform and a compelling vision. As communicators we need to ensure that both components are reflected in our communications.

We need senior leaders to sign up to that case for change – one of the biggest causes of cynicism is leaders who have different or even conflicting versions of the need to transform. Invest time in working with leaders to get them to say the same thing, perhaps by getting them to agree a statement that they can all sign up to.

Involve me...

Explaining the need for change is not always enough. As far back as the 5th century BC, Chinese philosopher Confucius said: 'Tell me and I'll forget, show me and I may remember, involve me and I'll understand.' Now it seems widely-accepted wisdom that people are more likely to transform if they have some sort of control over how that transformation is to be implemented. This concept is at the heart of Quirke's escalator model that was mentioned previously.

John Smythe has long made the point that involvement comes in many forms and that a communicator should take care to distinguish the particular form they have in mind. At one extreme there is a model of involvement where employees are asked to consider a strategic question and develop responses based on a clean sheet of paper. This model was most famously used by IBM in online 'jam' sessions where colleagues were invited to design everything from business policies to shaping strategic decisions.

At the other end of the scale is the most usual approach which is where employees are asked to decide how a particular policy, procedure or plan is implemented in their workplace.

The lesson for the internal communicator when considering the Excitement stage of change is to ask what scope exists for involvement in the conception or the implementation of the change and to be clear about the extent of the licence being given to employees: if they are being asked to consider the final details of implementation, make sure you do not imply that the whole strategic direction of the organization is up for debate.

Is it about everyone?

Throughout any change, but particularly during the Excitement phase, it is worth asking how wide a population we need to focus on. Do we need to reach absolutely everyone or is there a subset we can concentrate on energizing?

Subgroups are potentially interesting for several reasons. First, you may only need to talk to super-users of a particular process or system. For example, there may be a major change in an IT system used by marketing, which on one level touches the whole organization, but only in a small way. However, there may be people such as planners or data managers who will be affected more than most. You may want to concentrate your efforts on them.

Super-influencers and early adopters

In recent years, writers like Herrero[7] and Gladwell[8] have drawn our attention to a naturally occurring phenomenon. Some people have better networks and are more influential than their peers. Regardless of social status or position in an organization's management structure, some people just make a bigger difference when it comes to spreading the word.

This is a similar phenomenon to that identified by Everett M Rogers in his work looking at the adoption of technology in his famous *Diffusion of Innovations*.[9] Rogers saw that people embrace new technologies at different rates, an observation that most us will recognize. We all know a small number of people who absolutely must have the latest smartphone or gadget and we all have friends or relatives who seem to take pride in being the last person to join Facebook or update their PC. The labels given in the research have slipped into everyday language: we talk about 'early adopters' and 'laggards' often without knowing that Rogers coined these terms.

For communicators, early adopters or super influencers provide a significant opportunity. If we can enthuse these people at the start of a change programme, our task becomes considerably easier. If we have people throughout the organization talking positively and credibly about our message, it will carry more weight than something that the management has decreed on its own.

Essentially our challenge is to find a way to reach these people, perhaps through internal social media or by having our own well-developed network.

Step 4: are they able to deliver?

A communicator who believes that they alone can deliver lasting change is probably deluded and a consultant who promises that a particular channel or tactic can bring about transformation is probably to be treated with suspicion. The truth is that while we might be willing to do things differently, if we don't have the right tools or skills there is not much we can actually do about it. Anyone who has ever facilitated a focus group will have heard people say things like 'I'd love to deliver better customer service but the IT system won't let me,' or 'If we're so keen to be leaders in our field why are our services so poorly designed?'

Thinking about the change curve, this is the point when people need support to test new behaviours and when a transformation programme moves fully from needing information sharing to showing colleagues how to work differently.

The internal communicator has two roles at this stage of the transformation process.

First, we should be asking hard questions about the practical steps that are being offered to help people undergoing change. What training is on offer?

Does the technology actually work as promised? When will people be shown the new processes?

Asking these questions at an early stage ensures that wild promises are not made by the project team and will influence things like the timing of our communication plan. Seeing the change process in terms of the staff experience can help us prevent senior leaders making fools of themselves and causing lasting damage to their credibility.

Second, we can help by making sure that the support on offer is properly signposted and that people understand how to get the most of it. This might involve advising HR on website design, helping the IT team design roadshows or gathering testimonials from colleagues who took part in pilot studies so that their experience and reassurance can be shared.

Step 5: does it feel like the right thing?

In Kotter's change model, the author talks about 'consolidating' and 'institutionalizing'. At a certain point in the journey we have to help people understand that the change has become business as usual, stop them slipping back into old habits and remind them that their hard work so far is showing results.

In our planning at this stage we should be highlighting the reality of change by reporting and celebrating what has actually happened.

Reporting is all about showing people the progress that is being made. At its most basic this could involve posting stories on the intranet as important milestones are reached. Perhaps sharing reactions from customers, service users or stakeholders could be helpful as people can see the difference the change is making.

Essentially, we need to show colleagues that progress is being made and, importantly, that their peers are making headway. The aim is to maintain a sense of momentum and remind people that after the initial excitement behind the launch of the programme things are still happening.

Possibly the most potent way to do this is through the sharing of stories of real people rather than through dry, technical reports from the project office or yet another exhortation from the CEO. As we have said elsewhere, people are most engaged by people: if they can identify with the characters sharing their experience so much the better.

So look for opportunities to put real people in front of their peers in addition to written articles. Video testimonials, problem-solving groups or recruiting 'ambassadors' to walk the floors and help people solve problems are possible solutions. Social media, with a little stimulation, gets people talking in a very potent way.

Celebrating achievement and progress is essential for recognizing the behaviours that matter and encouraging others to act the same. We talk about 'catching people doing the right thing' at this stage and making sure everyone else knows it.

Celebration can take many forms – from small celebrations within the team to full-blown corporate awards ceremonies to simply telling the stories of the teams that are being successful. The aim should be to show that real people are making a genuine contribution.

In your communications plan you need to give careful thought to the way you will celebrate when results come through. Including ideas early on helps you consider how you will find out about the noteworthy actions and avoid the embarrassing situation where you start scratching around for candidates to recognize at the last minute.

Often you can uncover inspiring examples by looking in unusual places or asking colleagues who are normally not seen as the heroes of your organization. If you are struggling to find the illustrations you need, a little lateral thinking may be needed. Are there support functions who can give you examples of where change is actually happening? Perhaps procurement can tell you that the organization is wasting less money? Maybe facilities have tales to tell of the changing patterns of work in the organization because fewer people are staying late?

Remember also that these stories won't just be of interest to other employees. Make sure you share them with the leaders too. This will provide them with examples they can talk about during meetings and briefings and it also gives them the realistic personal perspective of how change is impacting the workforce.

Preparing leaders

How your people perceive change will be greatly influenced by the behaviour of leaders at all levels. A communication manager will want to spend a lot of time thinking about how well prepared they are to handle the journey.

Announcements

As a basic step you should prepare clear instructions around announcements that set out what is expected of individual managers on the day any announcement is made.

A typical guide will follow a basic structure including:

- What happens and who is accountable, eg:
  - briefing external media;
  - handling regulatory announcements;
  - briefing suppliers and customers;
  - briefing senior leaders;
  - when the staff e-mail is sent;
  - what team leaders need to do;
  - when feedback will be collated.

- Key contacts and their details, eg:
  - press desk;
  - human resources;
  - internal communications;
  - regulatory affairs.
- Background.
- Core messages.
- The announcement timeline, eg:
  - when the announcement is agreed;
  - when managers are to be briefed;
  - when the CEO's e-mail will be posted;
  - when team meetings are to be held;
  - when feedback will be collated and a response provided.
- Copies of statements:
  - press releases;
  - customer letters;
  - CEO e-mails;
  - intranet articles.
- Questions and answers.

When drafting sample questions and answers, take care to stress that you are not writing a script to be followed word for word but that managers are expected to adapt their responses and localize them.

Questions and answers do not need to be exhaustive but they should be realistic and honest. It is always likely they will end up being circulated, even by accident, so beware of preparing sample responses that sound evasive or patronizing.

An exercise to help managers handle difficult questions

When faced with the need to discuss difficult change, managers will need support and encouragement to handle questions. If you have time to prepare managers, the following is a useful exercise to help them anticipate the needs of staff, build their confidence and reassure them that their peers are saying the same things as they are.

On the eve of an announcement, bring the group of managers together.

Step 1

Introduce them to the idea that when faced with a question they need to include three key elements in their answer:

- **Acknowledge** the intent and emotion behind the question, eg 'I can see why you'd be concerned about your job.' or 'I think what you're asking me is whether we'll need to move offices.' This reduces the likelihood that they might sound evasive or political.

- **Respond** to the question being asked in the most helpful way with as many facts as they know. It is normally acceptable to say that they don't know the full answer at this stage – a promise to come back at a later date is normally preferable to speculation.

- **Bridge** to the key message, eg '...but we should not lose sight of the fact that we are hoping to grow the business and that means opportunities for you all...' or 'The aim of this development is to give service users a better experience.'

Make sure these elements are visible on a wall or big screen throughout the exercise.

Explain that this formula enables them to show they are listening *and* get their point across without sounding like a politician on the campaign trail.

Step 2

Ask everyone to think of the toughest question they are likely to be asked and to write it down on a piece of paper. You may want them to include what type of employee that they think would be asking this question, eg sales, operations, etc. Make them write down two questions. When they have done so, put the paper in a hat or a bowl.

Step 3

The hat is passed around the room and in turn each participant asks the person standing next to him a question from the hat, who then attempts to answer. A full round like this is to be completed without comments to the responses delivered. Warn the group that the answers in the first round are always clumsy and inelegant!

The second round is done in the same way, with the difference that as each question is answered, the rest of the group discusses the answer given and debates how it could be improved. The facilitator ensures that the ACKNOWLEDGE–RESPOND–BRIDGE formula is being followed and that the group doesn't slip into giving hollow-sounding answers.

Step 4

Immediately after the meeting, write up the questions and the agreed answers and circulate them to the participants.

Keeping communications going through the life of a change

Transformation programmes never happen quickly. At the very least, they take several months and often may last years. Maintaining the flow of communications is a significant challenge over the life of the programme.

Planning for the long haul should be done on two levels – the long term and the six-to-eight week window.

The long-term plan should be matched to the phases of the planned change. For example, a change programme might be broken down by the project team into phases like leadership engagement, development of tools, HR intervention, training, testing and close out. As a first step, the communications plan should attempt to match each of these phases and reflect what behaviours are needed to make each phase successful.

This long-term plan will include things like feedback and intelligence gathering processes. When developing the long-term plan, naturally the communicator will be aware that the plan will change considerably over its lifespan. The transformation programme may change direction, need to respond to external pressures or reflect the feedback from participants. However, there may be multiple changes to the short-term plan that you will need to consider and manage also.

The six-to-eight week window is your statement of what exactly will happen in the coming weeks. It allows you the flexibility to respond as the change programme changes and develops. You will list out things like intranet articles, manager training dates, focus groups and other tactics. The aim is to keep a tight focus on delivery and to reflect sudden changes of direction in the change programme. Most of all, it helps the communication team manage through the frenetic level of activity that normally accompanies change programmes, especially in their early stages.

Where possible in the short-term plan, the programme should be updated weekly. Tasks that did not happen last week should either be dropped or rescheduled.

The key learning points from this chapter

Change and transitions are exciting opportunities for any communicator. Most great careers in our profession have been established during complex change programmes. These are the moments where communicators with skill and competence can truly step up and become that strategic resource an executive team can trust and rely on.

When the change is urgent or important it often allows the communication team the licence to experiment with new techniques, opens access to new resources and most of all allows us to see a real difference to the business as a result of the work we can do. Skilled communicators are able to remove a great deal of uncertainty, which is what most people fear, not the change itself.

When we do a great job we are able to move people quickly through the change curve and thereby reduce the period in which an organization is exposed to low morale. These are the moments when we get noticed and that has benefits for how we get to do 'business as usual' communications.

The key to adding value is simple. We need to keep asking two central questions: 'What do we want people to *do*?' and 'What can communications offer to get people doing the right thing?' Being consistently practical always works: understanding the human motivation and the business strategy are important, but successful communication depends on things actually happening.

Great communicators know that their core skill is to make things of value happen – a skill that is often in high demand and short supply when a transformation programme is launched.

Notes and references

1 Bridges, W and Mitchell, S (2000) Leading transition: a new model for change, *Leader to Leader*, **16** (3), pp 30–36

2 Kotter, J P (1995) Leading change, *Harvard Business Review*, March–April

3 Kübler-Ross, Elisabeth (2009) *On death and dying: What the dying have to teach doctors, nurses, clergy and their own families*, Taylor & Francis, London

4 Smythe, J (2007) *The CEO: The Chief Engagement Officer – Turning hierarchy upside down to drive performance*, Gower Publishing Ltd, London

5 Based on Schmidt, O (2005) The 10-point guide to effective employee communications during a company crisis, *The Business Communicator*, March 2005.

6 http://www.sinicom.com/

7 Herrero, L (2008) *Viral Change*, Meeting Minds, Beaconsfield

8 Gladwell, M (2000) *The Tipping Point: How little things can make a big difference*, Little, Brown, London

9 Rogers, E M (2010) *Diffusion of Innovations*, Simon and Schuster, New York

10
Research and evaluation for internal communicators

What you will learn from this chapter

A previous boss of one of this book's authors used to have a sign sitting on his desk saying:

> In God we trust – everyone else brings data...

This leader is typical of our age. In June 2013, recruiters Korn Ferry published a list of the core competencies of CEOs before and after the financial crisis.[1] Being data-focused is increasingly becoming a sought-after competence in the boardroom. Why then would a communicator not want to bring data to conversations if that is what leaders value?

Organizations are run on data and managers are above all else numerate. Think about your own senior leaders: there's a strong chance that they'll include a number of accountants or engineers. And when you think about your executive team making decisions, who is delivering the input? Most likely it is the strategy and financial teams who talk the language of growth scenarios, peer comparisons, SWOT analyses of markets and models of how to mitigate threats and capture opportunities.

Successful communication teams know that they need to talk the same language when they sit at the executive table.

This chapter is all about the collection and use of data by communicators. We'll look at where it fits into your strategy before and during a campaign, how it can be used to improve your channels, where it can save you from the problems of inappropriate messaging and how you may go about reporting to start building your credibility among your key stakeholders.

We'll look at a number of the main collection techniques and talk about the importance of sharing your results.

Why do internal communicators need data?

Few of us got involved in communication because we wanted to play around with numbers. We often like to think of ourselves as creative types or as 'people people'. Spreadsheets and graphs are the realm of accountants and statisticians – they certainly are not the concerns of clever writers or smart leadership coaches, are they?

Actually, it is getting harder and harder to maintain that belief.

Without a strong business case it is a challenge to win the budgets and resources needed for large-scale campaigns. You need to be able to describe in factual terms the situation you want your communications to change, what value it will deliver to the business and objectively set out clear, business-relevant goals that can be evaluated.

At a minimum, you will need to explain the proportion of staff who are unaware of a particular policy and what might be a reasonable target at the end of your campaign. Then you will need to think about what value this target will bring to the business (eg fewer leaks of confidential information), following which you can debate your intended resourcing and whether it seems like a wise investment.

Imagine how potent it might be in an oil company to say that a campaign promoting innovation could save a day of drilling costs. In a consumer business would it be difficult to justify a customer service campaign that helped acquire new clients?

Every investment needs to show that its results are worth the resources involved. Showing your 'return on investment' or how you add value to the business is as much an obligation for communication managers as it is for colleagues elsewhere in your organization.

Further, data helps you understand the actual scale of the task facing you and can suggest how it might be tackled. Data telling you that the least awareness of a message is among mobile workers might suggest you put less effort into the intranet and more into depot meetings. If you notice differences between staff at various sites perhaps you might be prompted to further investigate what is causing misunderstandings – maybe local management needs some personal coaching?

A data-gathering and intelligence-led approach will allow you to test and refine messages.

Perhaps most importantly, managers who bring evidence to meetings with their peers have greater business impact – simply because decisions are then based on deeper insight and less on working in the dark.

We operate in a world where everyone has an opinion about our work and they are not afraid to express it. While senior colleagues might be reticent about lecturing other specialists such as lawyers or finance people, there is no perceived barrier to voicing partial or ill-informed views about employee communication.

By contrast, when communicators own their expertise and are trusted as the experts on what employees think, organizations are able to make better decisions. When those decisions work out as they should, the communication team grows in stature and respect.

The simplest way to be acknowledged as the expert is to become the monopoly supplier of fact about communication. Our message is: take your data seriously and you'll be taken seriously.[2]

What should you measure?

Broadly speaking, a communicator needs evidence and data to help them understand:

- What is the lay of the land? What are people saying and thinking? How might we expect them to react? Where are there hotspots and where should we be putting our efforts? We call this descriptive data *intelligence*.

- What are we trying to achieve? What are our goals and how do they support the wider objectives of our organization? We call the process of data analysis that allows you to predict what you need to do to get results *targeting*.

- What is working and what is not? What is it that we actually do that makes a difference? Are there tools that are delivering what they should be? Are there refinements we can make to our messages? Are we doing what we set out to do and are we spending resources wisely? We call this *tracking*.

We are using the term 'data' to mean any evidence or facts that can help you shape your communications as distinct from simply your professional opinion or the judgement of the team. Clearly experience and judgement are important, but in this chapter we are focusing on the information you need to help you form, develop and support those judgements.

We'll explain this more later, but we are not just talking about numeric data. Some of the evidence you might collect might be subjective opinions, insights into how people form opinions or understanding about which information is actually reaching staff. You might gather this data by analysing statistics or simply by having a strong personal network. The aim though is to place the gathering of information in the management of communication and try to remove the guesswork.

Outcomes, outputs and drivers

An important point is the need to make a distinction between measuring activity (outputs) and results (outcomes). A communication manager needs to look at both but output metrics like the number of stories published, page views or satisfaction scores with events tell you how technically effective you are being.

Outcome metrics such as changes in customer service behaviour, understanding of safety rules or improvements in sales can be harder to establish but speak powerfully to stakeholders who are concerned with the performance of the organization and ultimately the value of their communications effort.

Drivers help you to understand how to improve the performance of your organization – and which aspects of IC have the greatest leverage.

Intelligence

Throughout this book we have stressed the importance of knowing your organization and the dynamics at play among your audiences. We say that being recognized as the people who really know what is going on makes the communication team enormously valuable to leaders. In addition, having an intimate understanding of what is happening outside the confines of your office helps you make choices in your planning and decide on the right tone of voice to use in your messages and the stories that you want to build into your forward pipeline for the intranet.

There is no substitute for getting away from your desk and meeting people and we often say that communicators who have lunch at their desks are probably not doing their jobs! Seeing things through the eyes of your audience is only possible when you talk to them frequently.

A communicator gathers intelligence in a number of informal and structured ways, not just eating in the canteen or hanging around the coffee or kitchen area.

Common approaches include:

- having a 'panel' of contacts who you call from time to time to sound out for reaction and feedback;
- asking your network of communicators to pose one or two questions either on a periodic or a regular basis;
- monitoring comments on internal discussion fora to track recurring themes;

- creating a rolling programme of focus groups around the organization to gather opinions and views;
- setting up a simple pulse survey (more of which we will cover later) to track attitudes to a standard set of questions;
- using social media channels to gather a live flow of unstructured data.

It is important to find a way of collating and assessing the intelligence. Effective approaches we have seen in the past include producing a single page of *verbatim* comments which can be shared with leaders or including some form of temperature check (with suitable caveats about the science behind your collection methodology) in your regular progress reports. More on the idea of a running balance sheet will follow later.

Targeting

Sometimes it is obvious what result you need to achieve and how you will get there. Informing people about a site closure for example might just need a staff meeting and a letter from HR.

But such occasions are rare.

Even taking our example of a site closure, your objectives may go beyond simple awareness of a piece of news such as the date and impact of the site closure. You might want to ensure that people understand the reason for the site closure and feel that the company is acting fairly. You might need an objective target for levels of understanding or a measure of the sense of fairness you hope to create. You might set a target such as a closure without strike action or the number of skilled employees applying to transfer to a new location.

If you have an objective set of targets, you then start looking for communications tactics that will help you achieve those results. If you want people to consider moving to a new site, will a town hall meeting and a letter from HR be enough? In order to explain the rationale for the closure you will need clear messages about the competitive situation and a fresh way to explain operational costs.

You must never assume that everyone automatically sees the connection between communication and its potential to drive engagement and performance. Setting clear targets for what you know can be achieved is the first step towards demonstrating the business impact that communications can make.

Looking ahead, having evidence paves the way for your arguments in favour of a particular course of action. Naturally this means you have to be confident about what you can achieve and encourage your stakeholders to have faith in your professionalism.

Tracking

If you set yourself a goal you need to know not just when you have reached it but also how you are progressing towards it. Are you moving too slowly?

Are you managing to deliver the tools you set out to? Are your messages being misunderstood and in need of refocusing?

As a manager you are interested in seeing how you are performing, spotting opportunities to improve and capitalizing on your successes. You need data gathering to help you run an efficient function.

You might rely on a mix of process or output measures and result or outcome measures.

For example, you will want to see if you are doing the things you set out to do, like publish material on the intranet at a set frequency, get a set number of people to attend town halls or improve the number of participants in social media. You will want to see how fast (or slowly) you are spending your budget or understand why some of your colleagues seem busier than others.

If you have clear outcome targets, how close are you getting to them? Perhaps you want all staff to say that they understand safety rules, so do you need a small pulse survey to tell you each month what proportion of the workforce is getting your message? Maybe monitoring customer satisfaction scores quarter by quarter will tell you if you are on track to build excitement among your customer-facing colleagues about the service promise of your company.

You may want to start by creating your own balance sheet for your function. Begin with a strategic performance assessment to see if people understand the business strategy on a basic level. You can also build regular measures in about activity and specific outcomes for business priorities.

Audits – creating the communicators' balance sheet

Most communicators, at some stage or another, will want to conduct some sort of audit. Taking the temperature of the communication system is an essential first step for someone new in the role and will probably be something a communication manager will want to do as a periodic health check.

Having some kind of a communication balance sheet that you review often makes a lot of sense for the following reasons:

- **Alignment issues.** Perhaps the communication team is scattered around or located in different divisions, areas or locations making alignment of communication priorities challenging.
- **Focus issues.** Maybe it is not clear to the communication team what the priorities are and people are therefore not working on the right things.
- **Team issues.** The line of sight for the communication team might be unclear even when they sit together and solutions are not always joined up. Alternatively you may have performance issues in the

team and want to use your metrics as way of underlining what outcomes are important and what activities are irrelevant.

- **Stakeholder issues.** The executive team and other leaders are asking questions about what the IC team actually does and what the organization is getting out of it.

In general, a communication manager needs to know a number of standard things, a summary of which is set out in Table 10.1 below.

TABLE 10.1   The standard things an IC manager needs to know about

What	In detail	How can I find out?
Role	**What is the role of IC in my organization?** Connecting people? Explaining instructions? Creating advocates? Supporting change?	• Desk review of objectives • Discussion with senior leaders
Leaders	**What do leaders think of our role?** Do they think we do a good job and why? What value do they expect from us?	• Asking what do they value and what do they think we do well? • Review of business performance data
Audience	**How well do we know our current audience? And what are they up to?** Do we know our demographics? What evidence is there about morale (eg sickness or staff turnover) or performance	• HR and performance data • Walking about • Casual research
Channels	**What do we have, who do they reach and how well?** Do we have a mix of push, pull, community building and dialogue media? What levels of usage do they have? Do audiences trust and value them? What is the quality like?	• Subjective review • User statistics • User surveys/Focus groups • Costs per user • Does content reflect organizational agenda?
Messages	**Are core messages getting through?** Do employees hear messages from the organization? Do they believe and trust them? Does communication promote the right behaviours?	• Surveys • Focus groups/Panels • Data modelling/Correlating survey and performance data

TABLE 10.1 *continued*

What	In detail	How can I find out?
Performance	• **Is the communication team working right?** Are there clear responsibilities and processes covering planning messages and campaigns, approving materials, evaluation and reporting? How does the communication plan link to the business strategy? Are we doing what we say we'll do? Do we know how our work changes behaviours? – and can we show it?	• Desk review • Feedback from senior colleagues • Historic records and budgets • Observing processes from start to finish • Subjective evaluation of outputs

Based on the answers to the questions in Table 10.1, a communication manager can start thinking about the challenge of pulling together a running balance sheet.

The balance sheet can be designed and structured in a million different ways. A good rule of thumb is not to make it too comprehensive, but more of a simple overview. The key principles to follow when building it are:

- Why do we measure (ie to assess performance and improve it)?
- What to measure (ie how strategic messages reach and are understood by each employee)?
- How do we measure (ie quantitative/qualitative methods, sources)?
- When do we measure (ie the resource issue)?
- How do we analyse (ie how do we create insight and add value to the basic data)?
- Who owns measurement (ie assigned task to someone)?
- Where do we keep it (ie public or hidden)?
- Who is this for and why should they care (ie consider this as a communication piece in itself)?

The main things to keep in mind are:

- Wherever possible, use outcome-based metrics, not process measures. You are interested in behaviours, not reach (although it is beneficial to audit your channels as part of your basics – see later in this chapter and also Chapter 6).
- If you cannot find satisfactory outcome metrics, think creatively about other indicators that might reasonably suggest a likely

resultant behaviour. A monitor of people downloading appraisal packs could point towards the strength of the performance culture. Attendance at customer service workshops might tell you something about the experience being given to clients.

- Make the research actionable. Not opinion-based questions, but ones that will prompt results you can do something about.
- Act on the results and act quickly. Tell people you have acted and how.
- Have benchmarks from baseline surveys, external research and by piloting with defined groups.
- When you share with leaders, as far as possible suggest what should happen next rather than just talking about problems.
- Keep it 'explainable'.
- Don't be afraid to include selected *verbatim* comments to add colour and bring the evidence to life.
- You're a communicator, not a boffin, so rather than pages and pages of tables, pull out the four or five facts that matter most. Understand your data well enough to answer questions if they arise but get managers used to a few, easy-to-understand items of data.

So, get your team and your stakeholders used to seeing a regular report from you. Try to keep it as simple as possible but design it in such a way that it tells a story. The narrative you will want to share will revolve around:

- what your overall communication objectives are and how they link to business or organizational needs;
- your recent activities – including successes and learning points;
- the feedback you are hearing;
- what has changed as a result of individual tactics or the overall campaign;
- what next steps you propose.

This is an essential tool for you. It should be helping your stakeholders understand your objectives, see how you are committed to supporting them and building their respect in your deep knowledge of the organization.

Where can you find your data?

Knowing exactly what to measure and monitor is one of the fundamental challenges of research and evaluation. It has seen some of the hottest debates in recent years among communicators.

The problem is that outcome measures are not often clear cut. There is rarely a neat cause and effect between a communication action and a desired employee behaviour. People are influenced at work by a whole range of things – most of which are outside the control or influence of the communication team. Salary levels, attitudes to colleagues, the behaviour of senior leaders or the effectiveness of training all shape the actions of staff: it can be hard to decide which is the most significant influence and isolate the contribution made by communications.

This is not to say that we shouldn't try. Managers tend to know that communication is important, it is for communicators to show them how it makes a difference and so guide them to be increasingly more effective. Developing a robust model for return on investment is challenging for everyone, not just communicators. If you are helping organize the town halls about the quarterly results together with the strategy or finance intelligence teams, you will come to know that their facts and figures are also based on assumptions. If you can make defensible assumptions and explain them with credibility then your data, intelligence and reporting will be listened to.

Three levels of understanding

We argue that there are essentially three levels of measurement when it comes to internal communication:

- Reporting and analysing your activity – did we do what we set out to do?
- Understanding whether people got the message (and how they are reacting).
- Seeing if anything has changed as an intentional result of the communication.

Each level becomes progressively more difficult to track but there is value at each point.

Look in the cupboard before you go shopping

We've all had the experience of returning from the supermarket to discover that we still have a cupboard full of the things we've just bought. If you're not careful you can repeat the experience when you set out to gather data for planning and evaluation.

Increasingly, our workplaces are full of data, if only we took the time to look. HR records information about sickness and absence, can tell you about voluntary resignation levels and will have a wealth of information about skills and the development of 'talent'.

A review of management reports will point towards information on performance, quality or safety – all things that communication can have a direct impact on.

Often, a little judicious asking around will uncover someone else who has recently commissioned their own quantitative or even qualitative studies.

In large organizations we've come across teams that are unaware of the data-gathering activities of colleagues. If someone has already asked similar questions of your audiences it may be a costly duplication to start your own research.

Sometimes you really don't need to ask certain questions. Before you commission a study about morale, take a look at the number of cars in the car park 10 minutes after the regular end of the day. A Google search for 'I work at [company name]' may tell you a lot about the levels of employee advocacy and five minutes looking at intranet data will tell you a lot about the conversations that are happening around your organization.

Why start your own complex data gathering when there could already be an answer to your question? Seeing yourself as an unofficial intelligence officer and applying a little bit of lateral thinking may remove the need for more formal research activity, or at least it can be an inexpensive start of your measurement efforts to collect what is already there and distil conclusions from there. That way you will quickly learn what data you are missing, you will structure your thinking more about what makes sense to report on and you will make a more informed decision about what else you need.

Reporting and analysing your activity

Earlier we said that a good communication manager needs to look continually for improvements and that is only possible if you understand things like whether or not a channel reaches people, what is stopping a tool working or what sorts of things get read on the intranet. This awareness enables you to shape campaigns and also equips you to advise leaders on the media that are most suited to the messages they want to deliver.

Table 10.2 looks at the sorts of tracking questions you might ask of individual channels. They form the basis of a simple audit of processes and are worth revisiting from time to time just to make sure things are working as they should.

The point of understanding the processes is to help you improve them and speak authoritatively when a colleague next asks you to help drive customer service or improve safety by handing out balloons or sending a beautifully-worded e-mail. Our professionalism should be based on knowing the reach or usefulness of the tactics that are available to us and advising accordingly.

Outcome measures

In previous chapters about audiences and messages we have talked about how communications have different impacts depending on your objectives, efforts and prioritization. Your aim is to create awareness, build understanding and acceptance, initiate excitement and hopefully drive behaviours.

TABLE 10.2 Knowing your channels

Channel or activity	Consider	Reality check
Team briefing	• Did you get it out on time? • Do employees report attending a regular briefing? • Are the leaders liking and using the format you provide them with? • Does it drive staff to other information sources (eg the intranet, HR)?	• Do leaders really find your support useful? • Are you swamping people with briefings because that's what you have always done? • Can you cross-reference in your employee survey people who have attended a regular meeting and understanding of core messages?
All staff e-mail	• Did it reach everyone? • Did it drive people to a particular webpage? • Using a marketing or direct mail programme, how many opened the e-mail or forwarded it to colleagues?	• Is it really just too easy to use? Could you do better?
Intranet	• Did you manage to update the system as much as you planned? If not do you know what got in the way? • How many updates were published? • How many people looked at specific stories? • How long do visitors spend on individual pages? • What proportion of visitors leave a comment? • How many users go on to other sites to which they have been directed? • Do users rate pages? • Do users say (in a survey) how useful they find it? • How much time are they spending on finding the information they need?	• Numbers of viewers as a proportion of your workforce can sometimes seem small – even for the most controversial or interesting subjects. • People tend to view intranet pages for a handful of seconds at a time – don't be disappointed by people flicking between pages – that's how we use the web. • Just because someone has seen something doesn't mean they understand!

TABLE 10.2   *continued*

Channel or activity	Consider	Reality check
Social media – networking (eg Yammer/Chatter) and broadcast/debate (eg blogs and forums)	• How many are using it? • What are they talking about? • What popular themes surface? • Which blogs/posts become popular? • Any particular times in the week, in the month, in the year where activity goes up?	• The space might be occupied be a few vocal employee groups, so don't always think that the sentiment is representative for entirety of staff.
Video, podcasts and internal TV	• How many really watched it? • Did they watch it in its entirety? • What do they think of style and tone? • Does it work for everyone regardless of culture? • For which type of topics do staff prefer video? • What is the cost per view?	• Making video is fun – but are you using it just because it's easier than the alternatives?
Newsletters, magazines and newspapers	• Number of editions published? • Was it delivered to everyone? • What feedback did you get? • Is the writing/production of a high quality? • What is the cost, per employee, per edition?	• Is there a way to streamline all newsletters based on the feedback? • Would anyone subscribe by choice?
Noticeboards	• Are people actually stopping to read them? • Do they make notes or take a slip? • When you ask around in the office have people seen it and remembered what the message was? • How many notices date back to ancient times?	• Unless someone is giving away money or free Ferraris, noticeboards rarely make our hearts go faster, so think about tracking awareness and not behaviours.

TABLE 10.2   *continued*

Channel or activity	Consider	Reality check
Text messaging	• Do we know if employees are actually reading SMS messages? • Do we know how up to date our contact lists are?	• Perhaps you should be tracking effectiveness via behaviours or the numbers of people clicking through to websites?
Events: town hall meetings, open fora and roadshows	• How many people attended? • The number of questions asked? • Exit surveys asking about key messages, quality of delivery and usefulness of the event?	• Is it always the same people in the audience being active? Are the questions changing from time to time? Who is asking what?
Workplace accessories (eg mouse mats) and desk drops	• What is the cost per employee? • What anecdotal feedback are you getting?	• Are the trash bins filled with your give-away?
Gimmicks, incentives and competitions	• How many participated? • What are the benchmarks compared with earlier years? • Can we track a changed pattern? • Is it the prize rather than the issue that gets people interested?	• Can you honestly see any change in behaviour or are you just trying to inject some fun?

When you are thinking about planning and evaluation, all data-gathering exercises should begin and end with this simple model – what do we want people to know, what do we need them to understand, what level of enthusiasm, excitement or personal commitment is necessary and finally what do we want people to do differently as a result of our communications? If you ask these questions you will very soon get to the data-gathering process that you should follow.

However, there is a simple problem with outcome measures. The more ambitious we become with our communications, the greater the number of influences you have to take account of. Making someone aware of a piece of information is in fact quite simple. You have to make sure they can see it, put it into terms that they can grasp and perhaps repeat yourself enough times.

But as soon as you start trying to create understanding you hit problems – many of which are completely or partly outside your control. An individual's past history, the behaviour of local managers, the opinions of friends outside work, social expectations or education levels all come into play. Getting someone excited about an idea may have more to do with the benefits on offer from HR or the perceived value of the suggestion.

People won't act or behave differently just because of communications – they have to have the right tools, skills, knowledge and collaborators, things that communications alone cannot deliver.

The challenge faced by the internal communicator is to find suitable measures and think laterally about these issues.

Importantly, because communications alone may not drive behaviours, you should not baulk at gathering insights and data about these issues. It's your job to point out what communications can and can't achieve and to highlight what other management actions are needed.

Typical approaches to testing outcomes tend to rely on a mix of surveying, qualitative approaches and tracking specific behaviours. However, increasingly organizations are investing in their analysis, bringing together different types of data and building predictive models that connect the influences that drive behaviours.

The main ways of gathering output data are described below.

Return on investment – holy grail or fool's gold?

In recent years there has been a lot of talk in communication circles about demonstrating return on investment (ROI). Managers want to see the connection, often in financial terms, between communication activity and the performance of the business or organization where it happens. People argue that, in the same way as an investment in new machinery or advertising has to prove its worth, employee communication should be able to demonstrate its value.

Writers such as Angela Sinickas have done a lot of work in this area. Critics of ROI methodologies tend to raise objections about the assumptions that are needed to make the numbers work.

For example, how do you decide the relative importance of different factors that might be driving behaviour and value? Think for a moment about salespeople promoting a new product: would they do it more because they understood its features or because they earned more commission to do so? How would you value the contribution to greater sales volumes made by good communications about the product compared with the impact of the commission structure?

However you calculate ROI, there will be difficulties about your assumptions but the same is true for an assessment of ROI on a piece of capital equipment or a new facility. Because there is no perfect methodology at the moment, should we give up trying to explain the link between communication resources and business results?

Start with the leaders

Before conducting any research or evaluation, a smart communicator asks senior leaders what value they think communication should add to the organization. We cover this in Chapter 2 on organizing the communication team, but the essential point to note here is that whatever you decide to track or evaluate it should align with what the leadership of your organization sees as important.

If you are in an organization obsessed with costs you are unlikely to do yourself any favours if you miss cost control from your reporting on communication. Where leaders are concerned with safety you will need to have metrics which help them understand the impact that communication is having on the issue.

Quantitative measures – surveys and tracking

Everyone around the boardroom table loves numbers. That's a lesson that has been learnt in recent decades by our colleagues in marketing and HR and which has seen the rise of the employee survey as a tool in most organizations.

Most organizations today have an annual or biennial employee survey. Some workplaces do them more frequently and they are known by a variety of different names. As well as wanting to understand communication effectiveness, the reasons for doing surveys vary: measuring employee engagement, understanding workplace stress, combating bullying or promoting staff welfare are common motivations.

The danger with annual surveys is that they can be seen as an end in themselves. In conversations with employees we often hear the criticism that nothing ever happens as a result of the survey. This is because it may take many months for the results to be digested by top management, the essence is not extracted for each manager for them to action, the data collected isn't actually very useful or people are so embarrassed by the results that they hope everyone quietly forgets about it.

The other common criticism is that surveys are a snapshot in time. A few months after they are completed the world may have changed so much that they may be a poor guide to future action.

A communicator needs to decide whether they are going to rely on the major annual survey or conduct their own research to provide insights that help the communication team. The availability of simple online tools such as Survey Monkey make this decision easier.

However, before you start on any research process there are some simple questions that you should consider:

- **What exactly do I need to know and why?** If you are not clear about the issue that you're addressing, you are likely to find the whole experience frustrating. You need to start in a genuine spirit of discovery – if you already know the answer, want to confirm your prejudice, prove someone wrong or just fancy doing a survey, the probability is that you'll learn little and annoy your colleagues in the process. People tend to be happy to share their opinions as long as they think someone is going to listen to them.

- **What do I want to happen with the information after I have gathered it?** There are two main issues here. First, your results have to be fit for purpose. If you want to build a detailed statistical model you will want a different approach from simply wanting to report on the effectiveness of a short campaign.

  Second, if you are hoping to challenge senior managers with your findings it is often wise to involve them at an early stage in the data-gathering process. If they have been consulted before you gather data, you are less likely to waste time defending your results and more likely to concentrate on the actions they need to take.

- **Will I need to ask everyone or will a sample suffice?** Sometimes you will need to consult everyone who works for you on a specific subject, while on other occasions you can find out all you need to know from a small, representative sample of your audience. The beauty of the sample survey is that you can do it more frequently, for reasons of costs and avoiding survey fatigue.

- **Does the information (or something like it) already exist somewhere?** As we said before, there is normally a great deal of information available in organizations that could answer your question if you know where to look.

- **What resources do I have?** The majority of communication teams are actually quite small and few of us have massive budgets. Conducting big studies can be expensive. Furthermore, it is easy to underestimate the time it takes to analyse survey responses. If you don't want to work through too many weekends and late nights you'll need to restrain yourself in the data you gather.

- **How detailed?** When you have worked through a few nights and lost weekends interpreting open-text questions you start regretting your desire to give people a space after every single question to write in their comments. When the head of marketing asks you to compare results from five different sub-groups in a poorly disguised attempt to avoid responsibility for weak engagement in their area, you'll wish you'd stuck to a five-question pulse study.

  By contrast, if you want to build a detailed segmentation model of employees you'll need multiple demographic questions exploring nuances in their attitudes and the ability to cross-reference responses to each other.

  It is likely that once your need for complexity takes you beyond a handful of questions that can be e-mailed to a small sample, you will need specialist help.

The annual engagement survey

Annual engagement surveys are commonly the domain of the HR department. The IC team gets asked to help with publicity beforehand and the reporting of results afterward. Often communication will merit a few narrowly-defined questions, probably about channel usage.

This can be a significant missed opportunity and, where possible, becoming involved with the survey design team at an early stage is generally a good idea. Remember that a communication manager will almost always want to supplement the data from the annual survey with their own research if they want to get anything insightful or really useful.

Survey managers are normally wary of changes to questions in existing surveys. It makes it hard to make comparisons year on year if questions have changed and survey costs will go up if more information is sought. Additionally, some survey vendors use standard questions so that they can offer comparisons between companies: asking them to change things can make life complicated.

If you are not able to change much in the survey, try to ensure that questions are asked in such a way that you can see the relationship between things like how satisfied employees are with their company or their job and how content they are with communication.

Where it is possible to make broader changes, ask less about specific channels and more about levels of awareness, understanding and excitement. The aim should not be to see how satisfied employees are with communications, but rather to see if the IC team are doing their job of delivering results for the organization.

Some organizations favour a short type of survey – a common model is Gallup's G12 survey.[3] This tool touches on issues such as being trained to do the job or having strong relationships in the workplace. The questions can be viewed on Gallup's website along with some very interesting resources looking at employee engagement.

Getting your responses up and avoiding survey fatigue

Many people get put off running quantitative studies because of a fear of 'survey fatigue', a supposedly untreatable condition much beloved by managers who think communication can be best managed in the dark!

The symptoms of this condition are actually very common – low response rates and employee cynicism that their views would ever get listened to. Imagine a situation where colleagues believed that everything they said in a survey was acted upon: the levels of enthusiasm for questionnaires would be incredible.

Response rates for employee surveys can be helped by four simple tricks:

- **Make sure the survey is simple and quick to fill in** – ideally within moments of receiving it. Avoid long questionnaires, complicated question formulations or asking for facts that have to be checked elsewhere. We talk about the 'I'll do it later' test – if respondents think they should set aside a time slot to do the survey, the response rate will suffer.

- **Perceived anonymity**. Even for the most innocuous subjects, employees like to think that they can answer without being identified. This isn't just an ethical issue (and most professional bodies for researchers have specific rules on this point), it's good sense. If you believe that your answers are going to follow you around it is easier to forget to respond in the first place. The UK's Market Research Society[4] recommends that results are only reported for units or types of employees where the number is 10 or more – this prevents you inadvertently identifying someone's opinions just by producing ever more detailed analyses.

  The perception of anonymity doesn't only depend on the statement on the front page of the survey. Think carefully about the personal details that you collect from respondents – if you ask more than a couple of demographic questions people might think you have enough information to identify them.

Remember that anonymity is particularly important in some cultures where criticizing the boss is considered very inappropriate. Giving people comfort that their direct manager is not going to be able to take offence at them personally is always wise.

- **Is there any point in this?** If people expect nothing to happen with the results, they probably won't waste their time helping with your enquiries. If it is the first time you're conducting the study, consider having your most senior leader promise to report back the results. For regular studies take time to tell people how their comments in the last study have brought about changes. Don't leave it until the month before the next study, but find ways to do it all the time – in the CEO's presentations, in intranet stories or through the team briefing system.

- **What has this got to do with my day job?** If the questions seem removed from someone's daily reality, they are less likely to invest the effort required in filling in a form that looks like it won't benefit them greatly or address the issues which matter to them!

Supporting the annual survey

Regardless of who owns the survey process, there is always a communication job to be done in support of it.

There are broadly speaking two challenges for internal communication – maximizing a good quality response and helping report the results (and hopefully supporting individual manager actions).

Getting a decent volume of honest answers will involve some form of campaign alerting people to the impact that the survey has made previously, highlighting senior leadership's commitment to listening and explaining the process and deadlines attached to the field period.

Much of these can be done through regular channels – intranet stories, articles in the house newspaper or posters – and you should think carefully about the role of your CEO and middle managers. Perhaps think about how you can promote role models, share experiences from successful teams and use compelling external case studies from well-known companies.

As far as possible, prepare leaders with concrete examples of changes that have happened since the last survey or give them talking points about what they will do with the results this year. Ultimately this is a trust issue and we know that people trust real people more than they have faith in official internal media, so make the most use of your internal advocates.

After the event, reporting the results needs to happen within a sensible time-frame. This isn't always easy when the findings are uncomfortable and leaders want to reflect on what actions they will take. However, delays undermine trust and credibility and should be avoided.

Many organizations like to issue a high-level report and look to local managers to conduct some form of action-planning. If this is the case in your organization, your communications will want to impress upon leaders the potential damage they can do if they mishandle the report-back process.

This stage can be a great opportunity to support managers with advice and guidance on communication skills. Potential ideas include simple manager packs or including a few minutes' input as part of the results briefing which they might receive.

Crucially in all this, leaders will need guidance on the central messages that they should deliver. These should be the same messages that the most senior leaders have agreed.

Finally, once the reporting phase is done, don't forget to continually remind people that a survey took place, was valued by senior leaders and that its findings are leading to actions. It is easy to forget, after a few months, what the initial drive behind a particular change in the survey was – it is our job to make that connection in speeches, presentations or intranet stories.

Benchmarks – are we as bad as everyone else?

Many survey vendors have databases of how their questions were answered by other organizations. Some build their databases on historic responses from all of their clients. Others, using modern online tools, develop bespoke benchmark groups from the population at large. This information can be very useful in helping management teams prioritize actions.

However, just because everyone gets a poor score for a particular factor shouldn't be an excuse for complacency. The challenge facing communicators is to put any results within the context of our own organization – we're meant to be the experts on how you talk to our people, so we should think about how the results will be perceived back home.

Our job therefore is to ask whether the results we are seeing are right for us. We need to make the connection between what the organization is trying to do and what employees are thinking. For example, a local council might have results similar to other authorities when it comes to employee understanding of customer needs, but perhaps a comparison with a consumer services company might be more illuminating?

Finally, if you are using analytics to tell you what shapes attitudes and behaviours in your organization, how you compare with external organizations is actually less relevant. Bringing this sort of insight to the conversation reinforces the role of the IC manager as someone who can help the organization meet its goals rather than someone who simply describes the world!

Small-scale studies

Being able to conduct simple research is very useful for communication teams. Change projects, campaign evaluations or message testing all benefit from some quickly-collected data.

If you are conducting a simple study, keeping your research focused is key, as is giving some thought to having a reasonably balanced sample.

Online survey tools enable a quick turnaround of studies, although if you have a significant offline workforce you will need to find an alternative route. One company we know used its service centre to call remote workers and interviewed them over the phone. In the age of smartphones, whole new possibilities turn up to reach a remote or scattered workforce, although paper questionnaires still have an important place.

Sampling need not be complicated. Try to reflect the main divisions in your organization – so, if geography is the main dividing factor in your organization, seek responses in proportion to the number of people in different locations around the world (ie if 10 per cent of your staff are based in India, aim to get 10 per cent of your responses from India).

More detailed advice on sampling can be found in a variety of sources, but the crucial point for sample studies is to have faith that the results are giving you a general indication of your direction of travel. Do not pretend to have more precision in your data than you really do have.

If recruiting a fresh sample every couple of months is too difficult, you might consider recruiting a panel of regular respondents. Limit the likelihood that they will become unrepresentative by replacing a proportion each time you survey them. Think about some form of incentive for their long-term participation: this might be some material present or it could be a chance to meet the CEO and talk about their views.

Example questions for a change project

These questions were the basis for a (once-every-two-months) tracking study for a company-wide change programme. We have included some subheadings to make it clear what was being asked and why (these were not included in the survey). Respondents were asked on a five-point scale the extent to which they agreed with a number of statements. Asking for attitudes on a scale gives richer insight than simply asking for a yes or no answer.

Over time the answers to this survey built up to show the journey employees were on from awareness through understanding and into familiarity with the changes being implemented.

Awareness questions

- I am aware that the company is implementing a new strategy.
- I think [company name] thinks ahead and plans for the future.

Understanding questions

- I understand the changes proposed in the new strategy.
- I see the need for the changes outlined in the new strategy.
- At work, I know what is expected of me.

Commitment/excitement questions

- I want to change the way I work.
- I think the company is implementing its plans in line with our values.
- I am passionate about the future of the company.

Capability questions

- I know where to find out more information about the changes that the company is making.
- I feel supported during organizational change.
- I have access to the resources (eg material, equipment, technology) I need to do my job effectively.
- I have the training I need to do my job effectively.

'Is it working?' questions

- I can see changes happening around me as a result of the new strategy.
- I feel the new structure lets me do my job better than before.

Drafting questions

Drafting questions for a survey demands care and thought. If you ask a flawed question you may ruin the whole study because respondents could be confused about what they are being asked.

'Does your manager brief you fully and regularly?' could be asking about the frequency of briefings or about the content of briefings. It also asks the respondent to make assumptions about what constitutes a 'full' briefing and the researcher could be more interested in the frequency (rather than the regularity) of briefings.

As well as generating unhelpful data, poorly-worded questions will undermine confidence in your findings. When presented with survey data, managers always speculate on what the respondents thought they were being asked. If there is any room for doubt it can make it impossible to get any sensible action plans agreed!

For your own surveys, a few simple rules will probably keep you out of trouble:

- **Only ask one question at a time.** Avoid questions such as 'Does the intranet give you accurate and timely information?' Accuracy and timeliness are different and should be separated.

- **Avoid jargon or exclusive language.** It is easy to forget that people very often don't share the same terms for things or might be unwilling to admit their ignorance – keep it simple.

- **Avoid terms that have different meanings in different places.** For example 'dinner' is an evening meal in the South of England – it can be the midday meal in the north of the country.

- **Avoid words that can be interpreted differently.** Obvious examples include words like 'bimonthly', which can mean every other month or twice a month. Other typical words or phrases that need to be defined when you use them include 'senior management', 'your location' and any jargon or abbreviations.

- **Don't imply a correct or most acceptable answer.** So be careful about asking them to recite back the main points of the CEO's speech (it will only kill your response rate!) and asking 'Do you think it is fair that we sacked your friends?' is probably going to cause a lot of angst!

- **You should not depend on important assumptions that could confuse or frustrate the respondent.** For example, 'What do you think about the planned closure of the head office?' assumes that they've heard the news.

- **Do not bore the respondent or be too obscure.** After all, you want them to help you.

- **Be clear when you want to collect facts and when you want opinions.** Questions like 'Is the new pay scale fair to everyone?' will often get the response 'How should I know?' If needs be, insert the phrase 'in your opinion'.

- **Always give very clear instructions about how questions should be answered.**

- **Be wary if you need to gather information about topics of legality, morality or rule compliance.** For example, asking smokers how often they leave their desks may not get a useful answer.

- **If you need a complex answer, think about having a rating scale.** For example, ask people to give a score out of five rather than a simple yes or no answer. This gives you a sense of the strength of feeling about an issue or an indication of how comfortable people feel with an idea.

● **Phrase questions in a way that doesn't force people without a legitimate, informed opinion to provide a response.** For example, if you ask if communication has improved, worsened or stayed the same during the last 12 months, you need to include an option that says, 'I haven't been here 12 months.' Otherwise, people who have been hired recently would probably choose 'stayed the same' and dilute the true results.

When you are drafting questions, keep in mind how you need to use the data. Are you trying to make a case to management? Maybe you want to help test some messages or understand whether certain communications are working? Imagining yourself presenting the findings to colleagues or senior leaders is a useful test to see if you are going to gather the right information. Challenging yourself now is a great idea as you don't want to discover when the survey is done and the results are in, that different questions would have been much more helpful!

You will find that many of the online tools that are available have a range of question styles that you can use. However, try not to change the format of your questions too many times in a quick survey – it is deeply annoying and makes analysis very painful!

Finally, when you think you have a good questionnaire, unleash some of your most stubborn colleagues on it. Ask them to fill in the form and then quiz them about what questions they thought they were answering – there is nearly always at least one major improvement you'll uncover in this way.[5]

Analysing your data

Collecting the data is only half the story. Once your questionnaires have been completed you'll need to plough through the answers to make sense of what you are being told.

A crucial element in how you design your survey questions is thinking about how you will analyse them. As a good researcher, you will take time when designing the survey to think about how you might correlate the results of different questions (ie see how people who respond positively on one question answer a second question compared to those people who answered the first one negatively).

If you have done a large-scale study you have probably hired a research company who will do the basic work for you. Normally you'll be supplied with a set of detailed tables or given access to a website where you can view the results.

Typically, this basic data will tell you the numbers and percentages of people who have answered your questions in different ways. You normally get simple correlation scores that show where there is a connection between how people answered different questions: in other words, the tables will start to tell you a story about how your respondents think. If you are working with an experienced researcher they will guide you on how to read this story.

There are commonly two main challenges facing you when you receive this initial report.

First, there are always gaps in your knowledge and it is tempting to speculate. You'll wonder why people answered a particular question in a certain way or you'll be intrigued by the relationship between different bits of information. Why did people in one part of the company see things one way, while their colleagues elsewhere have an alternative view?

You have to be careful about turning data into findings or conclusions based on your guesswork. If you knew the answers, why would you bother surveying in the first place? A research vendor will normally be very careful about being drawn into this sort of speculation – their reticence should be a warning to you.

The best thing to do is to plan for a qualitative phase – a few focus groups will quickly tell you why you are getting particular responses. If you have actually listened to employees you are in a more potent position to contradict the wilder theories that always come out when you present your research to senior leaders.

Second, simple tables can often mask more potent underlying trends in the data. For example, tables will probably present data according to pre-determined groups in your population – you might have a column for people at one site or another for people in a particular division. The trouble is that people don't always see the world in the same way as their immediate colleagues – there might be more interesting segments in your population than those that naturally come to mind. A statistician may notice that people are more defined by how they use certain media, their relationship to a line manager or by their attitudes to a particular project.

A deeper analysis can identify what is actually shaping attitudes. Maybe attitudes to change are influenced by things you wouldn't immediately expect or there are certain messages that could be more engaging or potent than others. Taking a deeper look pulls out insights that you may not expect.

In short, if you are investing any significant energy in collecting employee data, consider working with a specialist to find themes behind the tables. Ask a statistician or data miner to see what information is hidden in the database and take time to ask employees why they think their colleagues answered in a certain way.

Making it actionable

Collecting and analysing data is of little use if no one can see how to use the results to drive benefit for their organization. Without a focus on actions, the process could be a waste of everyone's time.

We normally recommend that communicators develop very simple reports which, in very few pages, tell a story covering:

- *What have we achieved?* What activities have taken place since the last report and how have they changed awareness, understanding (and ideally) behaviours?

- *What are the opportunities ahead?* What gaps are there in knowledge or attitudes that we can fill and what communications events might possibly help us close those gaps?

- *What risks can we see?* Are there forthcoming events or issues that we need to take account of? What might happen if we do not address misunderstandings or negative attitudes in the workforce?

- *Actions:* What specific actions do we propose that leaders and the communications team consider?

The aim of reporting in this way is to draw leaders into a conversation about the role of communications. Done well, it can change opinions among managers about the benefit of good communication and present a powerful opportunity to promote effective solutions, as long as we keep our ideas linked to the needs of the business.

Qualitative approaches

One of the core skills of an IC professional is often the ability to conduct employee discussions. If our role is to be the expert on how to communicate with workers, it is essential that we are skilled at understanding how the audience thinks and reacts. One of the simplest ways of gaining that understanding is through qualitative research.

When people talk about 'qualitative' research they are referring to methods that give you a sense of the thinking of a particular audience group. These methods could be group discussions (or 'focus groups') or perhaps in-depth interviews.

The aim of these methods is to get under the skin of an issue rather than to gather numeric data. Skilful questioning will reveal why people think in certain ways, enable you to test the appeal of particular messages or get invaluable feedback on the tools and channels you use. If you are attempting to understand culture or explore attitudes to a controversial issue, you will do well to consider a qualitative technique.

Qualitative approaches have a number of advantages over quantitative methods. These include:

- it is easier to target a specific population;
- they allow you to modify your research as you proceed to explore areas you hadn't originally anticipated;
- a small number of conversations can be had reasonably quickly;
- carefully selected, a small number of participants will often give you similar results to larger scale studies;

- they can help develop solutions to problems;
- they can tell you things you never anticipated.

However, before you abandon the annual employee survey, beware that focus groups or interviews won't solve all your problems.

- If managers need numerical data or 'facts' to convince them, you will struggle to get much from qualitative approaches.
- There are times when everyone expects to be consulted on an issue – focus groups, for example, tend to work on relatively select samples.
- Finding people to take part isn't always easy – often the most interesting people are the busiest. Managers can be unwilling to release employees to take part if there are staff shortages.
- Facilitating group conversations or running a probing interview is a skilled task. It is not something that is easily delegated.
- External facilitators can sometimes get insights that your own team can't. Researchers from outside the organization can ask 'stupid' questions, participants are less afraid of offending them and might feel less inclined to react to comments made in the group.
- You must be aware of the risks of qualitative research, eg only seeing what you want to see, leading the participants to express a particular opinion or failing to account for pressures on respondents to express a particular view. If you are blind to the potential pitfalls you are in danger of making a fool of yourself and wasting people's time!

Organizing a focus group

If you are working with an external expert you will probably be advised on how to organize a focus group. For simple projects you need to think about the following questions:

- Who are we going to ask?
- What are we going to ask them?
- How will we analyse the outcomes?

The aim of a focus group is to get a group of people talking about an issue and through their interaction provide you with insights. Your mission is to create the right conditions to get that conversation flowing while steering it toward the subjects you need to understand.

Who do you ask?

Simple focus groups might last about an hour and a half and people do tend to want quite a bit of notice for them. Think about sending an initial invitation a couple of weeks before followed by a few phone calls. Then a week or so before do another round of invitations, followed by final reminders the day before each session.

If people have to get permission to leave their normal work to attend the session, think about how you will tell supervisors and managers. Have you got the authority to summon people? What happens to work while your attendees are with you? And if people have to stay late or come in early, will they be paid for their time with you?

For relatively straightforward focus groups you will want about eight to 10 participants in each session. Six is probably the lowest feasible number – you do want a conversation to flow. Unless you are very skilled and experienced it can be difficult to manage groups of more than 12 in size. It is often wise to recruit a couple of reserves as people always pull out at the last minute because of client or other commitments.

As far as possible you should aim for a mix of functions and people. However, it is often wise not to mix up people and their managers and the sessions work best when there is not too much discrepancy between the types of people, ie don't mix security staff with directors!

Basic topic guides

Before any interview or focus group, you will need a topic guide – a simple *aide memoire* of the areas you want to discuss.

A good topic guide will ensure that you and any fellow researchers cover the same ground in each meeting, provide prompts to help you if the conversation stalls and remind you of the areas where you will want to probe in more depth. A written topic guide is also useful to win consent or approval from managers.

Simple topic guides cover:

- a preamble introducing yourself, explaining the project and setting out ground rules such as anonymity;
- a 'soft' initial question to get people talking;
- progressively more probing questions;
- for each question, a couple of possible alternative phrasings or prompts to limit the amount of ad libbing you need to do;
- where appropriate, probe questions to ensure that you can dig deeper;
- a reminder at the end to thank participants and explain what happens to their feedback.

Time invested in drafting the topic guide is rarely wasted. By anticipating how the conversation might unfold (or not!) the guide allows the facilitator to concentrate on the conversation and removes some of the worry of thinking up questions on the spot.

Recording focus groups

How you record focus groups is a matter of taste and depends in part on the subject in hand. Using a tape or digital recorder rarely causes problems unless the subject matter is highly sensitive. However if time is short, organizing a transcription can cause delays. In most cases a facilitator and a scribe will be sufficient to capture the main points. Experience suggests that writing up notes soon after meetings is wise – it is surprising how quickly your handwriting becomes illegible!

Facilitator tips

Although facilitating focus groups is a skilled task, beginners can get very good results by following a few simple rules.

- Remember it is not a group interview – you are there to listen and spark conversation.
- Avoid reacting every time someone says something – it makes you the focus of the conversation.
- Draw quieter attendees out by making positive eye contact and making a point of inviting them by name to speak if a more vocal participant is dominating.
- Ask open questions as much as possible – if you are struggling try starting each question with 'how'.
- If the group is slow to respond resist the temptation to clarify – count to 10 in your head after asking a question, few people can bear the silence that long and someone always chips in.
- Try to introduce a mix of activities to make sure everyone contributes. Try Post-it note brainstorms, pairing people to discuss an issue or even creating a collage as ways of recharging the energy.

Most good facilitators only learn through lots of experience. Finding opportunities to experiment is nearly always a good idea and anything that brings the communicator closer to their audiences has to be worthwhile.

The team ring-around

Often neither a survey nor a face-to-face qualitative approach is possible. Time might be short or logistical difficulties get in the way. A suitable compromise is the team ring-around.

Using a simple topic guide of three or at most four questions, members of the IC team call a small number of contacts in a single day. Respondents are asked their opinion on a set number of questions and the interviewer takes the opportunity to probe or explore the answers being given.

Online tools such as Survey Monkey make collation of the comments quite easy. A team conversation about the comments enables a quick analysis before the creation of the final report.

This approach can be used in a day and is a powerful way of gathering reaction to significant events or announcements as well as working as a regular tracking measure. Additionally, this approach provides a potent way of connecting the communication team to their audience: this always improves the quality of their work.

CASE STUDY   Maersk line

From 2008 to 2013, Klavs Valskov worked as Global Director of Communication and Branding for the world's largest container shipping company, Maersk Line. He wanted to show senior leaders how his function made a difference to the organization as it was journeying through tough times. He ended up with a quarterly reporting format assessing how his team's efforts impacted the workforce and also gathered evidence of the value they brought.

Maersk Line was going through its most severe financial crisis, posting a loss in 2009 for the first time in its 100-year history. Before the recession there were 33,000 employees, but by 2013 that had dropped to 25,000 people.

Communication in this traditional company was never really seen as important in achieving business targets. In fact, communication was considered something to be scared of: being wrongly reported in the external media was seriously personally damaging.

Valskov set up an audit with the aim of learning and improving. How were communications working? Were they doing the right things?

The second aim was to explain to senior leaders that what the communication team were doing made a difference.

The tangible results for the team itself were that during the tough recession it grew three times in size and their budget increased ten-fold. Furthermore, the team increasingly got involved early in strategic projects (one year they even wrote the business strategy together with two other teams) and got a seat in the extended executive leadership team.

In Valskov's experience, speaking with data and bringing intelligence to the table had everything to do with the results.

The Maersk Line communication team identified a number of key principles for measurement:

1 **Why do we measure?**
- To demonstrate the value of communications.
- To assess our performance and improve it.
- To learn more about our audience so we can reach them more effectively.

2 **What do we measure?**
- How our communication efforts impact the business.
- How communications impacts employee engagement.
- How strategic messages reach each employee.

3 **How do we measure?**
- We measure how we are helping our key stakeholders with their strategic objectives through qualitative feedback on a regular basis (voice of the customer).
- We measure how communications is impacting employee engagement by focusing on the outcomes we are trying to deliver and by measuring 1) the impact we have had on those outcomes and 2) the effectiveness with which we have achieved them.
- Whenever possible, we seek to measure behaviour change, not just reach; however, we still do our basic measures (eg page hits, reader numbers, how many people heard/read/saw our message) whenever these are useful for us.

4 **When do we measure?**
- For us to measure our impact on outcomes, we need to embed the measurement in all our projects and processes, such that we always do a pre- and post-communications evaluation. The specific method may vary but the commitment is always there to plan out how we will measure success.
- We also do touch points throughout the year on how well we are executing to our strategy, and then we do more comprehensive mid-year and year-end evaluations.

5 **Who owns measurement?**
- We all do. We have a point person to remind us of the value of measurement, manage the format and repository, and collate our team's key measures, but we are all responsible for measuring the impact of our specific communications effort and documenting it.

6 **Where do we keep this data?**
- We have a team site where we track our measurements.
- We have a case study repository and we also have an Excel spreadsheet that captures the quantitative metrics throughout the year (eg video hits, article hits).
- We also store our survey results in the same site.

FIGURE 10.1 CIPR Inside Communication Measurement Matrix

Why measure? Internal communication is measured to: Establish the value of practice for organizational reputation and success | Generate insights that inform professional practice | Support insightful business decisions | Check progress against plans | Assess overall efficacy.

	What to measure	How to measure		Other forms of research
		Questionnaire		
Outputs	**Channels: are they working?** How effective are your newsletters, magazines, intranet, social media channels, e-mail briefings, conferences, 'town hall' type meetings, team meetings, project meetings and 1:1s? Is the channel appropriate for the content?	Access, usefulness, frequency, volume, preferences.		Content analysis. Ease of reading. Interviews.
	Content: are employees getting the information they want and need? Is communication timely, relevant, accurate and consistent? Is the tone of voice right? Is it open? Is it honest? What are employees interested in?	How well and how often information is provided. Message recall (for example, using marketing-style analysis). Interest and information levels by topic.		Content analysis. Interviews.
	Conversations: are people communicating effectively? How well do leaders, senior managers, middle managers, line managers and colleagues communicate, both formally and informally?	Frequency that people communicate at the level expected.		Content analysis. Interviews. Network analysis.
Outcomes	**Voice: are there adequate opportunities for people to have a say?** How seriously is employee voice treated? Are responses provided to comments and suggestions? Can people get involved in change management and contribute to decisions that support innovation and influence business outcomes?	Frequency of opportunities, frequency and quality of responses made to expressed voice.		Interviews. Content analysis (for example, comments in blogs). Focus groups.
	Sentiment: what do employees think and feel about the organization? Is communication helping to increase engagement? Are leaders and managers trusted? Do people identify with organizational strategy and values? Are they advocates?	Understanding and belief in strategy and plans. Perceived organizational support.		Interviews. Focus groups. Online communities.
	Behaviour: has employee behaviour been influenced by communication? How has it influenced their decisions or behaviour? Are they working more safely, talking more knowledgeably with customers?	Why did behaviour change, what influenced the employee's decision?		Pilot or control groups (purposeful or accidental). Network analysis.
	Return on investment (ROI): Have the benefits been identified? Can you isolate other factors affecting financial returns?	Were the benefits realized?		Cost (time and resources used), direct return (savings made or profit generated) in a specified time.

Fundamental principles of measurement

- Best practice goes beyond the inclusion of a few communication questions in an annual employee engagement survey.
- Research is part of everyday practice used to establish SMART communication objectives that are output and outcome based, linked to organizational objectives that enhance reputation.
- Regular and real-time reporting that includes going beyond basic data is used to find insights from deep analysis.
- Benchmarking helps to put results into context.

Developed by the CIPR
Inside Measurement
Panel (November 2012)

SOURCE: © CIPR. Reproduced with permission. The matrix was a CIPR Inside Group initiative led by past chair, Kevin Ruck, and developed with a group of internal communication measurement experts including Mark Applin, Dr Andy Brown, Nick Howard, David Iannelli, Scott McKenzie, Paul Roberts, Michael Silverman and Angela Sinickas.

Resources

The CIPR's Inside Group has developed a simple matrix, which is reproduced opposite because it provides a useful headline guide to the approaches you might apply when you want to track different impacts.

Anyone interested in exploring this area should look at the work of Susan Walker. Her book *Employee Engagement and Communication Research* is one of the most comprehensive and practical guides to the subject.

Peter Goudge's *Employee Research: How to increase employee involvement through consultation* is a good tour of the issues behind why research is needed and the value it can bring to a business.

Also, every practitioner should be aware of the work of Angela Sinickas – her writing is always informative and helpful. Her website **www.sinicom.com** should be a permanent link on every communication manager's desktop.

The key learning points from this chapter

IC teams must be comfortable managing facts and figures if they want to advise senior leaders, because top management is data-driven and organizations run on data.

The first step is to define why something should be measured. If the answer to 'why' is neither for proof nor for intelligence gathering nor for assessment then why do it? Connecting the objectives for your communications to what matters to the business is essential and helps you focus on establishing the relevant metrics that your stakeholders care about.

Communication audits are useful as regular health checks of an organization and also for someone new to the organization to get an understanding of how it works. The resulting 'balance sheet' will help a communication professional manage issues of alignment, focus, team and stakeholders. Remember the answers to some of the questions a communication professional might want to ask can be found from existing sources, including what employees are saying on LinkedIn.

What to measure will include both outputs – what communicators produce – and outcomes – the effects of those communications. How to measure them will include both quantitative and qualitative surveys, including the annual survey and small-scale samples. The success or otherwise of these measurements will depend on how well the questions are phrased so the communication professional can analyse them effectively.

And crucially, all this activity has to lead to action: action by leaders, action by communicators and action by employees in support of business goals. Reporting and suggesting change should be at the front of the communicator's mind from the very beginning of any process of analysis or data gathering.

Notes and references

1 Friis, L (9 June 2013) Topchefernes nye virkelighed, *Berlingske*, http://
www.business.dk/ledelse/topchefernes-nye-virkelighed

2 Peter Goudge's comprehensive book covers in some detail the need for
measurement: Goudge, P (2006) *Employee Research: How to increase employee
involvement through consultation*, Kogan Page, London.

3 Gallup's G12 employee survey can be read on the company's website and Susan
Walker provides in her book a very interesting discussion of the usefulness of
standardized questionnaires (see note 5).

4 The UK Market Research Society's guidelines can be accessed through its
website www.mrs.org.uk

5 Susan Walker's excellent book on research for employee engagement has a very
useful chapter on the issue of question design. Anyone planning very detailed
research or with an interest in this area should read Walker, S (2012) *Employee
Engagement and Communication Research: Measurement, strategy and action*,
Kogan Page, London.

11
Developing yourself and the team

What you will learn from this chapter

The rate of change in our profession is relentless. Within a generation we have seen employee communication shift in emphasis from being internal reporters and journalists to being a vital part of corporate decision making. A few decades ago a CEO may have given little thought to communication – today he or she is overwhelmed with advice exhorting the importance of good communication. The communicator of the late 20th century would need very different advisory skills to those of their contemporary colleagues.

Within a decade we have also seen the rise of social media and the growing realization that the skills needed to deliver value from tools like Jive, Chatter or even Office Communicator are very different to those needed to run an intranet. While few people actually know how to make a success of internal social media, it seems likely that all of us working in employee communication will need to learn how to work with it at some stage or another.

Throughout this book we have assumed that good practitioners are curious about finding better ways of doing things. The best in our field are continually asking themselves how they can improve and what they can learn.

If that wasn't, of itself, a wise attitude, developments in the last few years have proved time and again that internal communication people have to be prepared to reinvent themselves.

In short, the communicator who is not aware of the need to continually learn and develop is probably on an accelerating track to extinction.

This chapter looks at the careers available to people in internal communication, the skills that specialists in the field need and the routes by which people can learn and develop.

This chapter aims to help you think about two basic questions – what does a good internal communicator look like and how do I become one? These two questions should take you on an interesting journey!

What makes a great IC professional?

Many practitioners come to internal communication from other professions. It is very common to meet IC specialists who were previously HR managers or journalists or who hail from less obvious places such as engineering, quality or safety. Many tell a common story of getting involved in communications for a project and then catching the bug.

As the profile of the internal communication role has grown, as management teams have grown more demanding and as skilled professionals from other disciplines have seen IC as an attractive job, we have all started asking what the hallmarks are of a strong practitioner. What marks one person out as a professional? What is the base curriculum for a skilled expert? And how does a CEO hire someone who might actually know what they are talking about?

As a starting point we should look for people who take their own development seriously. For the CIPR, professionalism is defined by a commitment to invest time and effort in continually developing skills, knowledge and expertise.

In our profession, personal development is particularly important simply because of the diversity of roles involved and routes into it. Its practitioners include people working at the top of their HR function and people charged with compiling mailing lists and sticking up posters. It is a practice that includes people with great writing skills but who have no need to worry about corporate strategy and people who advise boardrooms but have no need to know how to produce a website.

For many people working in internal communication there was never a 'proper' career path. We all got here by different routes and attempts to define an approved learning and development path are bound to be frustrating simply because people with valuable experiences and insights from other walks of life will always be given jobs leading IC teams.

However, when you have arrived in internal communication – or want to break in – it helps to define the skills, experience and knowledge (or competency) that you need for the job you want to do.

There are two possible ways to look at this challenge:

- What is the role that I should be fulfilling?
- What specific skills do I need to add value to my organization?

It's about the role

In Chapter 2 we introduced the idea of 'value spaces': the spaces in which the internal communication team make a difference:

- delivery excellence;
- business partnering;
- strategic advice.

These spaces are equally applicable to individuals: as professionals we find that our work often falls into the areas of making things happen, developing plans to support the business or providing senior advice.

This is essentially the idea behind Bill Quirke's suggestion that professionals operate along a continuum that includes 'crafters' and 'drafters' (people who produce content), 'distributors' (the corporate postal workers who make sure that messages get to the intended audiences) and 'internal counsellors' (the wise advisers of senior management). It also rather echoes the approach outlined by Maister, Green and Galford[1] who have studied the practices and management of professional services firms, including lawyers, accountants and consultants. Maister *et al* talk about a hierarchy of roles that begins with service delivery and builds to advising and onto trusted adviser, where the professional will be talking about hard issues far removed from their base competency.

What skills, knowledge or experience do I need to do a good job?

Maister *et al*'s model intrigued Sue Dewhurst and Liam FitzPatrick when they started researching internal communication competencies. They wanted to understand what would be the right mix of skills, knowledge and experience for a professional communicator fulfilling different roles.

They surveyed nearly 900 professionals at different stages of their careers and asked what competencies people used in their current roles. The resulting data[2] suggested a number of surprising findings.

First, the respondents did not universally plump for a set of standard craft skills. They were not insistent that writing or event management were essential pre-requisites for internal communicators. Nor did they prescribe knowledge of certain disciplines such as HR or organizational development.

Second, respondents prized two essential attributes: *making things happen* and *giving advice*. Common to everyone in the profession is a commitment to delivery and to guiding colleagues and senior managers to making the right decisions. We should be judged by our ability to cut through obstructions and difficulties and so achieve practical results. We need to develop, even at the earliest stages of our careers, the skill of helping others make decisions, initially around communication issues and later about wider management concerns.

In this we see an echo of Maister *et al*'s thinking about the importance of both being practical and learning to guide others to make the right decisions.

Overall, the statistical analysis generated 12 standard competencies, within which, for the sake of clarity, the researchers identified three levels. The idea is that a practitioner should identify which of the 12 competencies are relevant to their role and, within each of the competencies selected, decide the level that is appropriate.

TABLE 11.1 The 12 core competencies of an internal communicator

Competency	Definition
Building effective relationships	Developing and maintaining relationships that inspire trust and respect. Building a network and being able to influence others to make things happen.
Business focus	Having a clear understanding of the business issues and using communication to help solve organizational problems and achieve organizational objectives.
Consulting and coaching	Recommending appropriate solutions to customers, helping others to make informed decisions, building people's communications competence.
Cross-functional awareness	Understanding the different contributions from other disciplines and working with colleagues from across the organization to achieve better results.
Craft (writing and design)	Using and developing the right mix of practical communication abilities (eg writing and design management) to hold the confidence of peers and colleagues.
Developing other communicators	Helping other communicators build their communication competence and develop their careers.
Innovation and creativity	Looking for new ways of working, exploring best practice and delivering original and imaginative approaches to communication problems.

TABLE 11.1   *continued*

Competency	Definition
Listening	Conducting research and managing mechanisms for gathering feedback and employee reaction.
Making it happen (including persuasion)	Turning plans into successfully implemented actions.
Planning	Planning communication programmes and operations, evaluating results.
Specialist	Having specific subject matter expertise in a specialist area (eg event management or intranet publishing).
Vision and standards	Defining or applying a consistent approach to communication and maintaining professional and ethical standards.

Detailed descriptions of the competencies are provided in Appendix 2.

How are you spending your time?

Take a few minutes to think about your working life. Are you really doing the things that add value to you professionally and to your company?

To help your thinking, complete the simple questionnaire overleaf, and discuss your answers with another friend or colleague whose advice you trust. The aim here is not to reach firm conclusions but to start thinking about what you can do to make yourself more effective.

What do you notice about your completed grid? Are you spending too much time on things that are of limited value? If you could change one thing what would it be?

(With thanks to Sue Dewhurst.)

TABLE 11.2   How are you spending your time?

	Percentage of your time spent on the activity	Value this potentially adds to the organization
	Estimated %	High/Medium/Low
1. Advising senior leaders or line managers about communication matters		
2. Understanding and reflecting on business issues and strategies		
3. Thinking about and developing communications strategies and plans		
4. Researching and understanding the attitudes and needs of your audiences		
5. Coaching line managers or colleagues to be more effective communicators		
6. Developing and managing communication channels		
7. Delivering collateral material – eg writing articles, managing events		
8. Measuring or evaluating communication outcomes		

TABLE 11.2   *continued*

	Percentage of your time spent on the activity	Value this potentially adds to the organization
	Estimated %	High/Medium/ Low
9. Fire-fighting/reacting to last minute requests		
10. Developing your internal network/building relationships		
11. Working to understand the needs of different departments around the organization		
12 Your own personal development		
13. Looking for new and innovative ways to do things		
14. Setting and applying standards to ensure consistent communications across the organization		
15. Other (write in)		

The emphasis in the model is on describing the behaviours that a practitioner will want to exhibit in their chosen role and on providing a baseline against which to plan training and development.

It is important to take stock of your current skills against job requirements – in Table 11.2 above we suggest a simple template for you to use to help you think through the competencies you currently need in order to add value in your organization.

FIGURE 11.1   The personal development pathway

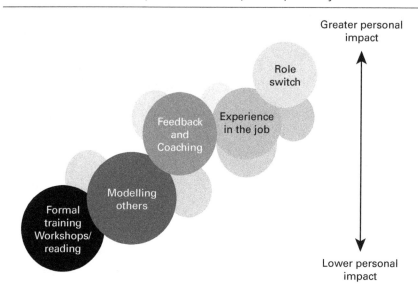

How do I get better?

So you have taken stock of your skills and abilities by assessing yourself against the competencies framework. How do you fill the gaps? In recent years, the availability of training for internal communicators has expanded considerably around the world. However, choosing a training course should not be the automatic first step in anyone's development planning. It is not just about formal training programmes.

The basic, intermediate and advanced level core competencies that will take you on your personal development pathway are detailed below. Here is a snapshot of what each step involves.

Formal training: courses, workshops and reading

Communicators do need a base level of knowledge. The syllabus of that knowledge will vary depending on the needs of the precise job being undertaken and the culture within which it is being done. Typically it will include things such as:

● the uses of different channels;
● measurement;

- legal and regulatory concerns such as copyrights, HR law covering diversity or collective consultation, financial market rules on the disclosure of information;
- writing, design, social media;
- planning.

Courses for many of these subjects are available through professional bodies such as the CIPR, the UK's Chartered Institute of Personnel and Development (CIPD) and the Institute of Internal Communications. The CIPR also offers a formal qualification at an introductory and an intermediate level as do academic institutions such as Kingston University in the UK.

The International Association of Business Communicators (IABC) is a not-for-profit trade association for business communication professionals with approximately 16,000 members, who, like commercial providers such as publishers Melcrum, also market programmes aimed at people seeking specific support in topics ranging from writing to running a communication function. Some skill areas such as coaching have their own specialist providers.

For all courses, the buyer should note that there are few agreed quality standards and that the experience of the student can vary enormously. Care should be taken to understand the skills and experience of the tutors (some may be highly developed practitioners, others may be academic specialists with limited hands-on experience), the academic or practical focus of the programme (not everyone thrives on reading journal articles or being fed old case studies) and who else might be participating (are they at the same level as you, will they bring diverse experiences and how much interaction will you have?).

A practitioner should also think about their continuing reading matter.

Online resources are produced by Melcrum and Ragan: both publish regular updates and insights. Members of the IABC receive the magazine *Communicate* and have access to an online resource centre and archive of past publications. Members of the CIPR also have access to an online resource centre including best-practice guides and toolkits, case histories, skills guides and live webinars.

Modelling others: changing your behaviours

Increasingly, practitioners are advised to think about development as something that happens outside seminar rooms or workshops. This can mean just attempting to imitate a behaviour that you have seen elsewhere or it can involve actively seeking the support of a colleague, coach or mentor.

We have said elsewhere that one of the hallmarks of a good internal communicator is curiosity, which is reflected in the number of networking groups and events that seem to surround our profession. In practice this means actively seeking out your peers from whom you think you can learn and benchmarking your work – either formally or informally.

Feedback and coaching

The value of a supportive coaching or mentoring relationship can be enormous if managed carefully and in a structured way.

To be clear, when we talk about a mentor we mean someone with direct experience that is relevant to you and who can give advice. A coach is someone who will help you set personal goals and help you find the resources within yourself to achieve those goals – they don't come with answers but their role is to think about the right questions. In practice, people use the terms interchangeably, but you will find that trained coaches concentrate on your understanding of a situation while someone in a mentoring role will bring their relevant experience to bear on your problems.

Several of the professional associations offer mentoring schemes and will help connect you with someone who can help you develop your career. Equally, mentoring arrangements are commonplace within organizations and your HR team can often help you find a colleague who can help you.

Interestingly, the CIPD makes the point that mentoring should be a learning opportunity for both parties – not just the mentee.

Broadly speaking, coaching tends to be done by two different types of people. Line managers will frequently see themselves as performance coaches and will accept that their role is to help individuals do their jobs more effectively and develop as professionals.

Additionally, in recent years there has been a growth of a skilled body of people who are experts at helping you understand the issues you are facing and exploring the approaches that you will apply to resolving them. In fact, in our experience there seem to be a great number of trained coaches who started their lives in internal communication – after years of helping senior leaders think about communication, becoming a full-time coach seems a natural step for many people!

In both cases the relationship should begin with an agreement about objectives – you decide what they should be – not the mentor or coach. Then you are off and running.

Crucially, you only get value from these arrangements if you are willing to work at them. That means being ready to listen to tough questions or go away between sessions and try new ideas and behaviours.

If you would like to find out more about either of these approaches, your internal learning and development colleagues are normally delighted to help. Alternatively, take a look at the resources provided by the CIPD.

Experience in the job

We have all had the joy of working with someone who claims to have many years of experience in a job when in fact they have had the same year many times over! Doing your job should be a continual learning experience, an experience that can be planned.

If you look at the backgrounds of the people you admire in our profession you will notice that they have experienced a wealth of different campaigns or challenges and have undertaken a range of roles over time. You need to consider what experiences you need on your CV and think how you might go about acquiring them.

If you go back to the Dewhurst and FitzPatrick competency model you have the beginning of a list of situations that you might want to experience.

You may want to add a range of situations or campaigns that you think could help shape your capabilities. These might include a crisis, a product launch, a site closure or a change of CEO.

Naturally you will not always get the chance to try all of your potential experiences, but having a list is an essential first step. You should share your list with your manager – if they don't know you are interested in a particular experience they may not offer you the opportunity!

Role switch

Finally, the most potent form of development is to switch roles.

This might be as simple as changing within internal communication, such as spending time as a channel manager, a project manager or a business partner. You might want to look at roles in other communication disciplines such as in the press office or helping marketing.

There is also considerable value in spending time as a consultant at some stage of your career.

Finally, your credibility as an adviser will be greatly enhanced if you can spend time in a role outside communication altogether – either in a function such as finance or in an operational role. Additionally you will gain insights that make you a better communicator, as you will understand the audiences and the thinking of senior leaders even better.

The key learning points from this chapter

We have shifted from being internal journalists to being a vital part of the corporate decision-making team. So, where in the past our role went to someone coming to the end of his or her career, today it goes to a professional and skilled communication adviser.

The best IC people recognise they need to carry on learning and developing throughout their careers because the ways we communicate change over time. Social media, for example, was not around at the turn of the century as an internal communication tool.

There is no one start point for our profession: we come from a variety of disciplines including engineering! But once there we need to upskill. That will almost certainly mean joining a professional body like the CIPR to develop skills, knowledge and expertise.

Dewhurst and FitzPatrick (one of our authors) surveyed nearly 900 professionals to produce a list of the 12 core competencies an IC professional should aspire to and the various roles they might fill. A questionnaire focuses the mind on which of our activities add the most value to an organization. A five-step career development pathway explains what is needed at each step, including mentoring and role switch.

Notes and references

1 Maister, D H, Green, C H and Galford, R M (2000) *The Trusted Advisor*, Simon and Schuster, New York

2 Dewhurst, S and FitzPatrick, L (2007) *How to Develop Outstanding Internal Communicators*, Melcrum Publishing, Washington

APPENDIX 1
The CIPR Code of Conduct

Members of the Chartered Institute of Public Relations agree to:

a) maintain the highest standards of professional endeavour, integrity, confidentiality, financial propriety and personal conduct;

b) deal honestly and fairly in business with employers, employees, clients, fellow professionals, other professions and the public;

c) respect, in their dealings with other people, the legal and regulatory frameworks and codes of all countries where they practise;

d) uphold the reputation of, and do nothing that would bring into disrepute, the public relations profession or the Chartered Institute of Public Relations;

e) respect and abide by this Code and related Notes of Guidance issued by the Chartered Institute of Public Relations and ensure that others who are accountable to them (eg subordinates and sub-contractors) do the same;

f) encourage professional training and development among members of the profession in order to raise and maintain professional standards generally.

Putting the principles into practice

Examples of good public relations practice include:

Integrity and honesty

- ensuring that clients, employers, employees, colleagues and fellow professionals are fully informed about the nature of representation, what can be delivered and achieved, and what other parties must do in order to enable the desired result;

- never deliberately concealing the practitioner's role as representative of a client or employer, even if the client or employer remains anonymous: eg by promoting a cause in the guise of a disinterested party or member of the public;

- checking the reliability and accuracy of information before dissemination;
- supporting the CIPR Principles by bringing to the attention of the CIPR examples of malpractice and unprofessional conduct.

Capacity, capability and competence

- delivering work competently: that is, in a timely, cost-effective, appropriate and thoughtful manner, according to the actual or implied contract; applying due professional judgement and experience; taking necessary steps to resolve problems; and ensuring that clients and other interested parties are informed, advised and consulted as necessary;
- being aware of the limitations of professional capacity and capability: without limiting realistic scope for development, being willing to accept or delegate only that work for which practitioners are suitably skilled and experienced and which they have the resources to undertake;
- where appropriate, collaborating on projects to ensure the necessary skill base.

Transparency and avoiding conflicts of interest

- disclosing to employers, clients or potential clients any financial interest in a supplier being recommended or engaged;
- declaring conflicts of interest (or circumstances which may give rise to them) in writing to clients, potential clients and employers as soon as they arise;
- ensuring that services provided are costed, delivered and accounted for in a manner that conforms to accepted business practice and ethics.

Confidentiality

- safeguarding confidences, eg of present and former clients and employers;
- never using confidential and 'insider' information to the disadvantage or prejudice of others, eg clients and employers, or to self-advantage of any kind;
- not disclosing confidential information unless specific permission has been granted or if required or covered by law.

APPENDIX 2
Dewhurst and FitzPatrick's core competencies

Levels

Each competency has three levels:

- Level 1 – Basic
- Level 2 – Intermediate
- Level 3 – Advanced

In each case, we describe the behaviours you would typically expect to see from somebody operating at this level.

The aim is not necessarily to be 'advanced' in every competency. Choose the level you need to operate at to be a strong performer in your role. Or, if you're looking further ahead to your next career move, choose the level you'll need for the type of role you're aspiring to.

There is also an 'ineffective behaviours' section for each competency. As the description suggests, these are the types of behaviour practitioners told us they see from less effective performers.

One final word of warning – take care not to discard competencies such as Craft (Writing and Design), just because you feel you're working in a senior role. People told us consistently throughout our research that senior practitioners must be strong in these types of fundamental skills, even if they spend less time using them from day to day.

TABLE A2.1   Core competencies

Competency:	**Building effective relationships**

Definition:

Developing and maintaining relationships that inspire trust and respect. Building a network and being able to influence others to make things happen.

Typical behaviours:

Ineffective behaviours	• Focuses purely on achieving own objectives. Fails to consider, or inappropriately ignores, other people's views.
	• Relies on force or hierarchy to push initiatives through.
	• Fails to engage or influence key stakeholders resulting in the failure to implement planned activities.
	• Afraid to ask questions or challenge decisions.
	• Being right matters more than getting the best result.
Level 1 – Basic	• Identifies individuals or groups that can help or prevent things happening and finds ways to work well with them.
	• Appears confident and comfortable working with people at all levels.
	• Respects and values other people's views. Tries to understand what's important to them.
	• Listens carefully, asking questions to aid understanding and clarification.
	• Seeks and uses feedback from clients.
	• Does what they say they will.
Level 2 – Intermediate	• Takes a structured approach to identifying their stakeholders and understanding their relative influence and importance to making things happen.
	• Builds a wide and effective network across their business area and invests time in cultivating relationships.
	• Seeks to understand and respect even the most difficult clients.
	• Can adapt their style to quickly inspire trust and respect from clients and colleagues at all levels.
	• Involves others in decision making and planning as appropriate to make sure activities happen as planned.
	• Stands up for their views without damaging relationships. Manages any conflict effectively.
Level 3 – Advanced	• Is a trusted and respected adviser to the most senior leaders.
	• Works well with colleagues at all levels.
	• Uses influence successfully to shape the strategic communications and business agenda.
	• Not easily intimidated but knows where to compromise.
	• Able to negotiate conflicting requirements from different stakeholders to build a coherent plan which is accepted by all.
	• Helps others to resolve conflicts or difficult issues.
	• Builds a strong network of relationships that can survive a change of direction, reporting lines or personalities.
	• Develops external relationships that enhance their knowledge and bring best practice into the organization.

TABLE A2.1 *continued*

Competency: Definition:	Business focus

Having a clear understanding of the business issues and using communication to help solve organizational problems and achieve organizational objectives.

Typical behaviours:

Ineffective behaviours	• Does not make the link between communication activity and the business/ organizational context. • Lacks understanding of their business area, its structure or its operations. • Has insufficient understanding of their core audiences. • Shows a poor grasp of the business priorities or challenges in conversations with leaders and clients.
Level 1 – Basic	• Has a sound basic understanding of their area's structure, purpose, products/services, priorities and key measures. • Makes an effort to understand their audiences, potentially through work shadowing or visiting different locations. • Thinks about and clarifies the business purpose of the communication activities they work on. Asks 'Why?' • Understands how their personal objectives relate back to the business objectives for their area.
Level 2 – Intermediate	• Demonstrates a good understanding of their area's business strategy, targets and performance and uses it to shape communication strategies, plans and materials. • Anticipates future developments or issues and is proactive about discussing how communication can help. • Challenges where she or he is asked to undertake activity with no clear business purpose, or which seems to work against stated business direction. • Regularly spends time with their core audiences to maintain their audience understanding. • Can discuss business issues credibly with leaders and clients. • Can identify the key issues from an annual report or set of financial results.
Level 3 – Advanced	• Seen as a credible businessperson who uses their communication expertise to help solve business problems. • Talks the language of business with stakeholders, rather than the language of communication. • Able to analyse complex business challenges and scenarios and formulate communication solutions. • Maintains a good understanding of audience needs and issues, either through personal contact or through the communications network. • Earns communication a seat at the top table and is seen as having an important contribution to make to business planning. • Routinely sought for advice about potential issues and complex scenarios at an early stage. • Financially literate. Understands and can debate financial measures, plans and performance.

TABLE A2.1 *continued*

Competency:	Consulting and coaching

Definition:

Recommending appropriate solutions to customers, helping others to make informed decisions, building people's communications competence.

Typical behaviours:

Ineffective behaviours	• Constantly carries out tactical activity themselves, rather than helping others to do it when appropriate.
	• Does not recognize or respond to opportunities to consult or coach.
	• Does not understand what coaching really means. Confuses it with telling, advising or giving feedback.
	• Fails to listen effectively to clients or customers.
	• Does not clarify expectations.
	• Afraid to challenge or question decisions and assumptions.
Level 1 – Basic	• Uses effective questioning and listening techniques to take a clear brief from clients or customers.
	• Sets clear expectations about their own role.
	• Provides sound advice about potential communications solutions.
	• Negotiates with clients to help them choose the most appropriate solution.
	• Can give basic advice and tips to help customers improve competence in specific scenarios (eg giving a presentation, holding a team meeting) or direct them to appropriate resources.
Level 2 – Intermediate	• Listens carefully to client or customer briefs, using questions to clarify understanding. Challenges the brief where appropriate to explore alternative communications solutions.
	• Is relied upon to provide sound communications advice and expertise and recommend appropriate solutions.
	• Is not afraid to say what people may not want to hear, and stands their ground when challenged.
	• Anticipates and prepares for questions or objections.
	• Sets expectations about their own role. Makes appropriate judgements about where they can add most value and where others are best placed to own actions and deliverables.
	• Has basic coaching skills and can coach line managers and customers to improve their communication competence in specific scenarios.
	• Gives feedback constructively and confidently when asked.
Level 3 – Advanced	• Helps colleagues and clients explore their wider business needs and explores options in anticipation of a discussion about communications solutions.
	• Quickly analyses complex scenarios to determine where communication can add value and recommend appropriate solutions and options.
	• Can present their case objectively and authoritatively.
	• Has well-developed coaching skills and the confidence to use them.
	• Identifies and takes opportunities to coach senior leaders and project managers to enhance their skills and improve performance.
	• Trusted and respected as a coach at a senior level.
	• Able to flex their style between directing, advising and coaching and identify which technique will be most appropriate in the circumstances.

TABLE A2.1 *continued*

Competency:	**Cross functional awareness**
Definition:	

Understanding the different contributions from other disciplines and working with colleagues from across the organization to achieve better results.

Typical Behaviours:

Ineffective behaviours	• Adopts an insular approach to internal communication and fails to make connections with the work of other departments. • Appreciates the needs of too few departments or may attend to the needs of one group or department to the exclusion of others.
Level 1 – Basic	• Understands the role of other departments and how internal communication helps them achieve their differing objectives.
Level 2 – Intermediate	• Understands relevant elements of law (including financial reporting rules) and local employment practice and the constraints they place on internal communication. • Can identify the implications for other functions from communication initiatives. • Can advise other functions or departments on communication issues.
Level 3 – Advanced	• Seen as a trusted adviser by leaders in other professions and is involved at an early stage in projects. • Keeps abreast of developments in HR, marketing, the law and areas of practice relevant to their organization.

TABLE A2.1   *continued*

Competency: Definition:	Craft (writing and design)

Using and developing the right mix of practical communication abilities (such as writing or design management) to hold the confidence of peers and colleagues.

Typical behaviours:

Ineffective behaviours	• Writes material that is inappropriate or unappealing for its audience. • Cannot brief or supervise a designer. • Produces or sanctions work which breaks identity standards, contains grammatical errors or is poorly designed or delivered. • Is not trusted by managers to deliver any communication activity without highly-detailed supervision. • Clients and colleagues use other suppliers for skilled tasks which should be done by this person.
Level 1 – Basic	• Writes simple items in a way that is engaging, grammatically correct and appropriate to the audience. • Can correct other people's writing. • Appreciates and follows visual identity principles. • Understands how to work with external suppliers and can prepare a simple brief. • Is trusted by managers and colleagues to deliver activities reliably. • Copes well working on a number of different tasks – sometimes with conflicting deadlines.
Level 2 – Intermediate	• Writes in a variety of styles for a variety of formats in a way that is engaging, grammatically correct and appropriate. • Can ghost-write for senior leaders in a way that captures their personality and spirit. • Can supervise specialists in different media (eg web layout, print design or photography). • Can quickly and sensitively sub-edit other people's writing for a variety of formats. • Is a reliable project manager, directing the work of other people and suppliers to deliver projects on time and to budget.
Level 3 – Advanced	• Writes and coaches less experienced communicators in writing in a variety of styles for a variety of formats in a way that is engaging, grammatically correct and appropriate. • Coaches other communicators in other practical areas where they are particularly skilled (such as design management). • Defines and develops basic standards for practical skills in the team.

TABLE A2.1   *continued*

Competency: Definition:	Developing other communicators
	Helping other communicators build their communication competence and develop their careers.

Typical behaviours:

Ineffective behaviours	• Does not allocate time or budget for development activity. • Fails to give feedback on performance. • Blocks access to development activity. • More interested in keeping individuals in convenient roles than helping them develop their career.
Level 1 – Basic	• Helps non-professional communicators such as communication champions develop basic skills and knowledge. • Invests time in helping them to build a network and share plans, ideas and best practice. • Commissions or delivers simple development interventions, eg training days. • Provides templates, toolkits and resources to help build competence. • Supports colleagues with their development needs.
Level 2 – Intermediate	• Supports direct reports in planning their personal and professional development. • Understands the organization's performance management process and their role within it. • Sets clear development objectives based on business needs and people's personal aspirations. • Coaches team members to enhance performance and build competence, giving constructive feedback as appropriate. • Develops improvement plans to support team members where performance is below acceptable standards. • Recognizes and publicizes good work. • Shares interesting and challenging tasks where there is a genuine development opportunity for colleagues. • Understands the range of development options available and the strengths and weaknesses of each.
Level 3 – Advanced	• Champions the development agenda within the team. • Allocates time and budget for team development activity. • Clearly defines the competences needed to operate successfully. • Chooses different approaches to development (ranging from coaching through to training) to achieve business results. • Ensures the team is kept up to date with best practice, new thinking and industry developments. • Supports sensible risk-taking in the interests of learning and is supportive if people make mistakes. • Develops the internal communication network, building capability and facilitating the sharing of knowledge, ideas and best practice across the team. • Ensures work is allocated with development in mind. • Is a highly-skilled facilitator and coach.

TABLE A2.1 *continued*

Competency: **Innovation and creativity**
Definition:

Looking for new ways of working, exploring best practice and delivering original and imaginative approaches to communication problems.

Typical behaviours:

Ineffective behaviours	• Consistently repeats old routines without taking account of changing circumstances or needs.
	• Produces dull or unengaging materials.
	• Lacks curiosity about best practice from inside or outside their organization.
	• Discourages others from exploring new ideas.
Level 1 – Basic	• Actively looks for ways to improve work processes and makes practical suggestions.
	• Looks for imaginative solutions to communication problems and ensures solution is fit for purpose.
	• Reads professional literature and is curious about how other communicators tackle similar issues.
Level 2 – Intermediate	• Initiates and develops new processes that work.
	• Is normally successful at presenting ideas and communications in a fresh and compelling way.
	• Advises on where to find ideas on good practice in their area (from inside and outside their organization).
Level 3 – Advanced	• Initiates and develops new ways of working which will still be in use after they have moved on.
	• Is recognized inside and outside their organization for extending established practice and developing fresh thinking.
	• Supports and encourages colleagues to generate new ideas or adapt existing ones in order to produce strong communications.
	• Looks outside internal communication for inspiration.

TABLE A2.1   *continued*

Competency: Definition:	Listening
Conducting research and managing mechanisms for gathering feedback and employee reaction.	
Typical behaviours:	
Ineffective behaviours	• Is not interested in gathering employee feedback and does not see its place in communications planning. • Presents their own views (or views of colleagues) as representative of wider employee opinion. • Accepts other people's claims about employee attitudes or experience without checking the facts. • Does not anticipate employee reaction to events or news or provide timely mechanisms to gather such feedback.
Level 1 – Basic	• Includes simple research or listening exercises in the planning and evaluation of communication activity. • Has a basic network of contacts around the organization which can be used as a simple sounding board. • Can present intelligence in a persuasive and credible way. • Supports other professionals in the conduct of focus groups (either as a scribe, logistics specialist or secondary facilitator). • Understands the legal framework surrounding consultation and information sharing in the territories where they operate – knows when to seek specialist help.
Level 2 – Intermediate	• Makes choices about research methodologies based on communication and business need. • Manages focus groups and depth interviews, including the selection of a representative and credible sample frame, the preparation of topic guides and the creation of reports. • Produces simple surveys which are credible to both managers and employees. • Manages stakeholders' sensitivities that arise when a study is proposed or designed or when results are delivered. • Presents findings and recommendations persuasively. • Reflects research in communications plans. • Ensures that communications are compliant with legal obligations to consult or inform. • Supports specialist colleagues in the smooth running of employee consultation groups or councils. • Has a robust informal network of contacts around the business which is used for ad hoc intelligence gathering.
Level 3 – Advanced	• Advises others on their research needs. • Builds management respect for data gathered and its use in shaping communication decisions. • Manages research contractors. • Understands different approaches to analysis and knows when to apply statistical tools. • Designs and leads programmes of qualitative research. • Coaches others in facilitation for qualitative research. • Presents findings and recommendations persuasively. • Contributes to professional good practice.

TABLE A2.1   *continued*

| Competency: | **Making it happen** |
| Definition: | |

Turning plans into successfully-implemented actions.

Typical Behaviours:

Ineffective behaviours	• Is not trusted by others to deliver activities as planned.
	• Develops impractical or unworkable action plans.
	• Does not keep to budgets or deadlines.
	• Fails to recognize the local implications of activities.
	• Lacks attention to detail.
	• Panics – and panics others around them.
	• Is easily frustrated or diverted.
Level 1 – Basic	• Can be relied upon to organize simple activities such as conference calls, open forums, mass e-mail distributions or executive visits, efficiently and effectively.
	• Appears calm and capable, giving an image of confidence.
	• Knows the right people, resources and processes to make things happen.
	• Anticipates potential questions or issues and ensures all angles are covered.
	• Keeps team members and other stakeholders informed.
	• Delivers on time and within budget.
	• Finds ways around obstacles with supervision.
Level 2 – Intermediate	• Successfully organizes larger events or initiatives such as management conferences or road shows.
	• Able to juggle a number of tasks and prioritize effort.
	• Produces comprehensive project plans.
	• Makes effective use of systems to store and organize information.
	• Forms effective working relationships with suppliers.
	• Negotiates competitive rates, possibly working with the supply chain function.
	• Deals calmly and efficiently with queries, requests and changes.
	• Handles poor service or unreasonable requests firmly but pleasantly. Stands their ground.
	• Is a calm and capable presence 'on the ground'.
	• Always overcomes obstacles or problems calmly without damaging relationships unnecessarily.
Level 3 – Advanced	• Organizes complex initiatives or events, potentially involving large budgets and multiple locations.
	• Manages multiple suppliers efficiently and effectively, involving the supply chain function as appropriate.
	• A good programme manager – co-ordinates complex programmes, tracks progress, identifies and manages issues and risks.
	• Identifies and builds relationships with key stakeholders, keeping them informed about progress and maintaining their confidence.
	• Anticipates potential problems and produces contingency plans.
	• Knows the project plan inside out and can act as an information hub, directing action as appropriate.
	• Inspires trust and confidence.

TABLE A2.1   *continued*

Competency: Planning	
Definition:	
Planning communications programmes and operations, evaluating results.	
Typical Behaviours:	
Ineffective behaviours	• Develops activities in a haphazard manner without due regard to resources, timescales or clarity of objectives. • Does not objectively evaluate communications programmes. Uses their own subjective judgement.
Level 1 – Basic	• Plans simple projects involving relatively few stakeholders and requiring simple deliverables. • Follows a simple planning model in all activities which sets out clear objectives, timescales and resource needs. • Understands the strengths and uses of different channels and can choose between them. • Tracks, as a minimum, whether communications reach intended audiences. • Is aware of other communications activity that is due to take place in their work area (using formal and informal means). • Learns from mistakes or experience.
Level 2 – Intermediate	• Develops complex plans for projects or divisions that include multiple stakeholders, uncertainty and risk. • Always plans work and includes audience segmentation, definition of messages and channel selection as well as making clear links back to business objectives. • Understands the different needs of change and business as usual communications plans. • Applies a methodical approach to crisis communication. • Ensures that channels are always fit for purpose and identifies improvements where necessary. • Can explain planning choices and options to stakeholders. • Has mechanisms in place to alert them to communication or other activity which might conflict or clash with their own plans. • Evaluates individual projects and whole programmes based on whether audiences understand messages. • Delivers projects or activities within defined resources. • Reflects learning from evaluation in evolving plans.
Level 3 – Advanced	• Defines communications planning standards for their organization. • Oversees the co-ordination of multiple programmes and manages complex organizational, cultural or operational change programmes. • Anticipates and mitigates crises. • Ensures that there is a suite of channels available in their organization to meet needs. • Establishes and maintains a framework for the co-ordination of plans to avoid overload, confusion or inconsistency. • Oversees budgets to assure value for money and the effective use of resources. • Is accountable for business results (rather than simply communication outcomes).

TABLE A2.1 *continued*

Competency:	Specialist
Definition:	

Having specific subject matter expertise in a specialist area.
NB Organizations should add in the skills, knowledge and behaviour appropriate to the nature of the specific role concerned.

Typical behaviours:

Ineffective behaviours	• Does not have the specialist knowledge or expertise needed to perform their role.
	• Is not trusted by other team members to provide a high-quality service or give good advice.
	• Has little or no knowledge of best practice, new techniques or current thinking in their specialist area.
Level 1 – Basic	• Has the specialist knowledge, skills and experience needed to carry out their role with minimum supervision.
	• Is trusted by other team members or customers to provide a good quality of service or give sound advice in their specialist area.
Level 2 – Intermediate	• Is respected as an internal expert in their subject area.
	• Is deferred to as the natural spokesperson/adviser in conversations about their subject area.
	• Has a good awareness of best practice and current thinking in their subject area and suggests ways of using it within the organization.
Level 3 – Advanced	• Is known throughout the industry as a subject matter expert.
	• Wins awards/has case studies published for their work.
	• Ensures the organization has access to the very latest best practice and new techniques. Constantly seeks ways to apply the thinking.

TABLE A2.1　*continued*

Competency:	Vision and standards
Definition:	

Defining or applying a consistent approach to communication and maintaining professional and ethical standards.

Typical Behaviours:

Ineffective behaviours	• Produces communications without any overarching goals on a purely ad hoc basis. • Is unaware of (or ignores) rules and standards for communication or visual identity. • Communicates information which is dishonest or misleading either deliberately or without care. • Does not apply consistent ethical standards appropriate to national or organizational expectations. • Can be pressured into issuing communications that are inappropriate for the audience, channel or situation.
Level 1 – Basic	• Understands their organization's standards around communications and visual identity. • Can articulate clearly role that internal communication plays in their workplace. • Maintains agreed standards for individual channels by not using them for inappropriate messages or compromising on quality. • Takes responsibility for the quality of their own communication. • Conforms to expected ethical standards and behaviours. • Where necessary, sets out simple standards for the team as a whole.
Level 2 – Intermediate	• Helps define quality and operational standards for communication in their organization. • Coaches colleagues in correct standards and values. • Takes responsibility for ensuring the quality of communication and channels in their team. • Develops with local managers a sustainable vision for the role that communication is expected to deliver in their areas.
Level 3 – Advanced	• Defines a sustainable overall vision for the role of internal communication and wins senior management support for that vision. • Is consistent in their pursuit of that vision. • Defines quality standards of internal communication. • Accepts accountability for the quality of communications and channels in their organization, but articulates clearly where the role of the internal communication function ends and the role of a line manager begins. • Models ethical behaviour within their organization.

INDEX

Notes: IC refers to internal communication(s).

Page numbers in *italics* indicate figures or tables.

CPSIA information can be obtained
at www.ICGtesting.com
Printed in the USA
BVHW04s1357180718
521945BV00003B/134/P